MY LIFE AND LIVES
The Story of a Tibetan Incarnation

Khyongla Rato

D1392778

Edited and with a foreword by
Joseph Campbell

RATO PUBLICATIONS
New York

Cover Design by Donna Swensen

Front cover, The Official Residence of Tulkus of the
    Khyongla lineage
    Photo by Elisabeth Benard

Back cover, Khyongla Rato
    Photo by Clive Arrowsmith

Library of Congress Catalog Card Number: 91-91189

ISBN: 0-9630293-0-4

Printed in U.S.A. by Book Crafters
        Chelsea, Michigan

10 9 8 7 6 5 4 3 2 1
Second Edition

Contents

Acknowledgments

Tibet, my native land, has always been inaccessible—its very geographical remoteness prevented people from writing firsthand accounts of Tibetan religion and society, and there is to this day very little authentic information about Buddhist lamas available in English.

Despite this lack of material in English, it had not occurred to me to write a book about my life until several of my Western friends suggested it, mainly because Buddhist teaching, especially as practiced in the Gelugpa sect, forbids the externalizing of one's achievements unless the purpose is to aid the spreading of the Lord Buddha's Doctrine. But since the Buddhist religion and the traditional monastic life have been effectively destroyed in Tibet by the Communist Chinese, I realized that the details of my life might serve to teach others about Buddhism, and so I agreed to write down some of them. I must confess that in my first attempt, I wrote down everything of interest in my life, and covered only one page.

In 1965, I began by dictating about thirty pages to Gautam Mohen in Holland, no easy task for him, since he had to teach me how to go about it. Later, Dr. Blanche C. Olshak, one of the leading Western tibetologists, made corrections to this short draft when I was in Zurich as her guest.

When I settled in New York, I dictated the major portion of the book to Charmion Von Wiegand, the distinguished painter and collector of Tibetan art, whom I met the first week I arrived in New York and who introduced me to the ways of Western life and herself became an ardent student of Buddhism. This writing took place over the course of many months, while she took valuable time from her own work. My dear friend, Marjorie Mortensen, then helped by rewriting the book several times, correcting the manuscript, and helping me to add much new material. Phuntsok Thonden, the New York representative of His Holiness the Dalai Lama, read it and clarified some of the historical information.

Other friends, including John Farber, Barbara Gauditz, Heather Stoddard, Sonam Wangdu, Phunsom, Donna Carlson, Thubten Tsering and Eric Dulberg, also read the manuscript and offered many helpful suggestions. Some of them also assisted in the typing.

Professor Joseph Campbell did the final editing and gave many invaluable suggestions for improving the book. He and his wife, Jean Erdman Campbell, were immensely helpful and encouraging over the last several years, and my life has been greatly enriched by the gift of their friendship. Joe's secretary, Marcia Sherman, then generously typed the manuscript several times.

I'd like to thank Richard Gere for his invaluable help and resources, as well as Elizabeth Avedon, Donna Swensen, Heinrich Spillmann, Dolores Cloward, Anne Cherry, Nicholas Vreeland, Sandra Vreeland, and many other friends who worked at making this second edition possible. Without the gracious assistance of my friends, this book would not have been possible. It is my sincere hope that the reader will sift through this mixture of gold and sand, to find whatever beneficial dust lies between the pages.

Tashi deleg!

Foreword

No one has given us anything like this full-bodied narrative picture of Tibet as it was known to its own people, to the very moment of that crackdown—described in the last chapters—which marked the end of its long history in isolation. Nor have we anywhere anything like this inward history of the life and disciplines of its great Buddhist monasteries and temples, heritages and mountain retreats—any such intimate portraits of its once numerous scholar-mystics. As I read with increasing fascination through the altogether astonishing manuscript, I presently realized that what I had in hand was a text of the greatest historical interest: a contemporary account, in detail, of the last decades of the native life and civilization of Tibet.

My chance first meeting with its author, Khyongla (the name is pronounced Chungla), was in one of those dismal "greasy spoons" that abound in the environs of American universities. I had been invited from New York to deliver an evening lecture on my favorite theme, mythology, and my faculty host had brought me to this disappointing spot for a quick dinner before the occasion. "It's the best we have," he said wearily as we took places in a booth and, unfolding our napkins, looked around. Across the aisle, quietly eating at another such enclosed table, was an Asian whom my host, in spite of the inadequate lighting, recognized. I was introduced as one who had published a number of books on oriental philosophy, and even though the hour of my lecture was pressing hard upon us, he paused for a brief exchange before leaving. The Tibetan, whose name I had not caught, spoke in a hoarse but gentle voice, with an accent I could scarcely understand, of some work that he had undertaken. Captured already by his personal charm, I suggested that if he should wish at any time to have a bit of help with his English prose, I should be happy to supply it; and with that and a general exchange of smiles all around, my host and I departed for the lecture hall.

"Truth comes," wrote Nietzsche, "on dove's feet." I had had no sense during that almost unintelligible exchange of intercultural courtesies of anything of significance having occurred. In fact, it was not until some three or four years later that my telephone rang and a hoarse voice reminded me of our all but forgotten encounter. Khyongla (and I still was unable to hear the name correctly) had moved to New York, and was living now in a walk-up on East 36th Street—a tiny two-room flat that no one but a seasoned monk could have regarded as a comfortable home. When he paid me and my wife his first visit a few days later, he paused, on leaving, before a fine Tibetan thangka in our foyer, which had been given to us some years before by Ananda K. Coomaraswamy. "That's the yi-dam of my order," he said; "Cakra Samvara Raja." And I think I heard at that moment, superstitiously, something like the sound of dove's feet coming into my life. He had brought for me to read the first chapters of his autobiographical message to the West, into which I presently plunged with a sense of real delight. For it was as though the fabled mysteries of the most secret fastnesses of forbidden Tibet were, at last, being opened to me by one whose entire life had been given to their interpretation.

Recognized in earliest childhood as the reincarnation of an abbot who had been returning to this world since the sixteenth century, Khyongla had been taken in his sixth year into a monastery for special training through the course of a truly fabulous lifetime—up to the very moment of the dissolution of his people's civilization in 1959—he had been intensively instructed in the lore of the Mahayana, as it had become known to Tibet during the fifth to the twelfth centuries, and where it was preserved to our own time, as though in a hermetically-sealed chamber. If a European scholar-monk of the period of, say, Abelard were to appear in today's New York with his whole life story in hand—the entire chronicle of his travels, debates, receptions in both palaces and peasant cottages, interviews with cardinals, princes, and the Pope, as well as eye-witness accounts of the great religious feasts and jubilees of his time—the miracle would be scarcely more remarkable or, finally as it seems to me, important for students of political and religious history, than this of the coming to us of Khyongla from the now desecrated and destroyed monasteries of Rato, Sera, Gaden, Drepung, and the great Tantric university of Gyud to in Lhasa. Intimate friend and protégé of the tutors of the young Dalai Lama, Khyongla had been himself among the number of recognized scholars appointed to examine His Holiness (hardly a week before that horrific day of cannonading, bloodshed, and fire, which terminated the history of his nation) when the Dalai Lama received, amidst a festival of acclaim, his lharampa geshe degree.

The final chapters of this remarkable biography, telling of the ominous approach and consummation of what has been called in Chinese versions of the terror, "The New Happiness"; the accounts of the author's last visit to his doomed family; his beautiful leave-taking from his father and escape; the night of the Dalai Lama's own flight from the bombarded and burning holy city; the author's dangerous transit of the Himalayas afoot and arrival, together with a multitude of other exhausted miserables, in India; his confinement there to a refugee camp until released; to what has become his life today as a displaced person in the modern world—these stunning narratives rank, in my opinion, among the best historical documentaries of our time. However, what has most impressed and instructed me, both in my study of the manuscript and in my association with its author during the four or five years that I have now known him as a beloved and profoundly admired friend, has been the absence of any word or implication of hatred, or even of righteous resentment, in his references to the Chinese. It has been from this that I have learned my deepest lesson—come to me on dove's feet—of what a life inspired by the teaching of the Buddha means.

Joseph Campbell
Bangkok
April 4, 1977

1.

My Home

As a child I liked to play behind our house with a number of other boys, along a small irrigation ditch that brought water to our fields. One fine day in 1928, when I was five and we were playing there under the willow trees along the water's edge, we saw four monks arrive on horseback. They dismounted before our door and after a little time my mother came to fetch me, to lead me into the house. As I entered, the four monks bowed deeply before me.

The two eldest, stepping forward, offered me with great ceremony five gifts: two long white scarves, a red-brown cloak, a little cap, and new brown leather boots. The youngest smiled at me and put into my hand a new plaything, a small white porcelain bird. All four then bent to serve me, kindly, and one declared that soon they would be returning to take me to their labrang. When I asked where that was, they told me it was not far away, only a half-day's journey on horseback, at a place called Gonsar; and even though I had no real understanding of what they were talking about, I became excited. They presented my father and mother with gifts of precious silk, and my parents then served them lunch. For a long time they sat drinking tea, discussing the labrang, until finally the four visitors rose to go. My parents went out to help them mount and I followed, watching as they rode quickly away into the hills to the northwest and disappeared.

My country, Tibet, had long been known as Khawachen, "The Land of Snows," for it is situated on the heights of the lofty plateau of Asia, enclosed on three sides by towering snow mountains that for centuries made it impregnable, shut off from the rest of the world. Only on our eastern border are there openings in the ranges, and there, among the northern lakes, four mighty rivers rise, the Huang Ho, Yangtze, Mekong, and Salween, which, after flowing through neighboring uplands, turn eastward and southward to the sea, offering in the great gorges of the Yangtze a barrier almost as impassable as our hills.

Though large, Tibet has always had a small population, perhaps no more than eight million or so. It encompasses three regions: U Tsang, in the west and center, Domed, or Amdo, in the northeast; and Dodod, or Kham, in the southeast, touching China. I was born in the last, the Kham, between the Yangtze and Mekong—or as we called them, Drechu and Zachu—in a tiny village named Ophor, south of Chamdo, the region's most important town. There were many districts in the Kham, and in some of them large towns, but in my district, south of Chamdo, called Dayad, there were in my day no towns at all. The people there, of pure Tibetan stock, dwelt mainly in scattered villages, farming, cattle-breeding, or herding, and in the remoter sections there were nomads dwelling on the pasture lands in tents.

Trading between China and Tibet went on regularly during times of peace, and so we frequently saw large caravans passing through Chamdo. Not only merchants traveled with these, but also monks and pilgrims visiting famous shrines. Sometimes the journeys lasted months, even as long as a year; since there were no wheeled vehicles, everybody traveled either on horseback, muleback, or on foot, transporting goods by mule or on the slower-moving yak, and generally in groups armed for protection against the highwaymen who infested the remoter sections. Thus there was always movement on our roads, and this kept our villagers from becoming completely isolated. Everybody in our district dreamed of one day visiting the holy city of Lhasa, which was more than a whole month's traveling away.

The people of my region, the Khampa, were a strong and virile race, fun-loving, and active sportsmen, at home on their sturdy horses. They were given to such competitive sports as racing, archery, and wrestling, and in earlier times must have been avid hunters. However, having adopted Buddhism centuries before, they had become the great defenders of that faith and our most ardent supporters of the Dalai Lama—as time and the events of history about to break upon us would soon show.

My little village, Ophor, was situated on a high plateau surrounded by rolling hills that rose tallest in the north and descended gently toward the south. The meaning of its name, Ophor, in Tibetan, was "a wooden bowl of milk," and that is just what the landscape suggested when covered with snow in the wintertime. In summer, though, it was green, with grassy meadows rolling up to the foothills where they blended into the higher forested slopes of juniper trees. Flowers blossomed in springtime in those meadows, and the village girls would come to pick and weave them into wreaths and crowns for their hair. On the upper slopes there flourished a variety of herbs and other plants that were the basis of most of our medical lore.

In Ophor it was impossible to buy anything at all, and so for supplies we had to go either north to Chamdo on an expedition that might take as many as five days, or south to a market in Yendum, the largest village of our district, a good six hours by horseback from Ophor. Up in Chamdo we could exchange our wheat and barley for tea, cotton, and other such goods from India and China as were offered in all the larger market towns of Tibet. We would travel either in single families or in village groups, but always with a caravan, riding hornless yaks or horses, and with donkeys, yaks, and mules to carry our produce. To protect such a caravan, which sometimes comprised as many as forty beasts of burden, the men carried guns and swords, using the latter also for cutting wood for the nightly fires. There were fierce watchdogs along for further protection. My father worked in Yendum, in the south, and since he could not often go himself on such trips, he occasionally commissioned nomads to procure for us our household supplies.

Our villagers liked to wear silk, especially richly brocaded robes. The women sometimes donned silk aprons of finely woven stripes sewn horizontally in gay colors; and they also wore elaborate ornaments proudly on their heads. In the Kham such ornaments were set above the forehead and fell back over the head in a long row of delicately worked metal pieces to the middle of the back. In Central Tibet, on the other hand, they were arranged in a high triangular shape, and in Tsang were placed in such a way that the women seemed to have horns, like yaks. When I first saw these last I thought, What a strange version of beauty! They looked uncomfortable, too. Most Tibetan women wore necklaces of coral, pearls, and turquoise with amulet boxes known as *kaus* attached; and since we had many fine silversmiths and goldsmiths in our country, the workmanship of the kaus was generally superb. The men's hair, trimmed short in front, was long and braided behind. In winter they pulled on fox-fur hats and wore coats lined warmly with lamb's fleece. For though our village had a somewhat milder climate than those further to the north, our winters still were very cold.

There were some sixty families in Ophor, most of them poor. Mine, however, was well-off—which does not mean, of course, that we were nearly as rich as a wealthy American family, but rich only by the standards of a tiny village. My father was twenty-five and my mother twenty when they were married, in a purely traditional way, of which I heard a good deal from my sturdy grandfather. It was his custom to recount repeatedly to all our friends and guests the whole chronicle of his triumph in the accomplishment of this fortunate union.

My father—as I heard the story—had been serving as private secretary to my grandfather's brother, my father's uncle, who at that time was the second highest official in the district of Dayab; he was living with that uncle in Yendum, surrounded by monks, since the district office was located in the monastery. His experience there had strongly inclined him to the monastic life, but since he was the only son of the family it was felt that he should marry and so carry on the name. His bride—as my grandfather insisted to my grandmother—should be of good family, good character, and attractive. For if her family were poor, ours would be disgraced and blamed for contracting a marriage below our station; if she were not of excellent character, she would not give my grandparents the respectful treatment they merited, and their son would soon find life so painful that the marriage would probably fail; and if, finally, the young lady were not beautiful their son would be ill-matched, for my father was very handsome indeed. It would not be, however, easy to find a match with all these qualifications, and, after much discussion, my grandparents decided that if any one had to be dropped, perhaps the least serious consideration should be the wealth of the girl's parents. People would tend, in any case, either to flatter or to criticize, and neighbors would always find something about which to gossip.

Many young ladies were suggested by my grandfather's intimate friends. Some of the proposals, he felt, were sincere; others, however, he thought motivated by a wish to help certain families. Yet he listened to all, giving little hint of his own mind until he had settled upon three, whom he had himself been considering all along. And though he occasionally consulted his son on this very intimate matter, the final decision—as was customary in our country—was to be his.

Now my grandfather especially favored one young lady, whose father was influential in our district, but he wrote to all three of the chosen families for permission to consult astrologers for horoscopes, and lamas for divination. After receiving affirmative answers from all, he reviewed the matter with his son, telling him everything he had learned about the young women under consideration. Next he sought the advice of an astrologer who for years had been his best friend, and this expert, casting first the horoscope of my grandfather's favorite prospect, found that while she would in the beginning make a satisfactory wife, the marriage, later on, would deteriorate. This displeased my grandfather greatly, who thereupon sent his head servant off for advice to the hermitage of a certain celebrated monk. The journey on horseback required two days, and when the man arrived he knocked a number of times at the hermit's door, but the monk, who was in meditation at the time, failed to respond. Our man impatiently waited until finally the door opened and the monk allowed him to come in. When asked who he was and for what reason he had come, the servant simply handed the holy man my grandfather's handwritten letter, along with some formal gifts, informing him briefly of the matter at hand—to which the hermit responded that he know nothing of the future and could be of no help. The messenger insisted, explaining that His Holiness was not being asked to decide upon the best bride for his master's son, but only to practice divination. The other replied that with all his daily religious duties he had no time for such worldly affairs. Our excellent servant then became angry and heatedly reminded the monk that he was meant to practice religion for *all* sentient beings, my grandfather's son being no exception; adding that if that monk was practicing only for himself his religious motives could hardly be admired.

That worked, and the monk began to smile. Refusing the gifts, save for a packet of food, he took the letter and disappeared into his cell, returning immediately with buttered tea and a bite for his guest to eat. Then while the servant, with his temper restored, went outside to admire the view (for the hermitage was on a high mountain and overlooked a wide landscape), the monk went to work on his divination. After about an hour he came out with a sealed envelope in his hand containing both my grandfather's letter and his own prophecy. Our good servant, receiving this, respectfully took his leave, and on arriving four days later at our home, let my grandfather know that he was not so sure that that hermit was a holy man at all, since he had seemed short-tempered and selfish. However, he had served such delicious tea and refreshment that our man himself would have liked to remain a few months at that pleasant hermitage and become as lazy as that solitary monk almost surely was.

When the envelope was opened and my grandfather found that this second advisor, too, had rejected his favorite candidate, he sadly accepted the inevitable and, writing to the parents of the first of the remaining two, explained that their daughter had been selected for his son by means of a horoscope reading and divination by a lama. The young woman's family had already inquired, meanwhile, about the prospective bridegroom's character, education, experience, and property, and had discussed his qualities with their daughter. An affirmative reply was therefore soon returned, and an auspicious day astrologically selected for the wedding. Our steward thereupon was sent with gifts to the other household, to read aloud there and to seal (together with one witness from the bride's side) a form of marriage contract guaranteeing that the bride would show respect for her husband's parents equal to that shown her own, and that my grandparents, in turn, would treat her as their daughter, the married couple themselves contracting to strive earnestly to live together in harmony. That settled, our steward, in my grandfather's name, gave a dinner for the bride's family and, all assignments accomplished, returned gratified to our home.

Three months later, however, the steward was again sent forth, this time with a number of our friends, all wearing their very best clothes, and for two days these emissaries rode the way to the bride's home, arriving one afternoon. Gifts again were presented, and early the next morning, before the bride's departure from her family, there was held in the reception hall a ceremony that our steward opened with a long, formal, and flowery speech. "The sun and the moon," he was supposed to say, "are bright in the sky," and the harvest on earth is good with abundant fruits. However, he was nervous and, instead, announced that "on earth the sun and the moon were good and, in the sky, the harvest and fruits." Everybody laughed, and for years thereafter he was teased about that blunder. But the ceremony was restored to order and our man, regaining his dignity, went on with his formidable assignment.

Touching an arrow ceremoniously to the nape of the bride's neck, he ritually gave notice that from that moment she belonged wholly to her husband. There had been brought along with the wedding party a young colt and stallion for her use, and she, now rising and proceeding to the door, mounted the latter with the blessings of her friends upon her, and accompanied by a large procession of riders departed from her parents' house.

The bridal cortege was led off by a man bearing an astrological chart, behind whom there rode the groom's entire welcoming party. Next came the bride, followed by the farewell retinue of her own relatives. Along the road the gala company passed a girl with a pitcher of water, and in token of the occasion she was presented by one of the party with a white scarf. Two days later they pulled up at my grandfather's door, and our steward, in another grandiloquent speech delivered before the bride could dismount, described this simple door of her new home as a portal "fortunate for all who passed through it," giving praise then to the exalted qualifications of her groom. That done, he finally helped her down—ceremoniously—from her mount to a platform arrayed with nine customary objects: a leopard skin, a tiger skin, five lengths of finely colored silk brocade, a white scarf, and a package of twelve bricks of Chinese tea sewn into a yak skin. Thereupon everyone dismounted and, along with a number of invited guests, entered the reception room, where the bride was conducted to a seat beside the groom, whom she beheld now for the first time. In back of the two were seated my grandparents, and at the end of their row a special troupe of singers began to sing the marriage song, to which all joined in for the chorus. An auspicious sweet-tasting herb, *droma*, was scattered in the air, and pure cooked meats and barley cakes were carried to the couple on silver plates.

Next the bride was escorted to the roof and conducted to an incense chimney situated there above the main door, where she planted an arrow decorated with a flourish of blue scarves, blue being the color of her zodiac sign. And since it was our custom that no monk should meet with a bride on her wedding day, the next part of the roof program—a ritual supposed to prevent hailstorms—was performed by an instructed layman. Chanting spells, offering incense, and giving praise to all the gods from the Lord Buddha and the local mountain spirits, that layman must have been a very busy man indeed! For while his two hands were occupied clashing cymbals, he also beat a drum with sticks attached by a thong to one thumb, and recited aloud verses that required him to visualize and meditate upon each divinity named. When he had concluded this remarkable feat the roof ceremony was ended, and the bridal company returned below, where the neighbors and friends of my family—not only from Ophor, but also from more distant villages—offered gifts and congratulations.

The members of the groom's welcoming party and the bride's farewell party, together with the whole company of friendly guests and neighbors, remained in our house and village for three days of continuous banqueting and celebration. Great silver cups of a sort of barley beer called *chang* were every evening filled and filled and filled gain, until everybody would go reeling and staggering out in the starlit night, singing at the top of his lungs. When this glorious drinking, dancing, and carousing had come to its appointed end, the whole retinue, presented with scarves, departed gaily to its variously distant homes.

Three months later, however, all the celebrants from the bridegroom's side reassembled to ride in festive style to the bride's parents' home, and there—just as formerly at my paternal grandfather's place but now joined by guests of the maternal side—the parties, dancing, and singing were resumed for a last fling of another few days—after which all returned to the sober chores of their daily village ways.

My paternal grandfather had made his fortune as a young man, traveling to China and India for trade. From China he imported tea and silk brocades; from India, sugar, cotton, candles, glass, and various manufactured goods, in exchange for which he exported sheeps' wool, yak tails, deer antlers, and musk. In the years of my childhood my family owned two houses: one built for my father in Yendum, since his work as my uncle's secretary kept him there most of the time, and the other in Ophor, our main house, much larger, with many guest rooms for visitors. There were no inns, restaurants, or grocery shops in our tiny village, and since ours was by far its largest house, important government officers and high lamas would always stop with us when passing through. The village was a farming settlement, and our staple food was a barley flour dough, *pag*, supplemented by potatoes, turnips, peas, and onions, some of which were dried for the winter and stored in holes in the ground. In the house we grew flowers in pots, as well as spices such as chives. Meat, butter, cheese, and yogurt were also included in our diet, and on rare occasions, sweets were a special treat.

When I was born my grandfather was already in his seventies, no longer traveling but living most of the time in Ophor. However, he assumed little or no responsibility for the household, and my father, although in Yendum, acted as the actual head of our estate. My father retained a steward in Ophor who took care of our business affairs, but on all other important issues he would come to consult with grandfather; for the old man, in spite of his age, was still the most powerful and respected member of our family. Every day he and his wife, my grandmother, were asked what they wished to have served for dinner, and only when they were way would my mother or father be consulted.

I have many fond memories of the old gentleman. He was a genial, outgoing man who enjoyed telling us about his early travels and exploits in the business world, recalling just how much he had made on every deal—he could recount at length the whole story of each successful venture. Our storage house was filled with brocades, rugs, and curios that he had brought back from his numerous trips, and on the wall of his sleeping room there hung a large map of the world, brought from India. I did not know that it was an English map, for I could not tell the difference between Indian letters and English. My grandfather enjoyed pointing out the large areas of China, Europe, and America, but since he knew no English himself, he could not name many of the smaller countries. We children used to point to a place on the map and ask the name of the country, and he would sometimes have to admit to us later that he had had to make up his own names. In India he had visited Calcutta and Bombay, where he had seen many Europeans and people from other parts of the world, and when asked to tell us what Englishmen looked like, he would answer that they had big noses and blue eyes. He had bought a stereoscope in India and with this showed us photographs, not only of Europeans, but also of English houses and gardens, which we thought were very beautiful. It was thus that my grandfather introduced me to the wonders of the larger world.

My grandmother had never accompanied him on his journeys for the caravan routes were hazardous, particularly in winter, and there was always danger of bandits. Letters were rare, and so she had often been very lonely when her husband was away for months in India or China. To us children she was always very kind, playing little games with us and jogging us on her knees. Every day both she and my grandfather read the scriptures, usually something from some sutra that they had pledged themselves to read, and frequently they could be heard intoning *Om Mani Padme Hum*, six syllables of the great national prayer of Tibet, the Mani, invoking the blessing of the great Bodhisattva known to us as Chenresig. I recall that whenever my grandfather was not feeling well, he would invite some old friend to come by and read aloud to him his daily passage from the sutras; and if by chance he ever missed a day, the next he would read double his required amount. My grandmother, on the other hand, who was not so regular in her daily readings, was continually muttering the Mani.

Indeed, everybody in Tibet, from the highest noble to the humblest beggar, recited religiously the Mani every day. I can remember even a beautiful parrot in my father's house in Yendum, who would recite the prayer whenever he felt hungry. He was particularly fond of walnuts, and we youngsters would hold up nuts in our hands and tease him until he recited *Om Mani Padme Hum!* Tibetans believe that if even an animal repeats this prayer, though not knowing what it means, in his next life he will be born in some higher form. For in the lives of all Tibetans religion played a much greater part than it does in the modern secular world of the West. Every daily task and occupation was accompanied by prayer. Housewives, when shopping, carried rosaries on their wrists, and at every lull in the bargaining sent up prayers to the Bodhisattva. At home the maids prayed between sweeping floors and washing clothes, and travelers, whether on foot, horseback, or riding yaks, lightened their weary journeys by continuously reciting prayers. Characteristic, too, was the use throughout Tibet of the prayer wheel—a simple hand-held device consisting of a circular head loosely attached to a handle, with the words of the Mani inscribed on the head, and a roll of prayers tucked inside. The wheel, when revolved by a little swinging motion of the wrist, would set the prayer in rotation, and the user would gain spiritual benefit as it whirled just as though he were praying. The humming of those little prayer wheels could be heard everywhere in Tibet though mainly it was the older folks who used them. At the temples there were huge examples to which people could give a few quick spins as they passed.

Perhaps the role of Christianity in medieval Europe might be suggested for comparison with that of Buddhism in Tibet right up to 1959, and even today that religion plays an important role in the lives of most Tibetan refugees, wherever they may be. As was the case in Europe, the Tibetan people knew mainly one religion, within which there had developed a number of differing sects, for every living religion is forever changing in its external forms in response to historical and environmental determinants. In contrast to the medieval Christian situation, however, there was never in the Buddhist world any sense of essential conflict or antagonism between sects; for, as a growing plant continually changes yet remains ever the same, so among our sects has there been generally recognized a fundamental accord in basic doctrine.

Buddhism was introduced into Tibet in the seventh century A.D., and in the course of succeeding centuries various methods were developed for reaching the one goal known as Liberation. These methods were popular, mystical, and esoteric, the last being based mainly on the study of a recondite body of teaching known as Tantras. Each of these manners of interpreting the Buddhist Doctrine, whether new or old, was based on words recorded of the Lord Buddha himself. The only aim in every case was to arrive at a deeper understanding of the original teaching, which had been carried intact to Tibet, and has been preserved in a pure form in our tradition to the present day. The disputes of the different sects, consequently, almost never involved essential doctrine. They were rather about methods, politics, or other such secondary topics. Moreover, no one was ever required or forced to accept the Buddhist faith. Buddhism has always been an essentially peaceful religion. Hence Tibetan Buddhists have never sought either to make converts or to constrain all believers to a single authorized dogma. Harmony in diversity has always been a feature of the history of religion in Tibet.

I mention all this to explain how it was that, although my grandparents and parents had quite different attitudes toward religion, there was never any discord between them or disagreement in the matter of belief. My grandparents had been initiated, at one time or another, into all four of the main Buddhist sects of Tibet, the *Nyingmapa, Kagyudpa, Sakyapa,* and *Gelugpa,* and had found in them no real conflict. As they often told us, every sect belonged to the one Doctrine. They illustrated this point for us with a parable that we could readily understand, saying: "Now what difference does it make if you cut a piece from the middle of a cake or take a slice from the side? Your piece of cake will always have the same sweet taste and so it is with the Doctrine."

My mother and father, on the other hand, unlike my father's parents, belonged only to the orthodox Gelugpa "Yellow Hat" sect, and it would never have occurred to them to accept initiation from any other. Yet they respected all, and had friends from all. Our household shrine room was a large, rectangular, two-pillared chamber, containing books and images from all four lines of our Tibetan Buddhist tradition. The altar, set against a long wall opposite the window, was made up of three sections and elaborately carved and painted. The center—the altar proper—supported a hundred silver offering bowls and numerous other ritual objects. These were all arranged beneath holy images, some of which were very old and had come from India and Nepal. There were all kinds of images of Buddhas and Bodhisattvas there: Chenresig, our national patron Bodhisattva; Padmasambhava, the great Indian saint who in the eighth century came to Tibet and founded the Nyingmapa "Red Hat" sect, the oldest of our native four; Tsongkhapa, founder of the Gelugpa; many other saints including Milarepa, the celebrated Tibetan poet and anchorite. Most of the fixtures were of gilded bronze, but the oldest were of a

lustrous, darker hue. Many were clothed in embroidered robes or brocade, and when the butter lamps were lit these garments glistened like
gold.

On either side of this main altar there were bookshelves to the ceiling,
and beneath these, cabinets with doors decorated in a Chinese style. The
bookshelves were supported by pillars with gilded carved dragons coiled
around them and laid out on the shelves was a full set of the Narthang
Edition of the Kanjur, the whole teaching of the Lord Buddha, 108
volumes. The paper for our edition of the Kajur had been ordered by my
father in Bhutan, where he felt the best paper was made, and the printing
was in black ink, with each title page illuminated in gold. The unbound
pages were kept—as in India—packed between stout wooden boards,
wrapped carefully in expensive cloths. And since the volumes were all
rather heavy, they were laid flat along the shelves.

Our chapel was the real center of our household, and our most solemn
and important occasions were celebrated there—New Year festivals,
initiations, and marriages, for example. Our resident chaplain, a very old
monk named Thondup Chophel, lived in the chapel itself. His principal
duty was to keep the sanctuary spotless, all the images dusted, polished,
and the butter lamps continually burning. He was from a neighboring
monastery and had been assigned to our house for a period of three years
by the college of the monastery. However, when those three expired, my
father petitioned the college to allow him to remain three more, and in the
end he remained with us for life. My family had a close relationship with
the monastery as regular patrons, giving large annual donations and
whatever additional help might be needed. In turn, when any one of us
required religious advice, or if there were sickness or death in the family,
the monastery sent its monks to conduct the appropriate services and
prayers.

Every day our chaplain swept the chapel with a yak-tail broom, and
with felt cloths kept polished its floor of long wooden planks. Then he
would fill all the silver bowls before the images with fresh water,
following a prescribed order. He would fill first the first cup to the brim,
then dip from this a drop into each of the others; after that, he set about
filling them all. We, too, when making water offerings, were never

allowed to leave a single empty cup before any image, for that, as we were taught to believe, would bring us poverty in our next life.

While attending to all his duties in our chapel, Thondup Chophel would show the utmost consideration to the images on the altar, making, as he moved about, all the proper ceremonial gestures of reverence and purification. Then, at the end, he would put powdered incense in the incense pots to purify the air; having next lighted a few incense sticks, he would prostrate himself before the altar while they burned and recite his prayers, counting with the aid of a long Indian rosary of 111 red-brown beads. Such a rosary, usually worn around the wrist, has as its sole purpose the counting out of prayers; and every day, thus counting, Thondup Chophel would chalk up ten thousand recitations of the Mani for the benefit of all sentient beings. We believe that prayers should be offered without pride, and that happiness comes when the established number has been recited. We say, furthermore, that there is reason for rejoicing in the accumulation of merit. Rejoicing over meritorious acts is an important part of Buddhist practice, since it moves one to continue in the performance of meritorious acts, whereas rejoicing over evil deeds leads only to more evil doing. If a person has no time for the performance of meritorious acts and so cannot gain religious merit for himself, he may nevertheless be saved if he admires sincerely and praises those who conscientiously perform religious works. However, if one envies such a person for his acquisition of merits, one only sins and does oneself much harm.

On the eighth and fifteenth days of each month Thondup Chophel offered up special prayers. On these days of the quarter- and full moon, it was believed, the greatest benefits were obtained. And on the days each year of the Buddha's birth, enlightenment, and final passing, we were taught to offer one hundred butter lamps upon our family chapel altar.

The kitchen of our house was on the same floor as the chapel, and it, too, was a large two-pillared room. On one of its pillars hung two wooden *dungmos* (mixing vessels) for the preparation of buttered tea. There were two kitchen fireplaces, one small, the other large, both insulated by stone slabs laid against the wall. We used the larger only on holidays, when there were many guests. For fuel we used dried cow and yak dung as well as wood, all of which, fortunately, was plentiful in our district. And every evening before going to bed, our old kitchenmaid laid the fire and filled the tea kettles with water so that in the morning she would have only to light the flame.

When father was at home, my mother would get up early and fetch him a cup of hot water, for he had a theory that hot water on an empty stomach in the morning was healthy. A little after that, we children could go to our parents' room for our morning cup of tea. The first cup, however, had always to be offered at the altar, when my father, placing our offerings there, would recite a little prayer. Sometimes, instead of tea, we had turnip soup with milk or meat. But in any case, no one was ever allowed to take even a sip before the morning devotion had been completed.

After our morning meal the kitchenmaid would go out into the courtyard to milk the cows brought in by our herders. Occasionally mother helped with this, especially when father was away. They would always put aside a small portion of the milk to be offered in the shrine room, after which our two cats would be given theirs, along with turnip soup or sometimes a bit of porridge in their own special little bowl in the kitchen corner. The kitchenmaid would then begin to make butter in the churn. Thumping the dasher briskly up and down, she would sing out cheerfully the holy syllables *Om Mani Padme Hum* in a voice so loud that the sound seemed almost to shake the walls. When the butter had formed she would pass out pieces to us children, which we then used to mold little barley flour dumplings eaten later with our tea.

The courtyard where the cows were milked was partly covered to protect them in the winter. When summer came they grazed in the meadows round about, together with the cattle of our neighbors; at nightfall they were driven home by two herders. The families of the village took turns providing these men, and we children took delight in going out with them to the pastures. Our own herder, when I was very small, carried me on his shoulders, and that was one of my greatest pleasures. Occasionally in the pastures we collected yellow mushrooms, stuffed the caps with butter and *tsampa*—barley flour—and then fried them over a fire. Becoming drowsy after such a feast, we would fall asleep beneath a big umbrella opened for us by the herder.

My family owned some four hundred horned yaks, divided into four herds and given over to the care of nomads, who were paid in wheat and barley and had the right to keep, besides, a certain percentage of the yak butter. (Actually, the Tibetan word *yak* refers only to the male, the cow being known as a *dri.*) If any of the animals were killed by wild beasts, the herdsmen had to bring us their horns, which was our proof and protection against stealing.

My parents in the summertime occasionally went to inspect the pastures, living there for a season in tents, and we children were always taken on these most thrilling excursions. My mother would ride with my little brother sitting in front of her; and my father would ride with me, the elder, on his shoulders. (My parents had, altogether, three sons and three daughters; I was the eldest child. The second, my first brother, died when he was seven. The others were born only after I left home.) When we entered the pasturelands and the old nomads came to welcome us with tea and their thick yogurt, we would dismount and, sitting on down, eat together on the grass. My father wore a little amulet box, a *gahu*, containing an image of the Lord Buddha, and the nomads would quickly prepare a little altar of bricks, and cut turf on which this amulet could be set. The same ritual would be followed as at home, with offerings of tea, milk, and yogurt placed before the image on the altar. Only after that would we begin our meal.

In the morning following our first night in the tents, my father would rise early and go out and check on his cattle, referring to a list that the had brought along, carefully counting the herd. The family mark, in the form of a Tibetan letter, was burnt on each yak horn as a brand. Having checked his cattle, my father would thank the nomads with a big meal and plenty of chang, they in turn treating us to their butter and cheese. The yaks were raised for their milk, butter, cheese, and yogurt; they were never slaughtered. (Our meats were all bought from the butcher.) Yak hair made a wonderful material for the felt tents of the nomads, and was woven by the women in winter into a sort of heavy sackcloth. But we had even more sheep than yaks and produced an especially fine wool.

In sowing and harvesting seasons my father hired men to work our fields, and we youngsters would play on the edge of the plots while the ploughing was going on. Two yaks would be hitched to the wooden plough and guided by the ploughman as it turned the earth. At noon, when the sun was already hot even in early spring, I recall how the ploughman would stop, pull off his shirt, walk over to where his beer was cooling in an earthen pot covered with blankets, take a long drink, and wipe his lips with his hand. At harvest time the women came out to the fields too, and would sing their happy songs while they cut the hay or thrashed the barley with long sticks.

During the summers my father could spend his holidays with us more often than in winter, since his work in Yendum was then less pressing. He was particularly fond of playing dice, and when he could get four neighbors together they would frequently play all day. One such crony was a witty old fellow who when winning kept cracking jokes, but fell absolutely silent the minute he began to lose. When he had won he would stand up, shout, and proclaim his luck to the world; but when he lost, he would have to cheer himself with one beer after another. We children adored his antics, but my mother disliked having us around him, watching the men gambling and taking snuff, so she would shoo us out, and we had to find then some other pastime in the fresh air.

2.

I Am Taken
to My Labrang

Now when the four visitors who had so mysteriously bowed to me when presenting their gifts rode away on their four trotting mounts and disappeared into the hills, my father took me by the hand.

"Norbu," he said, "my son, you are now a recognized tulku. To all our people and all the monks in Dayab the name of the Lama Khyongla [pronounced Chungla] is a precious gem in the crown of the Buddhist faith, and you are his reincarnation. Soon you must study to improve your mind, so that when you grow up you will be able to act for the benefit of the people of Dayab. May you learn to teach the words of the Lord Buddha as your predecessors did! If you can accomplish this, you will fulfill the most ardent wishes of your parents."

Clutching the smooth white porcelain bird that had been given me, I looked up, bewildered, into my father's face. I knew that something very strange had happened to me, but I could not understand his words; and in fact, it was not until 1956, when I was thirty-three years old, that I finally learned the full story behind the visit of those monks, and the background of the turn that my life had taken.

At that time, when I had returned from Lhasa to my labrang to check on its administration and to pay what proved to be my last visit to my parents, I chanced upon a box containing a packet of old documents and letters. I began to read these and as I went on, fascinated, pieced together gradually the whole story of my selection as the tenth incarnate Khyongla. I had already heard parts of this story, of course, at various times and in various places during the intervening years, but had never understood fully the reasons for my selection.

The first Khyongla was born in 1510 in a district then known as Khyong Yul (pronounced *Chung Yul*), which was one of three small rural areas that in the seventeenth century combined to form the one administrative district known as Dayab. His parents had named him Jigme, which is a word meaning the "Fearless One." At the age of twenty he went to Central Tibet, where he remained for some twenty years, studying principally at Rato Monastery, but also at Drepung. Then he entered Gyudto, which is one of the most important Tantric monasteries in Lhasa, and there so distinguished himself in study that he received many initiations from such famous monks as Gedun Gyatso, the Second Dalai Lama. Returning home to Kham, he retired to a hermitage where he remained in seclusion for years, until gradually the outside world became aware of him there, and his reputation both for sanctity and for learning spread throughout the district.

Over the years this sixteenth-century Khyongla acquired many disciples, who finally persuaded him to give up his long seclusion and preach the Holy Doctrine to the world—which he then began to do. At first his eloquence in expounding the Word of the Lord Buddha as interpreted in both the Sutras and the Tantras attracted only monks from the nearby monasteries. Presently, however, layfolk from all walks of life began gathering to hear him, and from that time on to the end of his career he taught freely, turning no one ever away. His fame spread far beyond the little area of Khyong Yul. People came from the remotest parts of the Kham to listen and to ask advice; and so it was that he became known as the Lama Khyongla, the lama of Khyong Yul—only those who knew him intimately ever calling him thereafter by his given name. He lived to the age of seventy-eight, and when he had passed away he was mourned through all that part of the Kham that was later to become known as Dayab.

Some time after his passing, that first Khyongla's disciples began the search for his reincarnation, and the child whom they discovered as the Second Khyongla grew up to become no less illustrious than the First, both in saintliness and in learning. He founded the Katog Gonpa Monastery, and built also the labrang in which I was (centuries later) to be raised. The word *labrang*, meaning "lama's residence," refers not only to the residence of an incarnation or abbot and the many members of his staff, but also to the whole surrounding property, of fields, pasturelands, and even, occasionally, villages. Some labrangs are attached to monasteries, in which cases the resident lama is given absolute authority over both and assumes the responsibility for supporting both. My labrang, however, was completely separate from the local monastery to which I also belonged; and although I was not the latter's abbot, I was nevertheless its most honored member, often consulted for advice. We had a good relationship of cooperation.

The Ninth Khyongla, my immediate predecessor, was born in a village only two days' journey from my family home in Ophor. He was distinguished for his high scholarship and eloquence in the teaching of Buddhist doctrine. In accord with custom, he was sent when very young to study in Central Tibet, but he remained there only three years, and so did not receive there his *geshe* — Doctor of Divinity—degree. Instead, he returned to the Kham, and in the Dugugon Monastery in Chamdo district continued his studies under one of the most learned scholars in Eastern Tibet, the distinguished Gyara Rinpoche. The middle years of his life the Ninth Khyongla devoted to teaching and in his later years, assuming new responsibilities, he became the supreme abbot of all the monasteries in Dabay, which placed him in absolute charge of no less than fifty institutions. After his passing his administrator held gift ceremonies for all the monks in the district, without regard to rank, asking all to pray for the fulfillment of the departed lama's wish that his reincarnation should soon be discovered. The administrator asked particularly that Dayab Rinpoche, one of Khyongla's chief disciples, should compose a prayer-poem to assist the search; this poem, when published, was distributed to all the monks. Again a gift ceremony was held, and the administrator then wrote to many of the most important lamas in Central Tibet—especially His Holiness, the Thirteenth Dalai Lama—again asking all to pray that the new incarnation might soon be found.

Two years later the oracles of both Rato and Sangphu monasteries were consulted for advice, and each replied that a search should be made to the west of the Ninth Khyongla's labrang. Accordingly, news was sought of boys of unusual character in that area, and particularly of those whose births had been attended by unusual circumstances. Three likely candidates were located. One was from the richest, most aristocratic family in Dayab. The second was a nephew of the administrator himself. I was the third. And it was finally I who was chosen.

My candidacy became known in the following manner. It was learned that during the time my mother was carrying me she had once dreamed that the protective deities were pouring water on her head, and this had been interpreted by those she then consulted as meaning that all defilements were being removed from her child, even before its birth. In another dream she appeared to be entering a temple during her final month of pregnancy. She was very heavy and stumbled, and would have fallen had not a protective deity caught her and helped her to stand. This dream at the time was interpreted to mean that the child in her womb was an incarnation, kept safe from harm by his protective deity. In a third dream she saw the moon and sun come together, and this was interpreted to mean that her child would be exceptionally intelligent. My mother told several friends of these dreams; and then, while she was giving birth, a rainbow appeared over our home. People saw one end of it actually touch the house, which was a very lucky sign. Word eventually reached the Khongla Labrang that a woman in Ophor had borne a child thought to be an incarnation, and the monks there became interested; for when the Ninth Kyongla had been cremated the smoke of his pyre had drifted westward, which meant that the next incarnation would be found in that direction. A messenger was sent to obtain more information, and he wrote down the names of my parents, my own name, and various facts about our family. I was then about two years old.

Several other boys besides the two already mentioned were being considered at that time, and when all the information regarding their qualifications had been gathered, the oracle at Rato Monastery was once again consulted. By that time I was about three. The oracle went into his trance, during which letters were placed before him describing each of the child candidates. He read them all and then declared in a loud voice:

"The son of Tenzin Lhamo, who was born in the Water Pig Year, is the reincarnation of Khyongla."

The oracle went on to say, however, that before the final selection could be made the Dalai Lama should be consulted. When His Holiness was informed of all the relevant details, he confirmed the oracle's choice.

For a full year following the visit of the three monks to our home I continued to lead a child's life and seldom thought about what had happened. My whole world consisted of our house, the neighboring pasturelands, the little monastery on the hill, and the nomad camp in the uplands. I knew in a vague but effective way that my life was destined to be different from those of other children, and that this had something to do with religion. Also I knew that I was soon to be taken away; but I did not grasp what this really meant.

One day I went into our shrine room, and Thondup Chophel playfully held up to me his closed fist. "What am I holding?" he asked; and since he often gave me sweets, I said, "Candy." He asked me what the color was, red or white. "It's red," I said. And opening his hand, he exclaimed jokingly, "Norbu, you are right. It seems you really *are* an incarnation!" Next time I saw him he did the same thing, and I again guessed red. But he opened an empty fist and, laughing, teased, "Now I am not so sure you are an incarnation." Another day he told me that if I was a real incarnation I should soon have to begin meditating. "Please," I begged, "tell me how." He sat down in the lotus posture showing me how to cross my legs; placed his hands in the Buddha position, and gazed at the end of his nose. I sat down beside him, trying to imitate his gestures, and when I had succeeded in pulling my feet up to my thighs, he laughed in his good-natured way and passed me a handful of red candies. When I later told my friends about this, they thought it a clever way to get sweets, and so the next day came in with me. We all sat down solemnly, assuming the lotus posture, then looked expectantly at the old monk. "Other people," he said "meditate to attain Buddhahood, but you boys are imitating us only to win sweets." And he chased us out.

I was having a wonderful childhood, but the time was fast approaching when the monks would arrive to take me away to the labrang that would thereafter become my home. The year, in fact, passed very quickly. There were signs already of spring, and soon it would be summer. My sixth birthday would come July 4, and although we did not celebrate birthdays, the event that year had special meaning.

The administrator of the labrang and the treasurer of Katog Gonpa Monastery had consulted an astrologer to ascertain the most auspicious day on which to take me away. The astrologer had chosen my birthday; and so it was that immediately after sunrise on the day that I became six years old, the treasurers of both the monastery and the labrang arrived on horseback at our home.

They presented me with a new silk garment in which the administrator of the labrang, a man named Dongye, dressed me. I was greatly pleased with my new appearance. The two then conducted me into our chapel, and I was asked to sit down on some cushions that had been specially placed there for me. The old chaplain, my parents, and my grandparents were present, together with many of our neighbors who had come voluntarily to present me with scarves. The little ceremony finished, we all took a short rest and then with due form set out on horseback for the labrang that was to be my new home—the two monks, my father, mother, and one man from each of the village families close to us, all in festive attire. It was the first time I had ever had to ride a horse alone, but there was a wooden frame around the brocade-covered saddle to which I was able to hold. There was also a man to lead the horse, which was decorated beautifully with tassels, and I was so pleased that I was not at all afraid.

As this procession moved out through our gate we saw that the roofs of all the village houses had been decorated with flags. Juniper boughs were being burned in the incense chimneys above the main entrance doors, and the entire population of Ophor was gathered in front of our portal. My two favorite playmates were standing near, and when I begged to take them along my parents explained that they could not come with me now, but would be allowed to visit me later. The boys cried a little, but understood in the end that they had to stay at home. And off we all rode.

After a number of hours we arrived in a pleasant valley where a tent had been erected by representatives of the labrang, who were all waiting there to receive us. Everyone dismounted, and I was lifted from my horse. Within the tent a kind of throne of cut turf had been set for me, covered with a rug and topped with a cushion of red brocade. I was placed on this throne while my parents and the representatives of our village settled down on floor cushions to either side. I was then offered *droma*—a sweet-tasting red herb boiled in water with melted butter and sugar, which it was

customary to present to dignitaries on auspicious occasions. This was
served to me in a little cup set upon a silver saucer. My father told me to
toss some bits of the herb into the air. I did so, not knowing why, but
feeling that it was a delightful game. I later learned that when droma was
served on auspicious occasions, the custom of tossing a few bits into the
air was intended as an offering to the Buddhist "Three Jewels": the
Buddha, the Doctrine, and the Order. We drank tea, after which Dongye
prostrated himself before me and presented a white scarf. My father,
standing beside me, whispered to me to touch my forehead to the
forehead of an old dignified monk who had approached, whereupon we
all left the tent and proceeded to the labrang. On the way we were greeted,
joined, and welcomed by representatives of every family in Gonsar—the
village near the monastery—as well as by a company of monks from the
labrang itself, our caravan by now remarkably grown in size.

I saw my labrang for the first time when Dongye pointed it out
ahead—a large white building with red turrets, set in a lovely green valley
that seemed to me more beautiful even than my own home. All the
villagers were assembled. All the houses were decorated with colorful
new prayer flags, while above the main gate of the labrang itself there
were four monks standing, blowing flutes and trumpets such as I had
never heard before. I frowned, thinking the instruments much too loud.
We passed beneath the monks, on through the gate, and dismounted in
the courtyard. In the center of the courtyard on the packed earth, eight
beautiful emblems were displayed: a Golden Fish, Umbrella, Conch Shell,
Lucky Diagram, Victory Banner, Vase, Lotus, and Wheel.

I was first taken up to my room on the top story of the building.
Everything there had been prepared for me, the whole place newly
decorated with soft rugs on the floor, white curtains with blue trimmings
at the windows, embroidered cushions scattered about, and a silken
canopy suspended from the ceiling. Beautiful old thangkas (religious
paintings on cloth) in wonderful colors hung around the white walls, and
from the center pillar of the room there were fluttering silken banners of
white, red, yellow, and blue.

After I had had a little rest, Dongye—who was now, clearly, my chief
guardian—led me down to the assembly hall on the floor below, where

I was seated on an ancient wooden throne that my predecessors had used for their public teaching. Many people, mostly from Gonsar, were there waiting, together with members of my own retinue from Ophor. Dongye then formally presented to me three traditional gifts: an image of the Lord Buddha, a book, and a *chorten* (a little reliquary shrine), symbolic respectively of the body of Buddha, the speech of Buddha, and the mind of Buddha. The same ceremony was then repeated by a leader of Gonsar in the name of all the villagers, who lined up and came before me. One by one they prostrated themselves and presented gifts. They had come to receive my blessing. I, however, did not know how to render this until my father, again standing next to my throne, whispered that I should touch the head of each with my hand as he passed by. When officials of the monastery or other important personages approached, my father advised me to touch my forehead to theirs, in sign of special respect. When all these welcoming ceremonies had been auspiciously completed, Dongye took me back to my room upstairs, where a festive banquet waited. People who had come from Gonsar for the ceremony stayed on late into the afternoon and returned to their homes for the night, but all those from Ophor who had accompanied me on my journey remained as guests of the labrang for three days.

The first night I felt very strange and asked my parents to sleep in my room, but I was told that they had a room downstairs and I would not be able to join them. However, two young attendants, one about seventeen, the other twenty-one or so, were introduced to me as those who would stay to keep me company. They were very kind and friendly, and did everything they could to make me feel at home.

When suddenly it grew dark, the butter lamps were lighted. Most of the labrang was lit by butter lamps and oil lamps. In my own room that night there were lighted also white candles from India. These, in addition to the butter lamps, illuminated my private shrine, where the bronze images of the Buddhas and gods gleamed. Then I went to bed, and after all the excitement of that long birthday had no trouble sleeping.

Early next morning some servants came in to tidy up. They first refilled the offering cups, then brought us our morning tea. Dongye appeared and, sitting beside me, told me something of his life story and something, also, of my own immediate predecessor.

It seems that when the Ninth Khyongla passed away, a dispute soon arose between his family and the administrator of the labrang concerning the disposition of certain properties. It took a long time to reach a settlement, and since the legal costs were high, the labrang was left in financial straits. Furthermore, in the course of the wrangle, the administrator had made enemies. One evening when he had ridden out to the nomads' pastureland to check on the cattle herd, he was attacked and slain while sleeping in his tent. The unknown assailant escaped, firing his gun as he galloped off, and the nomads who then hurried to the tent along with the administrator's servant found him dead with a sword thrust through his heart. The killer was never apprehended: out of fear, perhaps, no one dared to betray him. But the labrang kept the fateful tent with a large slash in it from the sword blade. And years later, neatly mended, this tent was used for my first trip to Lhasa.

According to Dongye's story, told to me that first morning, it was because of the sudden death of the Ninth Khyongla's administrator that Dongye had been brought to the labrang. He had been selected as the new administrator by a committee headed by the abbot of Katog Gonpa Monastery, by members of both that monastery and the labrang, and representatives from the village. Known for his sterling character as well as ability in practical matters, Dongye had administered the affairs of the labrang with as much energy as devotion, gradually returning it to its former state of economic well-being; his whole life was now dedicated to this task.

On the final day of the Ophor villagers' festive stay in Gonsar, they and my parents began preparing for their return home. When I saw that my parents were getting ready to depart, misery overwhelmed me and I begged them to take me along. They kindly promised to remain a little longer, until I became accustomed to life in the labrang. After that I watched them carefully, and whenever I noticed any sign that they might again be preparing to leave, I would again be overcome and cling to their clothing, begging them, please, to take me with them back home! I did not want to be left with all these grown-up strangers. For I already greatly missed my playmates, and now to part with my parents as well was more than I could bear.

Things went on that way for two weeks, but then the day inevitably came. My father and mother, gently but firmly, explained to me that the labrang was now my only home: it belonged to me, and I must obey Dongye, who was next below me in rank. Dongye was a highly respected man, they said, greatly experienced in administration, liked by everybody in the village, kind, friendly, and gentle, especially to children and to the poor, whom he always helped. Many people came to ask his advice, and it was he whom I should trust, they told me as they left.

Then to my surprise, only a very few days after my father and mother had departed, two of my favorite playmates arrived from Ophor to study in the labrang. That made me marvelously happy. The boys had been invited by the labrang, and were to pay no fees for either study or board. Dongye had arranged all that, and was doing everything he could to make my residence under his charge as pleasant as possible. In a month my parents returned as promised, and when I then knew that I could look forward certainly to my mother's visits once a fortnight, and to my father's only a little less often, I felt happy and content. Having my two little friends with me and becoming used to the monks as well, I did not miss Ophor so much.

3.

The Start of My Education

Time passed; soon I was eight, and the day had come for my education to begin. My teacher was to be Geshe Tsering Choephel, who had studied for twenty years in the Sera Monastery in Lhasa.

On a suitable day, therefore, two messengers were sent to accompany the geshe to the labrang. His arrival was attended by all, and while he was being received at the door, I watched apprehensively from my window above, for I had been warned that he would beat me if I didn't study. But when Dongye appeared with Geshe Tsering Choephel, I was suddenly very happy. The geshe's face was glowing and he seemed to me a man of great kindness. From that moment I knew that he would never beat me, and I was no longer afraid.

My new teacher presented me with a scarf and with a book about Tsongkhapa, the founder of the Gelugpa sect, then spoke to me gently. "Khyongla, you are not to be merely my pupil. I was myself a pupil of your predecessor, so please do not rise—remain seated on your cushion!"

I was puzzled and looked to Dongye for assurance. He motioned me to do as my teacher wished. But just the same, when the geshe left, I rose and walked behind him till he reached the door.

Three days later, I put on leather sandals and proceeded to my teacher's room for my first lesson. The day had been especially chosen by Dongye and was, again, my birthday, the fourth day of the sixth month of the year 1931. At the entrance of my teacher's room I respectfully removed my shoes, prostrated myself three times before him, and offered him four gifts; an image, a book, a chorten, and a conch shell. He accepted these with evident pleasure and asked me to blow the conch, which I did, for the sound thus produced is interpreted as signifying the expansion of unbounded religious vision. And it was thus that my schooling began.

My teacher sat on his cushion, and when I had taken my place on a lower one he handed me a piece of paper on which all the characters of our alphabet were inscribed. The first sign that I was taught to read was *lao*, a compound form meaning "easy." To commence with that was supposed to be auspicious for the beginner's progress. I was taught to recognize its elements and required to pronounce each of these three times. I was not yet to be taught writing; only recognition and pronunciation. The lesson was brief, and when it was over my teacher gave Dongye his impression of his pupil. "I am happy to say that Khyongla appears to be intelligent," he said. "He is quick to grasp and eager to learn." I returned to my room, where I spent the rest of the day practicing pronunciation. I was excited about my new studies and worked very hard.

At my second lesson, next morning, I was asked to repeat what I had learned, and immediately did so. The difficulty, however, lay in recognizing the elements of the signs, individually and out of sequence. With a wooden pointer my teacher outlined the elements of the letters on the cover of a book, and this helped me to see which part of each represented the consonant, and which the vowel. When that more difficult lesson was over I again returned to my room to study, but with the help now of a pointer. This elementary exercise, with a constant sounding of the syllables, was continued for the next three days.

The following lessons were still more difficult, for they dealt with the compound letters. I now had to devote two hours to my lessons every morning and two in the afternoon, with increasing periods of study in my room. What had begun as a game became work, and I soon lost my enthusiasm for learning, often having to be persuaded to go on. Indeed, sometimes my teacher even slapped me, for I had failed to study at all.

For my slate I was given a wooden tablet, known as a *jangshing*, along with a small bag of chalk dust, with which to dust its surface. Later on I was taught to write with a fine bamboo pen and a brown ink made from wheat fried until burnt and then mixed with water. A deep groove, about an inch long, had to be cut into one end of the bamboo, through which the brown ink easily flowed. I was to write my letters first in the chalk on the tablet, good and large, and then smaller, trying to keep each sign clean and well-formed. Only after that task had been mastered was I given paper and a bamboo pen with which to write in ink the letters I had practiced on the tablet. I was to write them a line at a time, folding the paper each time into a narrow strip to keep the line perfectly straight. When I was not using my pen, I felt very sophisticated carrying it, as Dongye carried his, behind my ear.

I had gradually come to feel at home in the labrang, making friends not only with the monks but also with members of the forty or so neighboring village families, most of whom were farmers. My two little friends from Ophor and our preceptor's two young nephews were of about the same age as myself, and when my classes ended we would play together for hours, caring nothing for anything else. I could also invite children from outside the labrang to visit me in my room, or to join us in the courtyard, playing our games out there.

On one occasion, one of my friends somehow got hold of a bow and arrow which he happily displayed to us, demonstrating his skill; we all gathered around, curious, each waiting his turn to shoot. It chanced that his first target was a bird, and the first arrow felled it. We all shouted excitedly and my teacher, hearing the noise, ran out to see what we were doing. He plucked the arrow from the dying bird and recited some hymns in its ear, calling on the name of the Lord Buddha. We all stood silent and astonished, for we had never thought that the bird would die. We were interested simply in sport, and had failed to foresee the result. Geshe Tsering Choephel roundly reproached my friend, told him to return the bow and arrow, and warned us all against playing such games. Life, he said, should be protected, and especially (as he looked at me) by an incarnation. We all must, he said, respect the laws of religion. I hung my head in shame.

I frequently heard talk of a certain cave not far away, where the labrang had once been located. It had been burnt and destroyed by the Chinese troops of Chao Erh-Peng, when they invaded the Kham in 1910, on their way to lay siege to Lhasa. I had been told that the Thirteenth Dalai Lama had escaped at that time to India, taking refuge there until we had regained independence in 1912 and he was able to return. The cave was situated on the highest point of a steep cliff, far above a river. Six of us one day decided to visit that place, and though we found the cave empty and desolate, there were a few clay images scattered about in the rubble. I carried one of these back with me to the labrang, and when we found my teacher talking with Dongye, I felt both happy and proud as I presented him with the image. I thought he would be pleased and praise me, but on seeing it, he asked excitedly where we had found it. When we told him, a peculiar expression came over Dongye's face. Dongye frowned sternly at my friends and warned them never again to take me to that place because of the risk involved. Both he and my teacher got up and went out to my teacher's room, and I, afraid of their anger but wanting to know what to expect, very softly followed and listened cautiously at the door. I heard Dongye say, "Please tell Khyongla not to go to such dangerous places." I was so relieved that they were not angry, as well as impressed with a sense of responsibility for my own important life, that I returned quickly to my room and set to work diligently to practice writing Tibetan letters.

In those years my parents would come at least once a month to the labrang to check on my progress. And they would always, on those occasions, remind me to show respect to my teacher, from whom I was learning not only reading and writing, but also manners, good conduct, and loving kindness to all living beings. Their visits were always exciting events. They brought presents—shoes, new clothes, honey from a cousin's hives—and I especially remember one pair of new shoes that felt so good that I jumped and hopped all around the labrang, showing them off. My lessons were shortened during those visits so that we might spend time together. At the labrang I did not have many toys. On one occasion my father made a top for me from a chopstick and a walnut, to be spun with a piece of string, and whenever he came we played with this. My brother, Palden, sometimes came along too, and his visits were always wonderful; but then one day, when I was about nine, my parents arrived to tell me very sadly that Palden had died of smallpox. We all wept together and for a long time after that I was greatly upset. I long cherished the hope that my parents would invite me to visit them, but they never did, and it was not until I was thirteen that I ever saw my home again.

Occasionally, when I became tired of trying to learn to read, Geshe

Tsering Choephel would tell me stories of famous lamas of the past. The one that he liked best to tell, and which I liked best to hear, was of Milarepa. Despite the hardships of his rough life and the extremely difficult tasks that his teacher, Marpa, repeatedly imposed on him (such as repeatedly building a nine-story house of stone), he had remained steadfast in obedience and in reverence for his teacher. In later life, when he had become a very great teacher himself, he opened every lecture with praise and words of thanks to Marpa, the man who had led him in such a harsh way to the Path of Enlightenment. I deeply admired Milarepa for all this but could never imagine myself as so perseverant.

Dongye liked to read the ancient epics of Tibet to me—the *Thé Dung*, as we call them—and occasionally I would invite my friends, who would sit with me, listening for hours. The epic of our national hero, Gesar, was our favorite. There were many manuscripts about him in our library, and one day we took one of these with us up the juniper hill to the hermitage. There, one after another, we began to mimic Dongye's manner of reading. There were many poems in this work, and one of the boys, Phuntsog, liked these the best. I however preferred the story parts and furthermore wanted to read the whole manuscript. But Phuntsog wanted to read too, and began to tug at the book I was holding. I tried to keep my hold, and in our struggle some of the pages got torn, others were destroyed, and most of the manuscript fell in disorder on the ground. Appalled by what we had done, we tried to gather up and arrange the pages correctly, but found that we could not do so. When we realized that the damage was irreparable, Phuntsog urged me to assume the blame, since Dongye was sure to be less angry with me than with him. Later on that day, I shamefacedly confessed, but Dongye's only reprimand was that I should henceforth be more careful and never do such a thing again.

My friends were allowed in Dongye's room only when they came in with me. One day we entered when he was out and began to play at a coin-tossing game. One coin fell against a very precious cup and knocked it to the ground where it shattered. Another time, when we were again in there alone, we began to push each other about, and Phuntsog knocked over the teapot. It broke, spilling tea over the floor. We escaped, and Dongye later reprimanded me very sternly, saying, "If you continue to engage in such nonsense, people will think you are not an incarnation." I was angered, and retorted, "I never said I was an incarnation, and I did not ask to be brought here. I have a nice home of my own and can stay there with my parents!" Dongye waited a moment, then said quietly, "Don't get angry!" and when I settled down, told me that whereas he and my teacher might criticize me to my face, others, though saying nice things, might be nasty behind my back. Then he laughed and said that even if I ran away the members of the labrang would come and bring me back—which ended that discussion. There was never an angry word again between Dongye and myself. I had gained a new sense of the inescapable nature and coerciveness of my high estate.

During the summer holidays, my friends and I would go off with the monks to a nomads' camp, only an hour's horseback ride away, to spend about three weeks. Our companions put up the tents—one for themselves and Dongye, another for my teacher, and a third for me, my friends, and a small dog that I always brought along (a Lhasa Apso named Kunga, meaning "well-liked"). Often at night it would rain, and we would lie in our cushion-beds listening to the drumming of the raindrops on the taut cotton of the tentcloth. The nomad settlement was in the midst of excellent pastures sprinkled with flowers that we liked to pick and fashion into wreaths. I brought a whole hat that I had made of such flowers to Geshe Tsering Choephel one day, and he immediately began to recite a poem, offering the flowers to the Lord Buddha. Sometimes he would go with us to the top of a nearby hill and sit there for a long time gazing at the mountains, the valleys, and the villages below, often looking as though he were meditating. I never asked for his thoughts at such times, though I often wondered what they were.

In the winter of my ninth year my guardians took me to the town of Yendum, which was about six hours away on horseback, and there we lodged in the college of a monastery known as the Mother of Monasteries, as it was both the oldest and the most important in the district. Early one morning, three days after we had arrived and settled in our rooms, Dongye helped me to put on for the first time the robes of a monk, then led me to the building where the Eighth Dayab Rinpoche resided. I removed my shoes in his attendant's room and, alone, approached the

Rinpoche's presence. He said nothing at first, but just looked at me. I presented him with a white scarf in the most respectful, polite, and traditional way and the usual three gifts: the image, the book, and the chorten. He then asked me to sit on a cushion by the window, and opened our conversation by asking such indifferent questions as when had I arrived and where was I staying. He then showed me the proper way to comport myself in the robes of a monk, which he declared he was delighted to see me wearing. After these considerable preliminaries, he proceeded to the ordination for which this whole expedition had been arranged.

First, he formally asked if I truly wished to be ordained as a monk, and I answered that I did. He next offered prayers to the Lord Buddha and cut a lock from my hair. He tossed this into the air, chanting something that I could not follow. Then he handed me a single piece of paper on which was written my new name, and while the Rinpoche looked on smiling I read with great excitement: Losang Shedub Tenpi Donme, meaning the "Noble-Minded One Who Illuminates the Doctrine by Teaching and Practice."

The Rinpoche told me that my previous incarnation had served as the *tipa* ("supreme abbot") of Dayab and had done much both for the people and for the enrichment of the doctrines, urging me to emulate my predecessor in these ways. He also gave me advice concerning various spiritual matters, all of which I was too young and inexperienced to understand. I simply agreed with everything he said, too polite to ask questions. When the conversation was ended, the Rinpoche took up a scarf and a protection cord, made three knots in the cord, and blew on it as a blessing.

I approached him, loosened the right and left ends of my *zen* (a type of robe worn as upper garment) and leaned forward while he put about my neck both the scarf and the protection cord. He then presented me with an image about nine inches high of the Lord Buddha. With a gesture of respect I accepted this in my two hands and walked backward slowly toward the door, careful always to keep facing the Rinpoche. My labrang then rendered gift ceremonies in my name for all the monks in Yendum, and during the rest of my stay a number of my predecessor's disciples came to visit me. These were people full of love and I was, of course, happy to meet them. I was also disappointed, for I was rarely offered gifts of any interest to a child. From the giver's point of view it would perhaps have been disrespectful to present toys; once I was presented with a tiny wooden elephant, however, and this gave me the greatest happiness. I kept it by me with great care and looked at it continually. Then, at last, the two weeks were over, and we all rode back to the labrang.

When I was eleven I was taken by Geshe Tsering Choephel on a two-day ride to the village of Kyidam, which lay in a fertile valley westward of Gonsar. There was a temple there where a saintly lama had fashioned a thousand clay images of the coming Buddhas—for we Tibetans believe that in the course of the present great cycle of time (the present *Kalpa*), a thousand Buddhas will become incarnate on this earth as living men, each to devote his body, speech, and mind to the spreading of the Doctrine, that we may all eventually achieve Buddhahood. The Lord Gautama Shakyamuni, it is believed, was but one of these thousand, the closest to us, since he lived in our own historic period. So when my teacher and I entered that temple with its thousand images we found that there was only one life-size figure in the central position on the altar: the Lord Gautama Shakyamuni. All the other figures—much smaller—were clustered around it like stars around a full moon.

My teacher and I were offered a room with a family in the village for the whole period of our stay, and having settled there, next day proceeded to the large assembly hall of the temple. A special throne had been set up there for the Lama Zonglo Rinpoche, who was to be our teacher. About four hundred people were there to hear him. All rose when he entered, and when we had settled down he began to speak. He talked of the life of the Lord Buddha; of how Buddhism had come to Tibet and spread; of how our scriptures had been translated from Sanskrit into Tibetan; of the proper attitude to have in studying the Doctrine; and of the necessity for listening attentively to lectures and assiduously practicing their precepts for the enlightenment of all sentient beings.

Then he opened and began to read from our 108-volume Narthang Edition of the teachings of the Lord Buddha. Commencing with the first page and verse of the first sutra, he read through the whole list and account there given of the series of the "Coming Thousand": four, already Buddhas of the past; the rest to appear in the future. The names, birthplaces, families, and races of each are given in this sutra, as well as the number of years of their lives. It was a long and, for me, somewhat tedious occasion. Nor was that the end of it. Next morning the lama, when all had again settled down, opened his text and continued from where he had left off the night before.

During such a *lung*, or oral transmission of the scriptures, no one is allowed either to talk or to doze, for the whole idea is that the sound itself should be heard and retained by the ear. The sound is considered a blessing in itself for it will help the mind to penetrate to the meaning of the sacred words, guiding one to the deepest understanding of the Doctrine. Every day, therefore, from morning to evening, the Lama Zonglo Rinpoche read on, completing about one volume of the Narthang Edition each day. Sometimes he would pause to explain passages, but the main thing was the reading—which continued for three whole months. At the end of that time all 108 volumes had been heard.

I was so young that it was extremely difficult for me to sit quietly through all those hours. I could not understand the text at all. But there were some other boys sitting near me, and we had brought along small wooden toys to play with, or dumplings, which we used to mold little figures of sheep, horses, and people. My teacher, sitting behind us, seldom reprimanded us for this play. Either he could not see or, more likely, was pretending not to notice. He was probably grateful that we could stay quiet so long. Finally, after three months, the reading was completed, and we returned to our labrang.

4.

Lhasa

In the Kham there were many monasteries, a number celebrated for sound scholarship and good rules, but none to compare in learning and importance with the great three of Central Tibet: Sera, Drepung, and Gaden. Some of the monasteries in Amdo and Mongolia ranked nearly as high as these scholastically; even so, many of their students preferred to complete their studies in the neighborhood of Lhasa, since it was there, in the great monasteries, the "Three Pillars" of the Yellow Hat sect, that the main sources of Tibetan Buddhist thought had resided from the time of their founding in the fifteenth century. Young monks everywhere felt it to be of the greatest importance to go to Lhasa. Not only would they have an opportunity to enter one of the major three there, but they might also receive their *getsul and gelong* ordinations from the Dalai Lama himself. Such ordinations were the same throughout Tibet, but to receive one's ordination from His Holiness was an occasion of the greatest honor. Moreover, many monks there from the different regions and various monasteries of the country provided constant stimulation, sharpening each other's wits. Great public theological debates in which the best scholars of the land participated were another important feature. No scholar in such an atmosphere could afford to rest on his laurels.

Accordingly, it was customary in the Kham for incarnations of the Yellow Hat sect to be sent to Central Tibet to enter one or another of the "Three Pillars." Some would stay only a few months, others longer, completing their studies there and taking their geshe degrees; a few might even remain as long as twenty years, or more. Since I was the Tenth Khyongla, and everyone of my predecessors had studied in Central Tibet, Dongye decided that I too should go there as early as possible. However, when he asked my teacher to accompany me, Geshe Tsering Choephel declined. "You will find far better teachers than I for Khyongla in Central

Tibet," he said. "One can choose there a hundred excellent teachers from a thousand." He added that although he would surely have found it interesting to visit Central Tibet again, what he was most longing to do was to retire to a hermitage and spend the rest of his life in meditation. He would therefore not be at my side as my teacher for the next stage of my education.

Long before my thirteenth birthday, Dongye was already making preparations. In those days the North Road to Lhasa required an arduous one-month journey by muleback through many uninhabited northern regions. Dongye therefore had to arrange both for the financing of the trip and for the ordering of provisions. Since most of the food for the journey would have to be carried with us, we would require many pack animals. We already had twenty mules, but he had to buy forty more. Also, he had to find out when other parties would be going, for nobody would venture on such an expedition alone. Many of the nomads in the northern great plains were bandits, supplementing their incomes by plundering caravans. We should have to take along, therefore, many servants and armed retainers, both for protection and to care for the animals.

Before I left, I was given much precious advice by my teacher. I had gone up to his room full of excitement and anticipation, wanting to discuss all the preparations, but he turned my mind to more serious things. He told me that when Tsongkhapa, later founder of the Gelugpa sect, had been sixteen, and about to leave for Central Tibet to continue his studies there, he approached his guru, Choje Tondup Rinchen, for advice, just as I was now approaching mine. Although my guru, Geshe Tsering Choephel, laid no claim to being such a great teacher as Choje Tondup Rinchen, he said he thought that perhaps because of his long experience, he might be able to give me some useful thoughts to apply to my life, as Tsongkhapa had applied those of his teacher.

"First of all," he said, "when you get to Lhasa you must try to find a good teacher, who is both a great scholar and sage. He must be of excellent moral character and have acquired the spiritual merit that gives awareness and compassion for all living beings." I should choose no teacher before testing him, yet not delay and hesitate long. It was sometimes possible, he said, to recognize one's teacher immediately, but not always. He also warned me against associating with people who would argue that the study of religion was useless and that, life being very short, one should accept its pleasures, enjoying oneself to the full. "Never listen to them," he cautioned, "but do not show them anger either, for anger will destroy both you and all those who come in contact with you. Rather, you must show compassion; for their minds are darkened with the dust of ignorance. It is your responsibility to try to undo the evil influence of that ignorance."

He went on very seriously and I listened. "You should never study merely for your own personal benefit and reputation. For you must know that all that you may ever gain through worldly living will amount to nothing at the moment of your physical death." He gently smiled. "There are many levels of thinking, but the one that we must embrace is the selfless one of achieving enlightenment for the benefit of all sentient beings. That should be our sole motivation for the study and practice of Buddhism." Then he abruptly changed his tone. "But, above all, you must now begin your study of the Sutras, and after that, go on to the Tantras. When you have finally gained your Tantric degree, you should seek out learned and saintly teachers, to receive from them initiation [*wang*], oral transmissions from the scriptures [*lung*], and explanations of their meanings [*tri*]." He counseled me, finally, not to hurry back home to the Kham, but to take every bit of time necessary to increase and deepen my knowledge and experience. "And may you grow rich," he said, "in experience through the splendor of your accomplishments for the Doctrine."

Dongye, who was present during this visit, was kind enough to write down for me all of my teacher's precious advice. Later on in Central Tibet, whenever I was alone, felt a bit too lazy to study, or had become angry with someone, I would be heartened by rereading his guiding words. When I felt at times that I might be studying only to enhance my own reputation, I would again reread my first teacher's advice and recall my proper goals.

In the labrang I had already learned by heart the text of a little book called *Guru Pancha*, in Tibetan, *Lama Ngachupa*, which deals with the correct behavior of a pupil toward his guru, telling why and in what manner, according to Tantric ideas, a spiritual teacher was to be respected.

I had also read edifying stories about Milarepa's behavior toward his guru, and so had come to realize the importance of establishing an effective spiritual connection. Besides, I really loved my teacher, Geshe Tsering Choephel, and before leaving told him that since he had expressed the wish to retire to a hermitage, my labrang would provide for all his needs. Smiling, he replied that in a pious country a man devoted to religion would never have any difficulty in obtaining food. But I insisted, and the matter was finally settled in a written contract sealed by Dongye and myself. I could never have left the Kham without assuring myself that the future of my beloved guru was provided for, and later from Central Tibet I wrote periodically to the administrators of the labrang, reminding them to provide for my teacher's needs. To this day I rejoice in recalling that action; for according to the Buddhist doctrine of karma, it is imperative to help parents and teachers no less than the sick and needy. Any prosperity that we may ourselves enjoy will be the result of our generosity in the past, as poverty is caused by past miserliness. And so it is, I believe, that even though I came out of Tibet as a refugee owning nothing I have always somehow managed to meet my needs, even without a Western education. I attribute this to my own support of my teachers.

Dongye had by now completed all the preparations for my journey. He was planning to accompany me himself but before we could depart an unfortunate dispute broke out in the labrang. One of the old servants, who had been attached to the place for many years, had been for some time nourishing a grudge against Dongye for some fanciful insult, and now that everybody was occupied preparing for my trip, he seized the opportunity to connive with a couple of other members of the community to have Dongye replaced as administrator. I was still a minor at that time, with as yet no voice in such affairs—nor, in fact, did I understand the argument. The old servant accused Dongye of misusing funds of the labrang for the benefit of his own relatives and, in general, of mishandling affairs. In response, Dongye asked for a meeting to be called of representatives of both the monastery and the village, certain intimate friends, and my father as well, so that he might reply to the charges. His accuser had gained the support of a number of others within the labrang, together with a few of their friends in the village.

I was present at the meeting, but understood very little of what went on. Dongye, who had given his whole life to the labrang, did not defend himself at all, but only asked to be allowed to retire. His opponents accepted the offer immediately, before anyone might talk him out of it, and a new administrator was appointed to replace him. The new administrator was a simple monk named Palzang, who had had no practical experience whatsoever. He had no known close relatives either, and there were people at the meeting who had thought that this "qualification," along with the fact that he was known to be an extremely pious monk, would make him a dependable administrator. They asked, quite formally, for my opinion, but I could only say that I liked Dongye. All the assets of the labrang were officially recorded at that meeting; one copy of the document showing the assets was given to the new administrator, another copy to Dongye, and the original to me. Dongye then advised the meeting that he thought it very important for him to go along with me to Lhasa, and to that there was general assent. So it was that when we left, I bore with me two unfortunate documents: one, my trusted Dongye's resignation, and the other, the formal acceptance of the pious monk Palzang—who, as it proved, was quite inadequate to the charge he had assumed of managing the practical affairs of my labrang. When I, years later, reached an age at which I could assume responsibility for the labrang (after Dongye had returned to the Kham and I learned of the disorganized state of my labrang), I summarily re-appointed Dongye to his former post, where he again served for many more years with the same devotion and energy as of old. I think of him now with gratitude and affection.

During my last days in the labrang, my friends and many of the villagers brought me presents for the journey, and such offerings as scarves and coins to be presented in the temples of Lhasa. At last the journey began. It was early September, 1936, full summer still; the meadows a lush green and the grain all ripened in the fields.

Our caravan was ready and every one of its members adorned with farewell scarves that had been offered by the villagers and people of the labrang. We had about sixty mules, every ten cared for by a man with a sword and a gun. Before the gate of the labrang all the villagers were assembled, and they begged me to return very soon. A company rode along with us the first hour, and then turned back with a last farewell.

Our immediate destination was Ophor, my home village, which I had not seen for seven years. Before leaving the labrang I had been told that I could choose a present for my parents, and had decided to bring them a horse, and to give one dri to each of my sisters. We left the beasts with our nomads, to be delivered to my parents later, and when we arrived and had been festively received, we remained in Ophor for a week.

I had great joy in seeing my parents and two sisters, aged one and four. The little girls had already been brought by my parents to the labrang and I had become very fond of them, especially the elder, the baby being too small to be of much interest to a thirteen-year-old boy. (My youngest brother and sister had not yet been born; my first brother, as already told, had died.) Some members of the household cried when I left and I myself was profoundly unhappy.

Our next stop, three days away, was at Chamdo. The villages from there on were very far apart, so that sometimes we would see no human habitation for several days at a time. And indeed, the earth along the way was so flat and devoid of vegetation that once on getting up in the morning, we were able to look back and see far in the distance three stones that we had laid down the night before to build our fire. There was nothing else to be seen above ground all the way to the horizon.

When we started out from Chamdo I felt we were now really on our way. In a few days time our caravan arrived in Chungpo Serka, and we rested there with a family for two days. We were joined there by an intensely religious monk who carried with him a heavy load of books, but only a few changes of clothing, all of which we were able to pack onto one of our mules. We invited him to share our tent and eat with us as well; we then found that due to his limited amount of clothing he was richly infested with lice. He treated the lice with the same compassion that he extended to all living beings. He never tried to get rid of them, but on the contrary, replaced them if they happened to fall off his body. Luckily his contented lice chose to remain with him and not take their chances with us, no doubt because of his consideration as a host.

Along the road, and particularly in Chamdo, our small group from the labrang had acquired more and more traveling companions until now we were a company of about sixty; when at night our tents were set up we were a considerable encampment. Our own party carried three tents: one for Dongye and me, another for our kitchen, and a third for all the mule drivers and servants. Many who had joined us had brought along tents of their own, but not all had. Since there was little room for all of these in the camp facilities available, a number had to sleep in the open all the way.

After another stopover at Chungpo Tengchen, the capital of the Chungpo district, and many long and generally quite dreary days riding over narrow trails and camping out each night, we came at last to the territory of Lhasa.

On a beautiful autumn afternoon, we finally arrived in the great valley of Tsang-po, where Lhasa is located. The sky was like a vast turquoise canopy overhead, and as we rode through the broad valley I could see off in the distance a light blazing from a high hill in the center of the plain. When Dongye pointed out the contours of a huge building on top of that central hill I could see that the blaze was from the sun striking golden roofs. The building was the Potala, palace of His Holiness the Dalai Lama, and the largest building in Tibet.

The Potala had been built in the seventeenth century without mechanical means and with no mortar to cement its huge blocks of stone. I asked Dongye how many years and how many thousands of workmen it had taken to build it, and he replied that he had no idea how many workmen had been employed, but that the building was in three parts. The central section, painted red each year, was thirteen stories high, and the two side wings, painted white, were nine each. The whole was like a city in itself, covering the entire top of the "Red Hill."

As we rode along Dongye told me also that it had been there on that same Red Hill that the thirty-third king of Tibet, Tsongtsen Gampo, had in the seventh century built his palace. Some of the foundations of that earlier building still existed below the present structure. A thousand years later when the Fifth Dalai Lama had reconsolidated Tibet and was recognized as the temporal as well as spiritual ruler of the whole country he selected this ancient holy hill for his seat, and began building the Potala there. It took so many years that when the Fifth Dalai Lama died in 1680 and the building was still unfinished, his prime minister, Sangye Gyatso, kept the death a secret for thirteen years, for fear that knowledge of it would promote disunity, thereby bringing work on the building to a standstill.

I asked how it could have been possible to keep such a secret for so long, and as we trotted on Dongye recounted to me the old story of how a moustachioed monk had been found who looked very much like the deceased Fifth Dalai Lama and was set up by Sangye Gyatso in the Dalai Lama's place. The man would beat a drum and ring a bell every day at certain hours, just as the Dalai Lama had done when performing his daily rituals. Sangye Gyatso let it be known that His Holiness had now retired from public life to devote his last years in complete seclusion from the world to meditation. But the retained monk presently became restless and told the palace attendants that he wished to leave the Potala and go down into the town. Sangye Gyatso decided then that it might be well to consult, at last, the oracle at Nechung about a reincarnation. However, he was afraid that the oracle might learn thereby of the Dalai Lama's death. For the visit to Nechung, therefore, the prime minister disguised himself as a beggar. He went first to the home of the oracle's mother, who received him, not knowing who he was, and served him food. As they talked she revealed that the oracle, her son, already knew that the Dalai Lama was dead, but had never told anyone but herself. She begged him not to tell a soul, for she was afraid of Sangye Gyatso's wrath and punishment and the false beggar, bowing, went his way. Next day both the oracle and his mother were summoned to the Potala, where they were immediately killed. When I asked if the prime minister had had them beheaded with a sword, in the manner of the Chinese in the Kham during our war of 1910, Dongye said laughingly that I was being childish—he had not been present at the time and had only heard tell this tale. He could not vouch even for its accuracy. But there was a legend that Sangye Gyatso had often wandered about disguised in beggar's rags, spying on the people to elicit their opinions of the government. Those who had had the misfortune to recognize him and had revealed the fact were severely punished when he returned to the Potala, but those who treated him as a real beggar and had given him alms, whether innocently or through cunning, were rewarded. He was a good scholar and an able ruler, but made many enemies by such conduct. And by those who disliked him he was called the Flat-Headed Prime Minister, since he had a large head that was quite flat on top.

It was now late in the afternoon, and we had come to a place called Dogu Theng, about four miles from Lhasa, where three small tents had been erected and there were people waiting to receive us. We recognized the president of the Benevolent Society of Dayab, accompanied by some old friends of my family who had come here from Lhasa to receive me, and they invited us to stop and rest by the three tents. We enjoyed a pleasant hour of rest, chatting, and refreshment, after which we all rose and hurried on. We were eager to enter Lhasa and could already make out in the distance the outlines of many of its main buildings.

The city rests in a broad valley, spreading out to form a white irregular circle against the fertile green of the plain. Within the valley the only high ground besides the Red Hill of the Potala is Chakpori Hill ("Iron Hill") to the west, where the medical college was located. A large river, the Kyichu ("Happy River"), comes flowing through the valley from the north. All about the city are gardens, while rising high on all sides are the mountains.

We were soon at the outskirts and with the president and his friends leading rode toward the center of the city. Near one of the oldest of the many monasteries, Muru, we were brought to a stop by a passing procession; it was headed by a very old monk wearing a yellow hat with extraordinarily long streamers. Above his head an attendant held a pale orange silk umbrella. People came out of shops and houses, running in front of him for a blessing. Parents were pushing their children toward him. I turned to Dongye. "What's it all about? Who," I asked, "is the old man?"

"Rinpoche, keep still!" Dongye ordered sternly. "Don't talk that way. That is the Gaden Ti Rinpoche, supreme head of the whole Yellow Hat sect. His throne is in Gaden Monastery, the throne of Tsongkhapa himself, its founder, but his residence is here in Lhasa." We walked our horses, skirting the crowd, and Dongye continued, evidently pleased with the opportunity he had been given to put a new idea into my head. "The Gaden Tipa," he said, "has to be an *old* man, because he must have studied for years and years. He must first have been named abbot of the Gyudpa, which is one of our highest institutes for esoteric Tantric studies. And only after he has held that post for some time can he become the supreme Gaden Tipa." My guardian looked at me with a curious smile. "And now," he said, "if I were in your place, I would give myself up wholly to intensive study here so that I could become, when old, the Gaden Tipa. If you can succeed in doing that you will confer a great honor on our district and particularly on your labrang."

He motioned me to stop. We reined in our horses and, dismounting, went forward to receive the Gaden Ti Rinpoche's blessing. All our companions followed suit. Since I was wearing Mongolian traveling garments at the time, the old man could not have known who I was. However, he looked at me with penetrating eyes and, observing my retinue, gave me a blessing by touching his forehead to mine; he then laid his right hand on Dongye's head. In the Kham dialect he asked where we had come from. "From the Dayab, Rinpoche," I answered. Then bowing to him, I retired, since there were many behind me waiting to receive his blessings.

A path opened for us, and when we were again mounted, the president of the Dayab Society rode up to us from behind to say that we were now entering the second ring of the city and would soon be at our destination. He had arranged lodgings for us in the home of a merchant named Lami who had come years before from Dayab, and had made a great fortune in Lhasa.

Our host was already waiting at the front door when we rode up. He was a gentleman of about fifty, known for his generosity, especially to people from Dayab; and in fact, he had invited all seven members of my labrang to stay in his comfortable home while in Lhasa. Very soon the president of the Dayab Society came in with three monks, the representatives from Rato, Drepung, and Gaden of our Dayab *khamtsens*, or regional fraternities, in those monasteries. Very large religious communities were organized on three levels. There was, first, the main overall body, called the *tsogchen*, which included all the colleges or *dratsang*; and each of these, in turn, was composed of fraternities of members grouped according to the various regions of Tibet from which they came. Each of these khamtsens had its own dormitory in which the college members from that part of the country resided. Sometimes a large khamtsen would be subdivided into *metsens*, but generally the khamtsens were the smallest administrative units of a monastery.

Each level of order of this complex organization had within each monastery its own governing body and special religious functions. The tsogchen was governed by the *lachi*, a council composed of all the abbots and former abbots of the colleges within that monastery—the lachi, however, did not exercise any control whatsoever over the colleges or khamtsens, but dealt mainly with matters of general administration. In the dratsang, or college, the abbot had authority in all matters concerning discipline, study, and administration, and the prior of the college, appointed by a college council, functioned under his direction. In the khamtsen, finally, the authority rested in a council of all those monks who had ever been appointed priors of that khamtsen. Such a prior, known as the *khamtsen gegen*, was the main disciplinarian of his domain.

Under the lachi of each monastery there were two main offices. One, the *chyiso*, whose function it was to provide incomes for the monks, took care of the many estates owned by the tsogchen, or overall main body. However, since the income from these sources never was sufficient to provide a living for them, the monks also had to depend on funds provided by their colleges and khamtsens, as well as by private donors. The other of the two main offices of the tsogchen had to do with discipline. Two priors nominated by the government were responsible for carrying out this duty, and those of the tsogchen at Drepung were not only powerful in Drepung but also acted as city magistrates during the two most important religious festivals of Lhasa, the Monlam and Tsogchod. The master of chanting in the tsogchen was likewise selected by the national government, in recognition of his vocal abilities.

The abbots of the three largest monasteries, Drepung, Sera, and Gaden, furthermore, participated in the National Assembly. But since they were religious scholars it was difficult for them to exercise any influence among politicians. Most of them were merely the puppets of secular government officials, and yet occasionally they successfully vetoed proposals—not always with the best results. For example, in 1945, when the government had established an English language school in Lhasa, some of the abbots protested, arguing that the study of Western ideas by students inadequately trained might endanger their Buddhist beliefs; and after a few months their opposition moved the government to close the school. Years later, when we were losing our country, we realized what a fatal mistake it had been for us to remain isolated and not to have formed alliances with any part of the Western world.

The order of life in a monastery was largely sustained, one might say, on buttered tea. The tsogchen started each day with a tea ceremony open to every dratsang and khamtsen; each dratsang began its scholastic day with a tea ceremony of its own and then held three debating sessions; and between those debating sessions, the khamtsens would more than likely hold tea ceremonies as well. In the case of Rato, which was not as large as the main "Three Pillar" monasteries, there was one college only and nine khamtsens; the largest of the latter, Nyare, was that of my own home district, Dayab. Nyare khamtsen had branches at Rato, Dagen, and Drepung. Its members at Rato were regarded as members also of the Nyare khamtsen at Drepung. The khamtsen at Rato was called the Lower Nyare, that at Drepung, Upper Nyare, and the two were thought to share good or ill fortune. In the Lhasa area Sera was the only major monastery that did not have a Nyare khamtsen for its students from our district. The very few from Dayab who were there had therefore to join one or another of the other khamtsens.

And so it was that the three representatives who had come from Rato, Gaden, and Drepung arrived in my room with the president of the Dayab Society to visit and to inquire about our journey. They brought gifts of mutton, whole sacks of tsampa flour, rice, and even fodder for the animals. Throughout the long journey we had lived chiefly on tsampa and dried meat, so that the prospect of fresh food was most agreeable. Dongye ordered the cook to prepare some of the mutton for us right away, and it tasted like ambrosia.

Next morning I wakened early. I knew that we were to expect a visit from an uncle whom I had never seen, my father's oldest brother, Kunsang. He had gone to Lhasa before I was born and was now a monk in Drepung. As a child in my labrang I had heard a good deal about him from my parents when they came to visit, and I had been looking forward to this meeting with curiosity; more so since he was sometimes spoken of as Kunsang Tepo, or "Kunsang the Midget," and I thought he must be very tiny. As soon as we had arrived in Lhasa, Dongye had sent him a message, and Kunsang had answered that he would call on us in the morning. So I was quickly up and dressed, watching at the window. And I recognized him at once as he approached, for he looked very much like my father, only much shorter, but not at all a midget.

When Kunsang entered the room he addressed me as Rinpoche, and I called him, simply, uncle. I was so pleased to see him that I no longer felt like a stranger in Lhasa. He seemed equally pleased to see me, asking many questions about home, my parents, and our relatives. Then he suggested that we should go up onto the roof and take a look at the city, and up we went.

Leaning over a low parapet I gazed long and eagerly about at the white buildings and the crowded streets with their people, and all the traffic going by; elegantly clad gentlemen riding ponies with gaily covered saddles, followed by their grooms; donkeys loaded with firewood and provisions; mules bearing travelers from India, together with their baggage; and—most astonishing to me of all—two Nepalese riding bicycles. I had never seen such amusing two-wheeled vehicles in my life and immediately wanted one. I turned eagerly to Dongye, but then, fearing that he might become angry, held my tongue.

I turned back to the panorama before me. I was in the holy city of Lhasa, the first real city I had ever seen. It was late September, and in the surrounding parks the grass was just beginning to turn brown. The mountains that ringed the valley were a tawny yellow against a cloudless sky, the yellow of a lion's pelt. How different all this was from the sight of our tiny village, nestling in the rolling foothills of the Kham!

My uncle explained to me that the city was built in a circle formed by three enclosing rings. The Lingkor, the outermost ring, ran around behind Chakpori Hill and the Potala and held a number of parks. Pilgrims from all over Tibet and many of the older inhabitants of the city walked around it daily as a path of pilgrimage. The Barkor, the second ring, enclosed the shopping and business center, with many stores and outdoor booths. It was, however, not really circular but square. The Nangkor, the third ring, enclosed the religious center of Tibet, most revered of all. There stood at the city's heart the great temple known as the Jokhang, containing an image of the Lord Buddha called Jowo Rinpoche that was the most precious image in Tibet.

My uncle asked if we had not already visited Jowo Rinpoche immediately on arrival. When I told him that it had been too late and we had all been extremely tired, he replied: "Then it is imperative that we go today; for it is said that on arriving in Lhasa, one should go directly to the Jokhang and touch one's forehead to the knees of the Lord Buddha before the perspiration of the journey has dried on one's face."

The great temple was the largest and most sacred in our country, and might indeed have been thought of as the center of our world. For all the roads and caravan routes from the most distant provinces converged there, and radiating out again, connected Tibet to the countries surrounding it. The Jowo Rinpoche, the magnificent image within the temple of which my uncle spoke, was a statue of the Lord Buddha as a young prince of sixteen years of age, seated in the lotus position. The word *jowo* can have a number of meanings, but in this case it signified "the precious, supreme one." The figure was seated on a high throne, wearing a tall crown of gold inset with jewels—diamonds, rubies, turquoises, and pearls. At its back was a great gilded panel of copper covered with figures and Buddhist symbols. At the top of the panel, just above the Buddha's head, was a large sun-bird, a garuda (*jachung*) with outstretched wings. Jowo Rinpoche's face had been lacquered so many times with gold leaf that one could not make out what it must have been like in the beginning.

The figure was believed to have come from India. Buddhist texts declare that it was fashioned during the Buddha's lifetime by an artist named Besho Karma, and brought to Lhasa by the Princess Wen-ch'eng, daughter of the Emperor T'ao-tsung (known to us as Gyasa, the "Chinese Wife"), when she arrived in 641 to marry our King Tsongtsen Gampo. His first wife, the "Nepalese," who inspired him to build the temple, had brought with her an image of the Lord Buddha as well, and this too was enshrined in Lhasa in the Ramoche Temple, which we were to visit the following day. (The King, by the way, had three more wives, Tibetans, who joined him in becoming Buddhists.) Both images were said to have been blessed by the Lord Gautama himself, and they were therefore especially sacred and deeply revered—but the Jowo Rinpoche was the most famous and sacred image in Tibet.

We arrived at the temple and, after contemplating the image, we toured the rest of the chapel along with a great crowd of people. The melted butter that we had brought along was presented to an attendant for the golden butter lamps on the altar—there were so many of these burning in this chapel that the room was as bright as day. I remembered the people at home declaring that this great chapel in Lhasa used more melted butter than we had water in our village. In fact, so much butter had been burned in those lamps that the heavy wooden beams above, as well as the carved pillars and all the walls of the chapel, had been thoroughly blackened by the smoke; many of the silken robes of the images were also stained. The chapel keepers, who constantly nudged us on, wore soiled robes too, some with the whole lower half stained black from butterfat.

After leisurely visiting the other chapels, we stopped for a special visit to the chapel of the Goddess Tara, where traditionally all the chapel keepers were from Dayab. They welcomed us with great pleasure and asked us to have tea, and being quite tired from standing in lines so long and then climbing up and down stairs, we accepted. For half an hour we remained chatting with them and telling them all the latest home-news.

The chapel itself was imposing. In the center was a life-sized, painted clay image of the seated goddess, the Green Tara, one of Tara's many emanations, and all about the curved walls were twenty-one other life-sized figures of her in the half lotus position. For this beloved goddess, known as the Merciful One, was one of the most popular in Tibet. And hundreds of tiny mice ran here and there over her main image, eating the grain that devotees had scattered for them. They caused a real commotion with their squeaking, chattering, and little squabbles, and I was surprised to see so many. In two other chapels I had also seen mice running about, and asked my uncle why the government tolerated them in these three places, but nowhere else in the temple. Dongye leaned and whispered to him, "I told you Khyongla would be forever asking why, why, and why." My uncle answered that he did not know, but had been told that even when the Dalai Lama or the regent visited this chapel, the mice were allowed to run about. Occasionally, a visiting villager would ask for a dead mouse from the shrine, for the peasants thought that if a dead temple-mouse were placed in a field it would protect the crops from insect pests.

The next day we walked to the Lingkor, the circular road surrounding Lhasa and the Potala, where we found a company of devotees circumambulating the city by prostrating themselves repeatedly. These were pilgrims, many of whom had come from the remotest parts of Tibet. All wore leather gloves with wooden boards on their palms and leather aprons over their clothes to protect them from the dirt and stones. Many were followed by their pet dogs. There were also a number of Lhasan townspeople, some with their dogs or with sheep that they had bought in order to save them from the butcher's block, and had then kept as pets. A number of the Lhasans distributed coins to the poorer pilgrims and to the beggars lined along the roadside waiting for alms, many of whose faces were so tanned that they were almost black. Some of the beggars lived there permanently behind low fences of yak horns in black tents made of yak hair, and cooked in front of their tents on little fireplaces of three stones. People gave double the usual number of coins to those beggars who were ill or blind.

The next day—our third—we went for our first visit to the Potala, which had been constantly, tantalizingly, visible during all our walks around Lhasa.

We climbed the great stair in front of the building and came finally to the main entrance in the central section—the oldest part of the building, which is painted red to signify power. Within were the many great assembly halls and chapels used for ceremonial occasions. We climbed and climbed, but when we thought we had gotten to the top, there were still more stairs. My uncle finally led us into a corridor where we clambered up eighteen steps of a ladder-like stair in complete darkness. This was a passage frequently used by pilgrims as the most direct way to the main shrines, though there were other more spacious stairways in the building that might have been used also. At last we came out into the light and went directly to the shrine of Chenresig, the All-Compassionate One, after which we continued on to other chapels, including that containing the tomb of the Thirteenth Dalai Lama, which was at that time the largest and newest chapel in the Potala, since he died in 1933.

The chapel containing the tomb had been completed only a year before our visit, and was three stories high, facing south, with an enormous glass window that provided much better light than could be found in any other chapel of the palace. The Dalai Lama's body reposed on a throne within its second story, surrounded by relics, books, and images that had been placed there before the ceremony of sealing took place. A life-sized gilded copper image of the seated Dalai Lama, holding in his right hand a lotus and in his left, the Wheel of the Law, was set against one wall of the chapel. In front of the chorten stood an offering table full of perpetually burning butter lamps, offering bowls, and other ritual objects. Two prodigious elephant tusks, standing at either side, formed an arch above this table. In the corners of the room square pillars with carved red capitals supported the chapel ceiling, and on the northeastern pillar, as the chapel keeper pointed out to us, there had grown a star-shaped meadow-fungus, now protected by a glass box. We all studied this growth with curiosity. Although somebody remarked that it probably had grown because the wood of the pillar had not been dry enough when set in place, its appearance was nevertheless uncanny. The people of Lhasa could not at that time understand it. Later we came to realize that it was an indication that the new Dalai Lama would be found in Amdo, in the northeast.

5.

My Entrance into Rato Monastery

I had only one week to spend in Lhasa and then left for Rato Monastery, where I was to follow in my predecessor's footsteps and become enrolled as a member. Being inducted into one's monastery is an extremely important event in the lifetime of a monk. I was only thirteen, yet aware of the solemnity of the occasion.

We left Lhasa early one sunny morning in late November, and heading southwest out of the city, rode leisurely alongside the yellow fields. We soon came to a temple not far from Rato. Three monks from Rato—one from my own khamtsen, Nyare, were waiting there to greet me. As we approached, each lifted from his shoulder the end of his upper robe and held this in outstretched hands in a traditional sign of respect. We were then invited into the temple, the monks inquiring, as we joined them, about our long journey from the Kham.

Two rooms had been prepared for us, one for Dongye and me, the other for our attendants. I was conducted presently to a throne beneath a canopy of silk, to be honorably seated there on a pile of five brocaded cushions. At my right was a high table, and as soon as I sat down a monk approached with a bowl of droma on a silver stand. He set it down by a silver teapot on the table, and then poured some tea for me into a white porcelain cup. Other monks carried in a large, heavy teapot and poured tea for my companions. I took from the bowl at my right a few morsels of droma, which I tossed in the air as an offering, and then we all drank tea. The administrator of the college that I was to enter presented a white scarf to me and a tray with the usual symbolic gifts: an image, a book, and a chorten, besides which there was also a small bag of coins. After touching each of these symbolic presents to my forehead, I accepted all and passed them on to my attendants, presenting in turn a white scarf to the administrator. Having received this, he addressed me as the representative of Rato Monastery, expressing (as he put it) the joy of all the monks that I had come to be among them. There followed a similar exchange of gifts, scarves, and civilities with the representative of my khamtsen. Tea was drunk a second time; after which we all left the temple of the Goddess Tara to ride swiftly (eleven people, now) to Rato Monastery, hardly more than a mile away.

Even in the distance I could see that the monastery was much larger and more imposing than my labrang in Dayab, and so beautiful that I at once felt that I wanted to remain there many years. There were a great many buildings, mostly white with red trimmings; and the whole was surrounded by an extensive garden of willow, peach, and apple trees, now showing only bare branches. A number of monks in formal array were standing before the gates, and when I asked Dongye why, he answered that he supposed they must be the monks from the Nyare khamtsen who had been disciples of my predecessor, waiting—out of respect for him—to welcome me. Ordinarily the arrival of a student was not such a high official occasion, he said—and warned me that if I did not now study hard and learn what had to be learned, I would be shamed before all these monks and a disgrace to my predecessor.

Some monks came forward as soon as we arrived at the gates and dismounted. They led our horses and mules to the stables and took charge of our baggage. The prior of my khamtsen (the khamtsen gegen), who had been waiting, led me after his greeting directly to an assembly hall, explaining on the way that most of the members of the Nyare khamtsen in Rato were from Dayab, and that even some of those born in central Tibet had parents who had come from Dayab. He conducted me to the altar. There the central image was again of the Goddess Tara, her ornaments all of yellow gold. On one side of her was an image of our great reformer, Tsongkhapa, along with his two chief disciples, Khedup and Gyeltseb, while on her other side was the deity, Se-trab-pa, protector of Rato, as of all institutions where *Pramāna* (Buddhist logic) is studied.

Following instructions that I had been hurriedly given by Dongye, I offered to the Green Tara some scarves that we had just bought (for a very low price) from the keeper of the hall (a very young monk whose lower garments were all spotted with the butter that he had spilled when filling butter lamps). When that little ceremony was concluded, the prior led us upstairs and I was shown a guest room directly over the vestibule of the assembly hall. To my surprise it contained a bed about seven feet long, which, when I was invited to sit down on it, proved to be quite comfortable. Its frame was covered beautifully, and it was lined with pillows.

A monk now appeared who had been delegated to act as my attendant during the probationary period that I should have to survive before being recognized as a full-fledged monastery member. Middle-aged and with a jovial face, he seemed to me witty and amusing. His name was Thondup Tseten, and he asked me if I was hungry. I was in fact very hungry, but told him I was not, since out of politeness we usually refuse the first time a host offers food. Fortunately, the cook of the khamtsen soon appeared with a traditional meal of eight saucers, each containing a different dish, and my new friend suggested the best ones to try first. Tasting and finding the food delicious, I went to it with the appetite of my age.

It was the end of October and that evening there was to be held a debating session in the courtyard of the khamtsen. My room had a balcony that faced the court and from there I watched the monks gathering. One monk sat on a throne, and when the formal debate got started, certain of the others challenged him with questions. It all seemed to me fascinating, and I listened with intense interest, but, truthfully, understood absolutely nothing of anything I heard; consequently, I could not even tell who had come out best. Thondup Tseten, beside me, tried to explain both the rules and the topics of the game I was observing, as well as the method of study at Rato and some of the regulations of the monastery. I thought he must be a scholar of great learning, but found out later that not a little of the information that he had given me that evening was incorrect.

Early the next morning, with Dongye at my side, I paid my introductory visit to the abbot, who looked to be in his early sixties, and not in very good health. He asked me about my studies at home and our long journey to Lhasa, finally saying that we should be seeing each other often.

On the way to his room I had beheld for the first time many parts of the monastery that I was to inhabit for the next eleven years of my life, and from which, on one terrible night in 1959, I was to make my narrow escape from the Chinese.

The main college of Rato was housed in an old square building of stone, four stories high, with white-painted walls. An assembly hall occupied the entire main floor, with a chapel at its rear; four large pillars supported its central nave and numerous smaller pillars—delineating the side aisles—were all wrapped around with blankets to keep them clean. On festive occasions these pillars would be covered with beautiful ancient Chinese cloths of rich brocade and embroidered silk.

The principal image on the chapel altar was of the Lord Buddha in the lotus position, made of colored clay mixed with medicinal herbs and powdered precious stones, together with sanctified earth and holy water from the Buddhist places of pilgrimage in India. Before it, as in all monasteries of the Yellow Hat sect, were the figures of Tsongkhapa and his two disciples, Khedup and Gyeltseb, these also made of colored clay mixed with medicinal herbs. Below these three there was another seated image, of Dagpa Zangpo, the founder of the college.

The four main pillars of that great hall were so tall that the central part of the room was two stories high with the windows of the upper story furnishing light. Its walls were covered with murals (said to be very old) illustrating the life of the Lord Buddha, from the *Jakata* tales. And outside, in the vestibule, on either side of the doorway, were pictures of the "Gods of the Four Directions." At one end of that vestibule was a huge painting of the Wheel of Life, and at the other, an acrostic poem enclosed in a magic square, praising Dagpa Zangpo, the founder of the monastery, and arranged in such a way that the letters of his name, interwoven with the words of the poem, appeared in three directions, vertically, diagonally, and horizontally. On either side of the massive door giving entrance to the chapel were bookshelves containing a one-hundred-volume edition of the Kanjur, together with two particularly precious old volumes of illuminated manuscript, handwritten before block printing was introduced into Tibet. These were the gifts, I was told, of a wealthy donor.

I was so impressed when I saw all these beautiful things that I whispered to Dongye, "When I return to Dayab I must rebuild my own monastery and make it just like this."

"You think too much of externals," he replied. "The most important thing about a monastery is the opportunity it provides for study, religious practice, and the acquisition of good rules of behavior. If you study hard and become a truly great teacher, that will give us all far greater happiness than any renovation of buildings."

Shortly after that we returned to my room, and the counselors of the khamtsen came to pay me a call. They explained that when a monk joined Rato he was asked to select three guardians: one to be responsible for his legal affairs, one to care for his food and clothing, and one to supervise his spiritual life. If he had no friends or relatives in the monastery, the prior of his khamtsen would help him find his mentors, though usually it would be relatives, friends, or monks from the same village, who would advise him. Generally, the guardian caring for the food and clothing was the one to be selected first, since he was the one most immediately required and, once found, would help select the other two. The neophyte would not be a full-fledged member of his khamtsen until his guardian had been found. Moreover, he was not to live alone, but had to share his room with this guardian, his *jigten gegen*, who would take care not only of his food and clothing, but also of his other practical requirements, including financial help when needed; so that with such a guardian to protect him, the student monk could devote himself exclusively to his studies. Any student later preferring to live separately would have to take care of these things himself.

It would not have been difficult for me to find such a guardian, since there would never be any need for him to come to my aid financially. However, it was the custom that incarnations should have their guardians chosen for them by the khamtsen, and an old monk called Norbu was introduced to me as my first, my *jigten gegen*. He was over seventy, short, small-boned and white-haired, nicknamed The Pigeon, and thought by some to be insincere. For example, when on one occasion he was eating with a friend who enjoyed teasing him, the friend tasted the first dish and remarked that the food was too salty. Norbu tasted and agreed. Again the friend tasted. "Oh," he said, "it needs more salt!" Norbu again tasted and agreed. But then, when the friend actually added salt to the dish, Norbu did nothing.

After this little old monk had been appointed to me, he and Dongye began consulting with each other to prepare my formal admission to the monastery. The formal ceremony is known as *Choshug*, which means "admitted for religious activity." As an incarnation, I would have to hold two gift ceremonies, one in my khamtsen and the second for my college, where the monks of all nine khamtsens would participate. If I did not do this, I would not be accorded the privileges of an incarnation, but would share the chores and duties of the other monks. My first Choshug was arranged for a date five days after I had arrived: the thirteenth day of the tenth month of our Tibetan calendar (November). That morning Dongye sent Thondup up to the prior's room with a message announcing that we should like to hold our gift ceremony for the khamtsen the following day. He then invited both the prior and the cook to meet with us in a guest room adjacent to mine, which we had been given for storage of the bulky supplies and gifts that we had brought with us from the Kham. There Dongye and I delivered butter, tsampa, droma, dried meat, tea, and fruit to the prior to be used in the preparation of the festivities, and invited some other monks present to help make the *tormas* that would be required. Tormas are dough cakes, usually brown, made of tsampa mixed with water, kneaded into cone shapes, to be placed on the lower part of the altar as food offerings to the "Most Precious Triad" or "Three Jewels": the Buddha, the Dharma, and the Sangha. Such tormas are often lavishly embellished with decorations molded of butter dyed the five symbolic colors: white (the peaceful color); yellow (the developing); red (the conquering); blue or black (the destroying); and green (the all-accomplishing). They are works of art symbolic of life, to be destroyed when they have served their purpose.

Several monks took charge in our storeroom of cleaning and polishing the silver butter lamps intended for the altar; others began refilling them with the butter we had brought from home. We were offering butter for more than one hundred lamps, and when ready, these would be carried down to the great assembly hall and there placed on the altar. Thondup Tseten, meanwhile, in another part of the storeroom, was occupied counting out the necessary silver coins for gifts to the monks of my khamtsen. Each was to receive two Tibetan dollars; but those who were personally participating in the preparation of our ceremony—the cooks and kitchen help, as well as those attending to the altar and to the hangings in the assembly hall—would receive double for their services. Gifts of money were to be given, also, to those monks of high position, each according to his rank, the abbot, the incarnations, the prior, the members of the council, and the chanting master (*unze*).

The prior appointed a good number of monks to prepare the assembly hall and that evening there was great activity there. They hung banners on the pillars and covered the monks' cushions with beautiful old Chinese rugs. Thangkas were fetched from the storehouse and hung on both sides of the hall, many of them old and rare and displayed only on such occasions. There was a fine series of sixteen portraits by a famous artist from Amdo, Lubum Lharipa, who in the nineteenth century had been a monk in Drepung. His thangkas were very large and in the style of Eastern Tibet. The drab white cotton curtains, that normally hung at the windows and doorways, were taken down, and brilliant new red ones went up in their places. Cooks were busy in the kitchen mixing the various sorts of tea leaves we had brought with us from home; in the early morning they would cook droma to be served to the khamtsen after the tea.

Everything having been thus well prepared, about ten o'clock the next morning I heard the thrilling sound of the great stone gong that hung from a beam in the courtyard. A stocky monk in an old patched robe struck it to signify that all was now ready for the ceremony and that the hour to assemble had arrived. Once, twice, three times, the gong slowly sounded in a resonant tone that could be heard throughout the monastery. Once, twice, three times again; then again and again. I had climbed early out of bed and was already dressed, a number of monks having helped to attire me in the new robe that we had brought from home. The prior appeared at my door in formal robes, bearing an incense stick, to conduct me to the assembly. Together, we descended and came to the door of the hall, where I left my shoes, to enter with bare feet, as did all the monks. The prior pointed out to me the colorful cushion I was to occupy; and all the time that deep stone gong sounded faster and faster in the yard. Two Rinpoches senior to me arrived, and standing together at one of the windows, watching through the new red curtains, we saw the monks assembling in the courtyard. There were about two hundred, and they arrived in absolute silence, standing with plenty of space between them: the senior monks erect, with their eyes held straight ahead; the junior monks with heads slightly bowed, to show respect for the elders; the young monks, to be formally admitted that day, with their backs bent and eyes focused on the ground; and the youngest monks, hardly ten years old, in the rear, whispering and nudging and pushing each other. The prior did not notice their antics, for he was standing at the main door. The quickening rhythm of the gong suddenly broke, followed by three slow beats; then all was silence.

The prior pulled the curtain from the entrance doorway, allowing the monks to come in. They solemnly filed down the aisle and took seats according to seniority. A hush fell over the assembly. An old monk whose braided beard wagged nicely began chanting a special prayer to the Goddess Tara, called Dolchog, and everyone except some very new members (including myself, who did not know the hymn) joined in. We others just sat there, trying to look as though we were thinking very deeply. I could follow certain parts of the chant because its prayer to the Goddess Tara was known to everyone in Tibet; it was almost a national prayer, as familiar as the syllables *Om Mani Padme Hum.* As chanted by the monks, however, it lasted almost two hours. Tea was served thrice during the period of chanting; first tea, then droma with melted butter, and then, twice again, tea. It was brought to us incarnations in a turquoise-colored teapot, and to the rest of the members in a large copper kettle. We raised our plain wooden bowls in both hands to receive it when it was poured, and when everyone had been served, the unze led the grace and we prayed that our lives should never be separated from the Buddha, the Dharma, and the Order. When all these long recitations had been terminated and the ceremony was over, the prior, again bearing an incense stick, conducted me to my room, where he brought me tea in a silver pot and a full cup of cooked droma that he set on a tall-stemmed stand. One of the elder monks, a member of the council, presented me with a white scarf and four little bags of copper coins, while the other members of the council also came to congratulate me on having become a member.

That evening there were more preparations for the following day when the ceremony of admission to the college was to take place. The kitchen was supervised by the same monk chef as before, but with many laymen assistants, for he was now to serve more than four hundred monks.

About ten o'clock the next morning one of his main cooks climbed up on the roof, and we soon heard a big drum being thumped in loud double strokes. An expert drummer, the cook was very short, with an enormous nose. I later saw some of the small boys imitating him—having molded from tsampa very big noses for themselves, they mimicked his energetic use of the drumsticks. And I too was fascinated by his curious appearance. When in Europe, many years later, I saw a circus for the first time, the clowns reminded me immediately of our drummer in Rato.

While the drum boomed, calling the monks to the great hall, an attendant of the college prior appeared to fetch me for the ceremony. I was required this time to take a ceremonial cloak with me, along with my yellow hat, my wooden tea bowl, and a tsampa bag. The attendant insisted, however, on taking charge of all these things for me until we reached the door of the hall. Once there he placed the long cloak over my shoulders. We were not to enter barefoot at this time, but to wear the regulation white shoes. I was handed my tsampa bag, and with the yellow hat on my left shoulder, entered the assembly hall. A few other incarnate monks came in with me; others had gone in before. Then gradually the older monks began coming in. They took their seats on dark red cushions, while the sound of the drum continued. The younger monks were still in the court, waiting for the signal to be admitted, when the drum beat would quicken, slow to three sharp beats, and then stop. It stopped, and we heard the piercing sound of a conch being blown by a strong young monk up on the roof. At the same moment the prior's attendant drew the curtain from across the main entrance and the rest of the monks began coming in. Each carried a tsampa bag and a wooden tea bowl. They found their places, and the *geko* (the prior of the college), who was wearing his customary robe with heavily padded silk shoulders, walked slowly back and forth between the rows, making sure that all the monks were present and that each had assumed the correct sitting position according to the rules of the *Vinaya*, the body of rules governing the Buddhist Order and the behavior of its monks and nuns. When the geko was in front of him, each monk would sit absolutely silent and still, without even moving his eyes.

The whole vast hall was decorated much as that of the khamtsen had been, only here the colors were more subdued, since only the most precious antique silk embroideries and ancient Chinese rugs had been used, and the very oldest and most sacred thangkas hung. The chanting master, the unze, who was seated on a high pillow in the first aisle, began the chanting in a very deep, mellow voice, rehearsing the twelve main events in the Lord Buddha's life. This chant, according to tradition, had been composed by the First Dalai Lama, and above the unze's seat, which was against one of the pillars, there hung a mask of the protective deity of Rato which had been made (also according to tradition) by the Fifth Dalai Lama. Whenever the monks of Rato went out together on tour, this mask was taken along. The sonorous chant continued while the geko walked to the main door and when the assistant geko again pulled back the curtain the abbot entered the hall, preceded by one attendant, and solemnly walked down the aisle. To show respect we took our hats in our hands and bowed to him as he passed. He mounted his throne, which was to the left of the aisle, directly across from the empty throne of the Dalai Lama; and when he was settled there we all placed our hats on the floor in front of us.

The abbot, wearing his official robe of embroidered silk above and yellow cotton below, surveyed the rows of monks, as though looking directly at each. After this symbolic count, the curtains of the main door were drawn closed and the geko, inspecting the rows of monks once again and looking very serious, walked with great dignity down the main aisle. When he arrived at the abbot's throne he bowed down low with utmost respect, and the abbot blessed him by touching his own forehead to the geko's. The unze, who had been chanting all the while, leaned slightly to the right at this moment, which signalled the young monks appointed to the tea service to go now to the kitchen. They were soon back with the huge wooden tea pots, pouring tea into the wooden bowls held out by the monks in both hands. The geko in a low voice told them to move quickly, and they rushed out so fast that one fell on the slippery stones. I was afraid he was hurt, but he got up smartly and chased after the others like a young colt.

We drank some buttered tea in silence and then, with the half-empty bowls on our laps propped firmly against our cloaks, mixed tsampa with the tea that was left. While we still were eating and drinking, the geko rose, prostrated himself, and asked permission for those who had been unable to attend the ceremony because of duties elsewhere in the monastery to share the tea in their rooms. He then performed the *khyabtho*—a reading of the letters written by those who had offered gifts for the occasion. But since in the present case the only donor was myself, the only letter to be read was mine. All such khyabtho were couched in formal language, which at my age I had not yet learned. Friends in Lhasa, therefore, had composed my letter for me, with the usual formal prayers for all teachers and holders of the Doctrine, for the great seats of learning at Drepung, Sera, Gaden, and the two Tantric colleges of Lhasa; for all members of the Sangha throughout the world; and with prayers, furthermore, that all those connected with learning and practice of the Doctrine should have long lives; that plague, famine, and war should cease forever in the world; and that the nations of the world should live in peace, as in the Golden Age. This then was followed by a personal prayer, that I might complete my studies and that they should bear fruit in practice; that I might be helpful to other beings and to the furtherance of the teachings; and finally, that my parents and relatives, my *chagzo* (administrator) in the monastery, and all those connected with me, might find fulfillment and enlightenment in their lifetimes. At the conclusion of all that, the geko, who had read the letter, sat down; and while Dongye and his helpers distributed our gifts, the abbot recited the Ngowa prayer in a deep voice. The purpose of this prayer was to dedicate the results of all meritorious actions toward the attainment either of desires or of Enlightenment (according to one's motivation). When that prayer was said, tea was served again, with a thick rice broth that the monks very much liked. Then the chanting ended, the meal was finished, and all rose and filed out to their rooms.

I returned to my guest room in the khamtsen, where the khamtsen gegen met me to say that the new quarters, which were to be my permanent residence during the years of my studies at Rato, were now ready. The next day I was moved into a fine fourth-floor apartment of three rooms: a living room, a guest room, and a kitchen furnished with a stove made of clay. (There was ample room in the kitchen to accommodate the young monk who would be my attendant.) The living room had two windows that opened on the courtyard, unglazed and hung over with cotton curtains; for glass was considered a luxury and not permitted in most monasteries. There were, however, inside wooden shutters that could be closed when it was cold, and in winter we could have fires in our rooms. My room was square, with a single supporting pillar, and not very large, but things could be stored next door, in the guest room. My labrang had paid to have the whole suite newly painted—the lower half maroon, the upper yellow-orange, and between them two stripes of red and blue, suggesting a rainbow. My bed, against the main side wall, consisted of a bank of solid high cushions covered over with orange and red Tibetan rugs, and above it hung a large thangka showing the Lord Buddha surrounded by eight great Indian scholar-saints. There were no flowering plants in the room; for in Rato, as in many other monasteries, monks were not allowed to keep plants privately. It was thought that caring for them might distract from study. We could have cut flowers, however, as offerings for our altars. On the side of my room across from my bed a large lacquered chest had been arranged as an altar ornamented with paintings of lotuses and other emblems. Above it a wooden cabinet with glass doors enshrined three painted images of Tsongkhapa and his two disciples clothed in yellow brocade robes, wearing yellow hats and tasseled aprons. Along the whole top of the altar, finally, there stood ten silver bowls which were to be filled daily with fresh water.

I had just settled into these quarters, which I found comfortable and very pleasant, when two administrators from the college arrived to offer congratulations. They presented me with scarves and with money in two envelopes, assuring me that everything had gone well, and that my ceremony had been most successful. Not very long after they left, the time arrived for the usual evening session, and from the windows of my new room I could look down and see the prior come out into the courtyard and begin loudly reciting the prayers that announced the beginning of the recitations. I left my room and went down to the yard where all we junior monks were assembling (all those who had been in the monastery for less than twelve years were considered to be junior)—there were about a hundred of us. When we had all sat down, six feet apart, the recitation began of the mantra of Manjusri, *Om Ara Pa Tsa Na Dhi*, repeated and repeated. This was followed by prayers by an Indian scholar in praise of learning Manjusri after which each monk recited in a loud voice some text that he had learned by heart.

Rato, specializing in the Sutras, gave no courses in Tantric Buddhism, and so, most of the books that we were to memorize this session were of the Sutras, either translations from traditional Indian works, or books by Tibetan saints on the same themes. When at home I had already memorized the contents of a number of our prayer books, but very little from theological works. I knew, perhaps, only two or three short texts of this kind, and when it came my turn I recited a few pages that I had learned by heart from one of these.

Meanwhile the prior walked back and forth through the rows, checking to see that everybody was present. Each student was required to sit in the same place each session, which made it easy to spot absentees. When the prior had finished this survey he retired to the assembly hall, but in about an hour reappeared with a fresh incense stick in his hand. (We did not measure time with watches in the monastery, but counted the passing hours by the burning of incense sticks placed in pots about the courtyard.) No one was permitted to leave an evening recitation session until after the second visit of the prior. When he left I got up, prostrated myself three times, and prayed, as was customary. I then rose and returned to my rooms. Many of the monks would remain there in disciplined study for hours; but I noticed, from my room, that some of the smaller boys had moved together and began to chat as soon as the prior's back was turned. I noticed too, looking out my window every now and then, that as the long evening wore on, the monks became fewer and fewer, until there remained only a small number—but these stayed on almost through the night, pacing up and down the courtyard, reciting the texts that they had learned by heart.

6.

The Beginning of My Study of Dialectics

The day after I moved into my new quarters, the khamtsen council met to choose a teacher for me. Three names had been suggested: Jampa Tashi, Kunga, and Konchog Gyatso. The council had decided that divination would be the best way to settle the matter.

There are many kinds of divination practiced in Tibet. The idea of the council was to place the names in question in tsampa dumplings and draw lots. This was a form of divination used on very special occasions, such as selecting a Dalai Lama, and I agreed that it would be a very good method by which to select my teacher. The members, having heard my opinion, left me in my room and returned to the courtyard, while I returned to my place of observation at the window. I saw them first write down the names of the three candidates on a single sheet of paper which a monk then cut into slips. Next the prior's assistant, having washed his hands, molded three good-sized dumplings from a dough of tsampa and water. One of his helpers weighed each dumpling on a little scale and, after that, inserted a slip with a name into each. He placed all the dumplings on a silver offering tray, which he covered with a cotton cloth. Then the members rose from their red cushions and went filing out of the court. Soon after one of them came to my door to ask me down with him to the assembly hall where the council had reassembled.

I found them all standing before the central image of the altar, the image of our patroness, the Green Tara. One held out the silver offering tray with its dumplings and all fervently prayed. A second monk stepped forward, passed a lighted incense stick around the tray, and rotated it slowly, then increasingly faster and faster. A third monk held out his upper garment to catch the oracular dumpling when it fell, which he did adroitly. A fourth then picked the dumpling up, and squeezed it tight to distinguish it from the rest. We all then went up again to my apartment, where a council member broke the dumpling open and read out the name: "Konchog Gyatso!" Dongye, Norbu, and one of the members immediately left the room to call the young monk, Konchog Gyatso. When they had gone, one of those remaining whispered to me that this had been an auspicious choice; for while all three of the named candidates were excellent scholars, Konchog Gyatso had the most humility and the strongest religious feelings.

It was arranged that Norbu, Dongye, and I should meet Konchog Gyatso the next morning, and in preparing me for the occasion, Norbu suggested that in going to my new teacher I should not appear empty-handed. He reminded me of the story of how Atisha, when approaching for the first time the great Dharmakirti, his main teacher in Java when he had gone to that island on a visit, offered a crystal *Kalasa* jar full of precious stones. "Of course we don't have any such precious stones," said Norbu humorously, "but we might offer a yellow hat to suggest that Khyongla hoped to become a great teacher of the Yellow Hat sect." Norbu himself, it happened, had an extra yellow hat, which he brought along for me to give to my teacher.

Konchog Gyatso lived on the same floor as I did, and when we arrived at his door, a student monk still busy in Konchog Gyatso's kitchen drew aside the curtain for us to enter. I saw a tall, thin man with a round face and moustache who rose from his cushion to greet us, and there was something very pleasant about his personality that I immediately liked. I presented the yellow hat which he received with a warm smile, and I was glad that it was he who was going to be my teacher.

His room was small but very clean and orderly. Instead of a table in front of his cushion, he had only a log, sawed in half; but on the bookshelves I noticed many volumes, perhaps a hundred or more. An incense stick of very good quality was burning and smelled delightful.

When we took our seats on the cushions, he asked me to tell him of my studies in the Kham. Actually, it was Dongye who gave most of the answers. Konchog Gyatso listened respectfully, and when everything had been told, he and Dongye looked at the calendar to select an auspicious day for the beginning of my work.

That day arrived, and, again very early in the morning, my new teacher came to my apartment. He was offered the high seat we had prepared for him, and when he had settled himself on this I presented him with a kind of scarf that we call *nyinmo deli*, into which an auspicious poem has been woven. I then sat down respectfully, and Konchog Gyatso began my instruction.

He opened a text on logic called *Dudra* (a glossary of important terms commonly used in debating), and clearly and slowly read three times the four introductory lines of homage, then continued with the text. I listened carefully. He would read a little, then pause, and I would repeat the words just heard, my task at that time being only to memorize, not to analyze and appreciate the deeper meanings of the passages. We went on that way until we came to a propitious passage stating that the topic next to be studied would provide religious instruction according to the intellectual powers of the student. "Tomorrow," Konchog Gyatso said, "you are to recite these lines to me by heart. It is important, first to learn, and then to practice what you have learned, so that eventually you may be able to be of use to others."

Now the work that I was studying was an elementary text in logic, or *Pramāna*, "the means or measure by which True Knowledge (*Prām*) is determined." The first chapter discusses the colors red and white in such a way as to introduce terms and principles that can be applied to any subject. For example, such an elementary question may be asked as: "Are *color* and *white* the same, or are they mutually exclusive?" The reply is that they are neither the same nor mutually exclusive: *white* is a color, but *color* is not necessarily *white*. This line of reasoning leads later on to complex philosophical insights. The beginning is very easy, but chapter by chapter, more and more philosophical terms are introduced. The chief Pramāna texts that I was to study later on would be the *Pramānavartika* and various commentaries upon this most extensive and fundamental of the seven logical treatises written by Dharmakirti, the great seventh-century Indian logician. I was led through these to an appreciation of the essence not only of Buddhism but also of the chief non-Buddhist Indian doctrines then flourishing, the Sankhya system, Yoga system, Nyaya-Vaisheshika, Mimamsa, and Vedanta. Pramāna, as understood in Tibet, was finally a comparative study of these religions, proving and establishing through logic the superiority of Buddhism over the rest.

Three weeks after my admission to Rato, my uncle Kunsang came from Drepung to see me. He told us that he had just heard that one of the most famous lamas in our land, Tagdag Rinpoche, who had been a teacher of many of the most distinguished lamas of the Yellow Hat sect, was going soon to be lecturing at his own small monastery about ten miles from Rato; and my uncle thought that I should attend. The lama was an old man, but his learning was immense, and it might even be possible for me to receive from him the *getsul* ordination, which is the first of the two stages of ordination of a monk, and may be given to any seven-year-old boy big enough to scare a crow. The second ordination, the *gelong*, on the other hand, is only for candidates who have reached their twentieth year. The Tibetan word *gelong* applies to every monk who has taken final ordination, its extended meaning being: "He who is searching for release from the world and living on alms according to the teaching of the Lord Buddha."

When I had become a little monk at the age of eight, I had begun to wear a monk's robe, but had not taken any vows. When my uncle now made his suggestion, therefore, I liked the idea and fell in readily with his plan. I would not be permitted to make a decision of such importance alone, however, and Norbu and Dongye on talking it over agreed that the first step would be to ask the abbot of Rato for permission. Generally monks were not allowed to leave the premises for more than a week at a time, unless on business for the monastery. Anyone wishing to be away for even a single day or night had to ask permission of the prior of his khamtsen, and if intending to be away for anything more than three nights, he would have to receive the permission also of both the prior of the monastery and the abbot. Incarnate lamas were given greater freedom in such matters, yet it was still required that we too should ask permission of these officials.

The next day, therefore, Norbu went to our abbot to consult with him on the advisability of my going to Taglung Dag. The abbot in reply pointed out that since I had been only a few weeks at the monastery, I had had little time to get acquainted with either my teacher or my work. As a rule, he reminded Norbu, a monk who had not received his degree would be required to be in attendance for some years before going to listen to teachers elsewhere. However, since Tagdag Rinpoche was such a highly qualified and extraordinary teacher, he would not withhold permission. Even though he knew that I had not yet learned enough to be able to understand the lectures, he said that it would probably be to my benefit to experience an atmosphere of such sanctity and that seemed to him in itself to be enough to justify the breach of rules.

As the lectures were scheduled to begin within the week, we began our preparations immediately, and soon departed.

After a ride of two hours, we drew near the monastery and I began to make out the buildings. They were not really old, but also not very new, and neither beautiful nor significant in their architecture. A large number of small, stone, brick-fronted cottages were scattered about the grounds under the willow and juniper trees. It was in those that the monks lived. The labrang itself was three stories high, and when we dismounted some little distance before it to walk up an approaching path, we had to pass between two rows of kennels built of stone like little houses; from the front door of each a huge dog yelped his greeting. And what a fierce chorus that was! They were for the most part Tibetan mastiffs, which are famous watchdogs. My uncle told me, as we walked between, that the Rinpoche was very fond of these dogs and every day came out personally to feed them. We arranged to rent a cottage there from a monk from Dayab, who was now the keeper of the chapel. He had a thick black beard, which is a little unusual for Tibetans, and was called behind his back the Old Black Bear, which he knew and took with good humor. His little house, we found, had a large living and sleeping room, an outside terrace, and a kitchen. It was comfortable, and we soon had made ourselves at home.

Tagdag Rinpoche began his series of talks the next day. They were to be on the Tantra. More than sixty monks had arrived from various monasteries to attend them, and among these were no less than seven incarnations, including myself. We all met at the assembly hall of the labrang early that first afternoon, and the Rinpoche lectured from a text that I had already memorized with my beloved teacher in the Kham, the *Guru Pancha*, which deals with the question of how the disciple is to treat his teacher. So I now found myself, to my own surprise and great satisfaction, following the text and for the most part understanding it. To tell the truth, I felt a little proud of myself at that moment, but the feeling was not to last long. For the Rinpoche on the following day took his text from a work of which I had never heard, and although I tried to listen attentively, I found it difficult to grasp the meaning of most of the words.

I was sitting next to another incarnate lama, only two years older than myself, and in front of us was a pillar, so that frequently when the Rinpoche moved, we could neither see him nor be seen. We spent those periods playing together, at first in a friendly manner, but then occasionally becoming irritated with each other.

I was still a pretty mischievous youngster and liked to indulge in all sorts of pranks. In the courtyard of the labrang a young monkey was kept leashed that would squeal loudly whenever I went near him. My friend and I agreed to play a trick on him. I held out an apricot on a stick to the monkey, which he took and ate. Then I held out another, but when he reached for it, I moved away quickly and my friend hit his arm with a stick. The monkey screamed in pain and we were given a sound scolding, which we deserved.

To tell the truth, I cannot say that I gained very much from those lectures. The Rinpoche elucidated and demonstrated in his talks the powers of the different deities of the multitudinous Tantric pantheon, and for a student to follow such a discourse requires that he should be able to experience, at least to *some* degree, the Great Compassion (*Karuna*) and the longing to achieve Buddhahood for the purpose of guiding all beings to Liberation (*Bodhicitta*). But I did not know at that time exactly what Bodhicitta and the Great Compassion were. Furthermore, to be eligible for Tantric initiations it is absolutely necessary for the student to follow and enact in imagination the instruction of the guru, and I could scarcely follow the Rinpoche's words. I was, in fact, nothing more than a presence in the room at that series of lectures.

At the end of our first week two boys from Northern Tibet and I received ordination as getsul. The ceremony took place in the Rinpoche's room and lasted about an hour. All three of us were given new names by the Rinpoche and the one that I received was Nawang Losang Shedup Tenpai Donme, the "Lord of Speech; [the] Noble-Minded One Who

Illuminates the Doctrine by Teaching and Practice." Curiously (as already told above) this was the name that I had been given when I first became a monk five years before, at the age of eight, with the addition of the word *nawang*, "lord of speech." Yet Tagdag Rinpoche had not known what name I had been given before, and I cannot think that my behavior at his lectures was what had inspired this fine title. It was rather something for me to aspire to than a dignity that I might plume myself on having earned.

This new name of mine was to be used in the future only on very special ceremonial occasions; for example, when bestowing ordinations, or assisting my lamas in official functions. My father had named me Norbu, but from the time I had been recognized as the reincarnation of the Ninth Khyongla, people called me either Khyongla Tulku or Khyongla Rinpoche. Some addressed me simply as Rinpoche ("Precious One"), which is a title employed in addressing both abbots and incarnations. And after my admission to the Rato Monastery people from outside would sometimes address me as Rato Khyongla Rinpoche, or Rato Khyongla Tulku. Finally, however, my proper name is Khyongla. There is no one else now living by that name, and all the other fine titles are the ceremonious honorifics of formal address.

With the series of lectures ended, I returned with Dongye to Rato and my regular order of life, leaving Kunsang, my uncle, at Taglung Dag. And it was only a few days after my return that a special memorization test was announced. These tests took place four times a year, their dates being set and announced in the assembly hall only two days before they were to occur, and the only monks not required to participate were such very new students as myself and those who had already graduated to the study of *Vinaya*. The tests were held in a beautiful walled garden to one side of the front of the main building, where lectures were often given and the monks debated religious questions. This was known as the *chora*, the "place where religion is studied," and was a garden of harmony and peace. The examinations held there, among fruit trees, flowers, and bird song, were supervised by the abbot, the four members of the council, and the nine priors of the khamtsens. The monks would arrive early in the morning, carrying their books on their shoulders, and presenting themselves before the entrance, find the abbot and council members seated on their cushions, with the prior striding back and forth, checking for absentees.

My teacher, Konchog, suggested that even though I was not required to attend, and had not yet even listed the texts I had memorized, it would be a good thing for me to participate in this exercise. He knew that in the Kham I had memorized one *Prajnaparamita* ("Perfection of Wisdom") text and one of the *Madhyamika* ("Middle Path"), and he suggested that I should recite from those.

I was afraid and reluctant to go with my two memorized morsels into the arena of this great testing, but since I was duty-bound to accept my teacher's advice, I took my two books on my shoulder and entered the chora with the rest; and in my turn I came before the abbot, bowed to him most respectfully, and handed him my two books. "Is it true," he asked, taking them and beaming at me, "that you know all this and aren't just going to be making things up?" He opened the Prajnaparamita text to the first page, and said, "Recite!" I was very nervous. I recited the first page in a loud but unnatural voice. The abbot skipped over several pages and read a line at the top of another, saying, "Continue!" I recited to the end of the page. Then he leafed through some more pages and read a few words. I was now gaining confidence and recited more naturally, trying to bring out the meaning of the text. So we proceeded through the book which is luckily a short one; he then indicated the final page by quoting a few words. I recited to the end, perspiring from the effort, but I came through.

That was our customary way of testing a student's memory. It revealed immediately to the examiner how much of the text the student had covered, how correctly he had memorized it and—above all—how well he had grasped its sense. When the abbot closed the book, he put up his hand to detain me and said: "Khyongla, you had a very good teacher in the Kham. I am going to write to him and congratulate him, for I am greatly gratified." Then he asked: "Now, how many pages do you want to list to be memorized for next session?"

I was breathing more easily, but still hesitant. "Perhaps, five."

He burst out laughing. "Are you sure, Khyongla, that you want to make it more than one?" Then he suggested that it would be best if I decided to list at least ten. "No one should ever bargain," he said, "over how much studying to do."

Right after me was a monk who had memorized three hundred pages, and when he passed his test successfully, he was given a scarf by the abbot. Next was one who recited from a text of over five hundred pages and, being word perfect, was rewarded with a new robe. If a monk took an Indian Buddhist work as his text and recited two hundred pages, it was counted as four hundred in these texts; for we believe the Indian works are the real source of Buddhism, and since they are greatly condensed, they are far more difficult for us to master than our own Tibetan works. Tsongkhapa's works, however, were also given double credit.

One monk at that examination who had never been much of a student had listed a number of pages from a certain text, found that he had brought along the wrong book, and in his confusion recited pages from still another book. He was severely criticized by the prior and as punishment, the next day, was ordered to do prostrations for one hour during the daily service in the assembly hall. He was a middle-aged man, rather heavy-set and quite bald, ordinarily a great joker, and it was an extremely mortifying thing for him to have to humiliate himself in this way before his fellow monks.

At the end of the session the abbot invited me to come by his apartment, and when I was ushered in by his attendant I found him seated, waiting for me, on his cushions. He offered me a place and inquired about the getsul ordination, asking how many rules a getsul has to abide by. Although I tried very hard to remember, I was confused and soon lost count.

"You didn't listen, did you," he chided, "when you took the ordination? But I don't blame you," he then said more kindly. "You are a new student here and very young." He warned me to study well all the rules of the getsul and to practice them now diligently, for they were a basic part of the Vinaya and the basic rules of the Buddhist Order. Later on in my training, he said, when the time came for me to begin my systematic study of the whole Vinaya, they would be reviewed more precisely and on a different intellectual level. "If these rules are not learned and observed exactly," he told me, "they will be broken and the monk will sin." Then he laughed and quoted a saying that he had heard of a Mongolian monk: "When I took the vows," this monk was supposed to have said, "I had no Vinaya. When I finished the Vinaya, I was through with my vows." We often joked about Mongolians being uninformed, and what this saying meant, as the abbot explained, was: "When I took my vows I did not know the rules that I was going to have to follow as a monk; and by the time I had learned the rules I had broken so many of them that I almost had to give up my monkhood."

7.

A Debating Session at Jang

In Rato, as in other monasteries devoted to theological studies with debates, there were two main types of work programs conducted in alternation through the year. There was first the *chora tsugpa*, a season of sessions held in the chora, where the abbots met with their monks for lectures and discussions and the monks themselves held debates daily. Alternating with these were the *choentsam* periods, when the students devoted their time chiefly to reading and memorizing in their rooms. Two or three successive evenings a week throughout these choentsam seasons, however, all the junior monks would assemble in the courtyards of their khamtsens to sit on the bare stones and recite as loudly as they could the passages they were memorizing—and since they were all memorizing from different texts, the noise was frequently deafening. Then the evening after such a series of nights a debate would be held, during which one or two of the monks would be called upon to answer challenging questions put to them by any of the rest. Rato held eight such chora tsugpa sessions a year, a winter session at Jang, about twenty miles east of Rato, a summer session at Sangphu, on the Kyichu River, about fifteen miles to the south, and six sessions in Rato itself. The sessions at each place ranged from two to six weeks, and all those who had not yet received their geshe degree were required to attend.

Since my guardian Norbu had decided against accompanying me to Jang, I turned to Konchog, who immediately decided to come with me. When I asked him to tell me something about the session and why it was always held, not at Rato, but at Jang, he replied: "During the Lord Buddha's lifetime he and his disciples moved about to many places in order to discourage attachment to any one place. That is one of the reasons why we also move about—to Jang and to other places. But also, even though Jang is not a wealthy monastery, it is famous for the many scholars and saints who have lived and studied there; and that is why it has become a sanctuary of learning. The whole environment is conducive to study and to religious ceremonial." Konchog added that since he would be going with me, we could wait until we arrived in Jang for him to tell me what my duties there would be.

At sunrise on the big morning, I left on horseback with a friend. There were many monks on the roads that day, all heading for Jang, from Drepung, Sera, and Gaden, as well as from Rato. We followed the river road most of the way, and on approaching Jang could see the monastery on its height, back away from the road. It seemed a bleak sort of place. But when we arrived a few monks came out to greet us and to carry in our luggage. They helped us from our horses and took us to our khamtsen, which occupied a house two stories high with an assembly hall that filled the entire ground floor; on the second floor there were eleven rooms around an open court where we might sit when the sun came out.

Each little room had a single small window. That in the room I would occupy was not more than two feet high, and was covered with paper that made it very dark except when the sun shone directly in. In the mornings the light was a deep yellow, and that was the best of the day. My teacher, one of his classmates, and I, had been assigned to this little room together, and when Konchog asked one of the building attendants if there were cushions, tables, and lamps about that we might rent or borrow, he said he would rent us only two pairs of cushions, two lamps, and a single square wooden block for a table. My teacher's classmate consequently was left with no cushion at all, and so he improvised one for himself by filling a gunnysack with straw. We had brought along our own bed covers, and a few drapes for the walls and ceilings, but had forgotten paper for the window, to keep out the draft. The caretaker could furnish only one miserable piece of printed wrapping, which we pasted up with some tsampa porridge.

The new monks who were to take turns at kitchen duty were that afternoon brought together in the courtyard for the purpose of choosing work groups. Sitting in a circle, each threw one of his shoelaces into the center. Since Tibetan shoelaces were handmade, each one was different and thus easily recognized by its owner. The oldest monk picked the laces up, mixed them together under his upper garment, and threw out five, then five again; he continued thus by fives until all the laces were back in the center. Each group of five monks chosen by lot in this way had special duties assigned to it, and the assignments were rotated, day by day. The oldest on a kitchen team would have only to make the fire and keep the stove. The others would have to fetch water from the little brook some distance off and help with the cooking, under supervision of the first cook.

Every monk during his first eight years in a monastery had to work his stint in the kitchen in this way, except incarnations and *chogzeds*—monks who had gained privileges by offering gift ceremonies—who were exempted. One day while I was watching the work groups being chosen, one of the young monks said to me: "Khyongla, if you want to work, you may. However, your labrang has arranged for you to be excused from all such duties." And then he quoted to me a proverb: "If a lion lives on the mountain, he is a lion; if he wanders in the village, he is a dog." I did not know that he was joking, and so was somewhat annoyed, but kept still and walked away. Still annoyed, I spoke of the event to my teacher's classmate and he told me that I was wrong in taking it that way. "If you know how to make use of his words," he said, "that can be very good advice." Then he explained, pointing out that in Central Tibet, not only in Rato but also in the "Three Pillars," less respect was shown to incarnations in the monasteries than in their labrangs, since, after all, the life of a labrang was centered around its incarnation, whereas in the larger monastery each incarnation was but one of several, or even of many and so not held in the same high esteem.

The next day, after our morning ceremonies in the hall, everybody filtered out into the courtyard for the first debating session, but since I had not yet had any experience of the art I remained in my room upstairs with my teacher, memorizing, and learning from him the proper way to conduct oneself in a debate. I did not find it difficult to follow his instructions. I had only to stand up and pronounce the syllable *dhi*, which in the tradition of Buddhist meditation is the seed-syllable from which springs the vision of Manjusri, who esoterically is thought of as the Bodhisattva of Divine Wisdom, and exoterically as the aggregation of the

Buddha's insight. I had to pronounce this in a loud, high-pitched voice, and then say, *jitawa shindu choje*, the sense of which was twofold: In this discussion we shall adhere strictly to the Lord Buddha's own teachings; throughout, we shall conduct ourselves—mentally, verbally, and physically—exactly as the Lord Buddha has taught. Mentally, we shall not think in terms of gaining a victory for ourselves and defeat for others; verbally, we shall avoid derogatory and abusive language; and physically, we shall avoid facial expressions of anger or condescension.

During a debate the questioner would stand, and the respondent sit cross-legged. There might be a large audience of monks, or none, but even if there were none, this convention was to be observed. If in the course of an argument the respondent was forced to retract some minor premise that he had put forward, the questioner would slap the back of his right hand sharply against the palm of his left, saying, "*Tsa!*" which meant that the other had lost a point. And if the retraction was a major premise, monks of the audience would sometimes join the questioner in shouting, "*Tsawai dhamcha tsa!*" which meant that the respondent had lost the debate altogether. My teacher assured me that this was not intended as an insult to the losing debater's intelligence. The aim in refuting a statement, he said, was only to overcome the ignorance in the minds of the two debaters. The point was not to win an argument, defeat an opponent, or increase one's own reputation. If in debate such thoughts arose in the mind, they were to be suppressed and the inner attitude changed. Personal insults were never allowed. What I was to learn, Konchog told me, was to think of overcoming both my own ignorance and that of others, so that eventually we might all realize our Buddhahood.

In Rato I had watched the monks debating and in my play had tried to imitate them; but now that it was really serious, it all seemed to be more difficult and I felt awkward, especially in front of my teacher. So I went out alone, the next day, to a corner of the building and practiced there by myself. I first tried shouting *tsa*, while slapping my palm that special way and at the same time stamping my left foot. It did not always come out together as planned and I kept trying, over and over. Instead of always bringing the back of the right hand, smack, onto the palm of the left, I frequently found that I had only clapped my two hands together, which was wrong. But I kept trying, and a few days later attended my first evening lecture in the courtyard.

I remember vividly the abbot arriving in his official yellow cotton robes. Before him came his attendant holding a paper-covered lantern that threw a small circle of light around him but left the rest of the courtyard in darkness. The abbot seated himself on his high throne against the wall and the monks of many classes remained standing. So many had come from the great "Three Pillars" for this session that the monastery court was crowded. The usual procedure for an evening of this kind was for the abbot to address his readings to one class of students at a time—to the advanced classes first and then the others, following in order, for the rule of seniority was applied to classes as well as to individuals. The abbot when giving a reading would repeat some passage from a text three times, reciting very slowly from memory without interpreting. He would then take off his hat and hold it in his right hand while the leader of the class addressed repeated the text very loudly in such a way that the abbot should hear and know that the class had been following his words.

These class leaders were appointed by the abbot, who would of course always try to select the most intelligent; but during the first two years at a monastery, when the abbot would not yet have become acquainted with a class of students, a temporary leader might be appointed to function until a considered choice could be made. This leader of his class often remained until all its members had earned their geshe degrees, and when the time came for examinations he would be given the privilege of receiving his degree first. Such a leader was responsible for overseeing his class, and making sure that in all its activities all general rules were observed; if unexpectedly he had to be absent on any occasion, he would appoint another classmate in his place.

In former times it was customary for an abbot giving a reading to recite his text only twice and then explain its meaning. The more intelligent students would get it by heart immediately; the class leader would then take them to another part of the courtyard and repeat the text three times, after which they would all recite together what they had heard. In my day, however, the procedure was different, for most of us already knew what text the abbot was going to recite and had prepared ourselves by memorizing it in our rooms.

In the course of my first evening in the court the abbot gave separate readings and lectures to each of the fifteen classes present at the session. There were, in all, about a hundred monks in attendance, and when the abbot had finished his second reading, the class that had been addressed rose and moved to one side of the court, taking their places in a circle. They clapped their hands three times, their leader clapped once, and each monk clapped once alone. All the monks then clapped together rhythmically and prostrated themselves in gratitude before the abbot. Rising from their knees, they then ran swiftly into the chora—I found all of this fascinating both to hear and to watch.

My own class, which included all the newest monks, came last; and when our reading was finished and we had gone into the chora, the prior of the college came to observe us in our studies. He found us seated in a circle reciting the passage that the abbot had delivered to us, our class leader in the middle, answering questions on the topic of the reading. First some of my friends asked questions. Then they insisted that I should ask questions, too. I had no idea what to say, but stood up and began a discussion of the colors from the *Dudra* text that I had memorized. I asked my opponent, "What color is green?" He responded, "Amoghabuddha's color is green." I said, "All colors are not white." He answered, "The conch shell of the Dharma is white." I knew that I could not keep this up very long and was hoping that someone else would get up to fire questions, for until that happened I would not be allowed to stop. At last, somebody did get up and turned the discussion to another topic. From that time on I regularly attended every debating event of the session, both mornings and evenings.

My teacher, Konchog, usually remained at the evening sessions and did not like me to leave before he did. Sometimes we only watched the discussions but then sometimes he entered into them. Many of the nights were windy and cold, and our feet on the bare stones froze. It was now December and those evenings were something of an ordeal. We wore no underpants, and so the lower parts of the body became numb. And when my teacher and I would at last be back in our room, we would brew ourselves some hot buttered tea and light a fire in our fireplace to thaw out.

One day Konchog asked me how I thought my studies were progressing, and when I answered honestly that I had not done much, he said firmly, but not severely, "You must try to work harder, Khyongla, from now on. In the beginning, no one is perfect. Even the Lord Buddha was at first like us. He reached Buddhahood only after working hard, very hard for a long time." He urged me not to be lazy or shy. "Join the others in debates," he said. "When you are invited to debate, stand up and say whatever you can. Jang, I know, is a pretty chilly place, and not everything here is well arranged, but it's a very good place in which to make progress in one's studies, for there is nothing else to do here."

Toward the end of the first month we all had to take a test, not of our memorizing, but of how much we had learned and assimilated of the subjects of the texts on which we had been working. There were no scholarly honors to be gained from this. It was simply a hard test and I worried about it greatly. Some of the other new students were also greatly concerned, counting the hours to the test; a few days before it came we all redoubled our efforts and spent every evening cramming. I said to one of my friends, "Perhaps we could ask one of the monks detailed to examine us to let us know, in a general way, what the answers ought to be like so that we might ask our questions intelligently." He looked at me with disgust. "That," he replied, "would be improper and shameful. To make such prearrangements for an examination would be so disgraceful that you would never live it down. Even after you died," he said, "they would remember that about you." I was sufficiently humbled. And then very shortly before the test one of the three examining monks who would be answering our challenges said to me in a joking way, "I'm going to cut *your* argument short." I replied with what I hoped would appear to be an air of confidence that whatever he did would be all right, but actually I was greatly frightened by that remark.

The examination took place in the courtyard of our khamtsen and occupied three afternoons and evenings. The first evening went on through the night, until sunrise; the second evening was shorter, and the last was shortest of all. The monk answering challenges through the whole first night was an older person who sat on his throne never looking straight at any of us, but staring off into space. We sat around him, as was customary, and the youngest monk asked the first question. The order to be followed was of inverse seniority, with the oldest questioner last. Some of the youngest were so nervous that they trembled. Others, when they stood up, could not arrange their questions consistently, and the prior scolded them, even threatening to beat them. I was very nervous too, since I had no idea when I would be called upon. The questioning went on and on, the monks rising, one by one, doing badly or well, and then sitting down. About midnight the prior called my name. I stood up and my heart skipped a beat. I addressed my question to the monk gazing off into space: "What are the colors of the four actions?"

He answered:

"The color of peaceful action;

The color of developing action;

The color of wrathful action;

The color of conquering action."

I asked: "What is the color of peaceful action?"

He replied:

"White is the color of peaceful action;

Red is the color of conquering action;

Yellow is the color of developing action;

Black is the color of wrathful action."

The prior at that point stopped me, and when I had sat down again, I fell into a half sleep and in a dream worried about the examination.

We had now been three weeks at Jang and the time had come to collect firewood. A number of monks would be assigned to the task, and when the gatherers then came back, heavily laden with the wood that they had collected, the other monks would come out to relieve them of their burdens, carry the wood into the courtyard, and stack it by the kitchen door. "Helping others," Konchog told me, "always brings good fortune. You must never allow yourself to feel pride in having been born to your high station. So go out there now and help your friends carry in the wood."

I went out and walked about a mile downhill to meet the monks still arriving with their wood. Most of the loads were very big. I selected a monk with a small one, but even so, since I had never engaged in that kind of physical work before, I found it very hard to carry even such a small load on my back uphill. It seemed to me impossibly heavy. And when I reached the top I found my teacher watching. "Khyongla, when you have a choice to make, you should not pick the easiest task. It was very wrong of you to make the choice you did. Having the name of an incarnation, you were born into this world to help people, not to make things easy for yourself."

Considerably chagrined, I deposited my little bundle in the courtyard, and straightaway went downhill again to find a monk with a larger load. I found my man, took his bundle from his back, and found it heavy as stones. The monk was laughing. "You can't carry that!" he said. I told him I could try. He gave me a hand and we carried the load together up the hill and, arriving in the courtyard, set it down. I looked around for Konchog, but to my dismay, he wasn't there.

Toward the end of the term the time came for a special kind of debate known as *tsog lang*, which in Tibetan means, "to stand up in debate before a congregation." Only two monks would take part in these challenges, both standing, in contrast to usual debating procedure where the answering monk sat either on a throne or on the floor. For the coming event, the monks were allowed to choose their own competing partners. I hoped for someone from my own class. But there was a geshe named Tsering Wangyal, a disciple of my predecessor, who asked me to be his match. I was surprised and said, "But you are a geshe and I am a new student. How can I stand up to you?" He admitted that he ought to know more than I, since he had been thirty years in the monastery and had gained his degree a long time ago. He had consequently not been required to attend this session at Jang, but it was for him, he said, a pleasure to be present at such a religious session. And he wished now to work with me, he declared, both because he liked me and in memory of my predecessor, Jampa. The fact was that, despite his being a geshe, he was not a very good scholar, though deeply religious. He was a man past sixty, rather corpulent and with stooped shoulders, who spent most of his time reciting the Mani and had a delightful sense of humor. He was fond of giving advice, and his favorite piece of advice, which he would give to us all frequently, was that it was not right to become angry when people criticized you. "Insulting words cannot hurt your body, so why be angry?" he would say. And with this he had gained a certain reputation.

The great evening came. We convened in the assembly hall of the khamtsen, with the prior calling out the names, and the teams standing up to contend. When Tsering Wangyal and I were called we stood up together and proceeded to the end of the row. We prostrated ourselves three times before the monks, then walked down the main aisle to the altar to touch the image of Tsongkhapa with our yellow hats. Having done all that, we returned to the main aisle. I stood in the middle, halfway, while Tsering took his place to my left, between the first and second rows of monks. He confronted me, putting his hat on, and in a loud voice cried "*Dhi!* at the same time clapping his hands. He had a very deep voice and was so witty that even his gestures were amusing. The questions he then put to me were those to which I had already learned all the answers from the text of my very first lesson. Nor did he press on any further, but continued to put to me questions from that text. Having memorized it all, I had no difficulty with my answers; then my turn came to question him.

I asked him to name the Eight Auspicious Objects. He answered correctly, and I asked him next: "Why is the conch shell auspicious?"

He replied, "Because the Lord Buddha blessed it as auspicious."

"When and how was this?"

"When Indra offered him a conch shell, the Buddha blessed it."

So we continued until the prior stopped us. In our khamtsen we had not taken this particular tsog lang very seriously, and if anybody asked a wrong question or received a wrong answer, we openly laughed.

The next evening we all took part in a playful luck-bringing ceremony. A burning incense stick was passed from hand to hand, from one monk to another, and when each one received the stick, he would start reciting a familiar verse from some poem that all together would then finish. For me the challenge that evening was not particularly difficult since I was sitting at the head of the first row and so was the first to choose a verse. But some of the younger monks were nervous; for if anyone began to recite a verse that had already been used, everybody laughed and called, "It is already finished." One from my class tried five different verses, all of which had already been used, before he hit upon a fresh one. The verse with which I had opened was from one of our most famous prayers:

"Lobsang Dagpa's seat of Dharma,

Where conduct, wisdom, contemplation

Are pure and perfectly applied,

Is crowded with throngs of yogi-monks

By their practice may the Lord Buddha's teaching endure!"

The next day we left Jang and rode back to Rato. We were all happy to return and my room seemed almost luxurious after our Spartan life in Jang.

8.

Our New Year Celebration and Monlam

New Year's Day was approaching, and before that we were to have a holiday of five days. At all other times of the year strict rules were enforced in our college and khamtsen; so we younger monks were now excited, counting the hours. The holiday began on the twenty-fifth day of our Tibetan twelfth month (January) when the rules were lifted and we could leave the monastery without permission and go wherever we wished. Also the prohibition against long and noisy visits in each others' rooms was lifted and the rule of silence not enforced. We were able to visit back and forth, and it could be quite late when we retired. Nor did we have to wear the upper garment usually prescribed, but were allowed to dress informally.

On the twenty-ninth day of the month and last of our holiday, we all cleaned our rooms to be ready for the New Year. Lhabu, my attendant, and I worked together and some of my other friends helped us clean the apartment thoroughly. We scrubbed the walls and floors; in the kitchen, swept out the chimney—which was actually no more than a hole in the ceiling covered with a porcelain pot that caught the soot—and polished the stone floor with woolen cloths attached to our shoes, skating diligently with our feet until the surface shone. The outside frames of the windows were plastered and painted black, but the rain and sun had caused much of the paint to flake off, so we repaired and repainted the frames. When they were dry, we polished them with handstones until the paint shone, after which we rubbed oil over the surface to keep the dampness out.

When evening came and we had finished our great labors the three of us gathered in Norbu's room and ate soup with small dumplings of wheat flour made by rolling the dough by hand and cutting it into sections. Nine ingredients were then added: rice, some meat, a radish, droma, herbs, cheese, peas, chili peppers, a lump of charcoal, and a piece of porcelain.

In my monk's robes when I was about twenty seven. I was invited to Katmandu to establish a monastery. Katmandu, Nepal, 1950.

BELOW: A recent picture of myself in front of a thanka of Buddha. New York, 1986. Photo: Ken Maguire.

The Assembly Hall of Rato Monastery. Nyetang, Tibet, 1987. Photo: Doc O'Connor.

Greeting Ling Rinpoche and his secretary, Losang Lungrig, on their arrival at JFK Airport. I gave him flowers and a scarf and he gave them back. New York, 1980. Photo: Ven. Nicholas Vreeland.

Serkong Rinpoche and me. Dharamsala, India, 1968.

The present Ling Rinpoche and me at Chopra House. Dharamsala, India, 1990. Photo: Donna Swensen.

Rato Monastery monks including photographer at top right. Mundgod, India, 1991. Photo: Ven. Nicholas Vreeland.

LEFT: *Pabongka Rinpoche, one of the most important Gelugpa teachers of this century.*

BELOW: *Kartak Monastery near my Labrang. Gonsar, Tibet, 1983 . Photo: Elizabeth Benard.*

Ling Rinpoche giving a Long Life Initiation at the first Tibet Center on 28th Street. New York, 1980. Photo: Robert Cox.

One dumpling was shaped like a sun, another like a moon. Getting either of these was an auspicious sign. Lhabu got the one with the lump of charcoal in it and we teased him about having a black mind.

During the course of the evening ceremony in the assembly hall tormas were made for the demons. Some were in the forms of little images of monks in their robes. Coins were placed in the hands of these and tiny lamps of dough filled with butter. When they were all ready, they were offered to the demons while we chanted—after which a company of the youngest novices, ten or twelve years old, was dispatched to carry the cakes outside and throw them into the fields. Meanwhile a monk with a lighted torch had been going around into every corner of the assembly hall, calling, "Come out! Come out! Come out!" as though searching for thieves. When he had finished this work he went out with the boys and tossed his torch away to show that all troublesome influences had been expelled from the monastery.

The next day was spent preparing New Year decorations. In our suite we hung new white curtains on the windows and, over these, new valances, striped dark blue, red, yellow, and white. We put new rugs down, hung numerous thangkas, set out our best tea cups on silver stands, and then invited two artist monks in, one to re-gild the faces of the images on our altar, and the other to make decorated tormas. The first removed every speck of dust from the faces with a cotton cloth, then mixed a pure gold powder in solution, which he applied very quickly. He then repainted the eyes and lips, and in some cases, the hands. The other spent the whole day making a number of large cakes of dough, which he decorated with colored butter. When they were ready, we placed them before the altar, on the right side of which we set also a sheep's head molded of butter, with its eyes and mouth colored realistically and its head crowned with wish-fulfilling stones.

Our khamtsen that day distributed to all our monks wheat-flour cakes fried in poppy-seed oil. Some were shaped like a donkey's ear and this shape has given the donkey's ears (*pongpu amichok*) to such cakes, though many are in other shapes as well. We ordered in addition a few special cakes made of a particularly fine-ground flour, fried in butter and sprinkled with sugar, which we placed on our altar. On top of these we put dried fruits and fresh oranges, which we ate later. That was the first time I had ever tasted an orange, and I thought it wonderful—particularly wonderful to have such delicious fresh fruit in midwinter.

To symbolize the renewal of life with the New Year most Tibetan households kept an old pot or jar of earth in which barley or wheat had been planted a few weeks earlier; by the turn of the year, it would be sprouting green. We placed such a vessel on our altar as an offering to the "Three Jewels," together with some rice and a few coins. In the kitchen, we set out big plates of a tasty mixture of tsampa with sugar and butter, called *chemar*, of which everyone coming to visit us might take a pinch to scatter as an offering, and have a small bite himself—it being considered very important that everybody should partake of at least a little.

Around two in the morning of New Year's Day, two monks came into my room. One carried a lamp, the other a big pot of thick, hot wheat porridge. They had just returned from the college, where they had paid the first visit of the New Year to our abbot, who had been brought nine bowls of such porridge, one from each of the nine khamtsens. As these two monks came in to pour some of their porridge into my bowl they sang in loud voices:

"Gathering auspicious blessings,
May you attain to eternal happiness;
And may the gods be victorious."

Lhabu came in behind them and we offered scarves and chemar at my altar. Each monk took a pinch, quickly scattered it about, and departed. For they had to visit every room in our khamtsen and by the time they had finished with all seventy, their necks would be bent with the scarves they had been offered and their legs thoroughly worn out from the climbing of innumerable stairs and rushing up and down of corridors with their heavy hot-porridge pots.

Lhabu, already dressed, went out now to fetch the first water of the New Year from a little mountain brook running down the hill about half a mile from the monastery. When he returned shortly, he was toting on his back a very large earthenware jar of the fresh water. It was still dark outside and the water was ice cold. Meanwhile I had gotten fully dressed in my gala robe: the time had come to make our water offering. First we ladled some into a pair of copper pitchers that had long, narrow, curved spouts. Dorje, a friend of mine, took one, I took the other, and as we were pouring the fresh clear water into the silver vessels on our altar we heard out in the courtyard the voice of a well-known beggar named Dekar. The sun would not be up until after six, but looking down from our window we could clearly see him in the light of all the lanterns that had been hung around the balconies over the courtyard. He carried a small staff and wore a cotton mask spangled with shells and little glass mirrors that glittered in the lantern light. A white goat skin draped his shoulders, and he improvised verses fluently in a loud voice, singing:

"What is my name?
My name is fulfillment of your wishes.
Whence do I come?
From east of India, this morning I have come.
Where shall I go from here?
I am on my way to the Western Paradise,
To Sukhavati, the Heaven of Amitabha,
The Buddha of Boundless Light;
To Him will I go!"

Next, Dongye and I went out to pay our New Year's visit to Konchog, on the floor below. When we entered his room I was surprised to see that he had not put up any New Year's decorations at all. Everything was, as usual, spotless, but all he had done was to place a few scarves on his altar and his books. "Peace and good wishes!" (*Tashi deleg!*) was his greeting as we entered, and he asked us to sit down. I had brought him a present of dried fruits. One of his other students had already offered droma and chemar, and we scattered some of this in the air. Then my teacher advised me: "This, Khyongla, is your first New Year's celebration in the monastery. You must pledge yourself to study hard this year and to make very good progress." Dongye invited him to my room, having also already invited some of Konchog's friends, and so we were about seven or eight when we assembled to begin the ceremony known as *Tsog*.

In front of the altar we placed an offering table on which a number of small offering cakes, also called tsog, had been arranged, with a large cake in the center, rounded on top, made of cheese powder mixed with melted butter and tsampa, with white and brown sugar added. Dyed purple from a coloring made of the dry roots of an edible plant, it was covered with Buddhist emblems: conch shells, a sun, fish, wheels, and the like. On the right was a platter of dried yak meat and on the left a mug of beer that we had gotten from the villagers and into which we had put brown sugar. First we all chanted, making offerings to the "Three Jewels," and then cut the big cake and placed the first piece on the altar. We continued chanting for a long time, accompanied by a flute, bell, drum, and conch shell, and it was beautiful. Only on such a high holiday were we allowed to play musical instruments in the khamtsen. My teacher, Lhabu, and a few other monks had very good voices, and we enjoyed this sacred concert enormously. During a pause, a prayer was intoned, and then we passed around the cakes, large and small, and the fruit. We only dipped our fingers into the beer, however, to taste it, for our monastery was very strict, and anyone who drank chang would be expelled.

Just before sunrise we all went down to our assembly hall, and although this was a very great holiday, we were not allowed to make jokes there, and recited our prayers as usual, after which there appeared in the courtyard the oracle's procession. With his many attendants he had come to us from the Chapel of the Protective God to circumambulate the monastery and pay visits. Many monks and villagers had been waiting at the door of the college to offer him scarves and greetings, and the abbot himself had come down from his room and stepped out to receive him.

His attendants stood holding banners, and while drums sounded and cymbals clanged, the oracle clutching in one hand his sword and in the other his bow, danced around and around in a circle. When he had finished he bowed three times in the direction of the main image of the monastery, and we formed a line to receive his blessing—first the abbot, then the members of the college staff and, finally, we incarnations. On the abbots and incarnations he conferred his blessing in the usual way, touching his forehead to theirs; but sometimes, because his movements were so jerky and quick, one or another got a real crack on the head. The staff members were luckier, and got only a touch of his hand. When the blessings had all been given, the oracle and his retinue hurried away and back to their chapel. It seemed they always went from place to place nearly at a run.

The second day of the New Year we began preparations to go to Lhasa for the celebration of the Monlam festival. I was very much excited, since this was the greatest festival of the year and every Tibetan dreamed of participating in it at least once in his lifetime. Officially it would last three weeks, from the third day of the New Year to the twenty-fourth. And practically all of the four hundred monks of Rato would be going, only thirty remaining behind as caretakers, to prevent the recurrence of an incident of the year before, when robbers had broken in and emptied a number of apartments.

The festival had been founded in the fourteenth century by Tsongkhapa himself, and its original intention had been to celebrate the anniversary of a legendary occasion, when the Lord Buddha defeated six heretical teachers by performing a series of miracles. Tsongkhapa has designed the carnival to last fifteen days, culminating the night of the first full moon of the year, but later the government increased the period of celebration to twenty-one days, the last week being the moon's waning and actually something of an anticlimax. Not all the Tibetans knew the reason for Monlam, but they did know that about twenty thousand monks gathered for its celebration, and this in turn drew thousands of lay folk, both to witness the many interesting spectacles and ceremonies and the festively religious atmosphere.

On the third day, early in the morning, Dongye and I set forth. We rode through the beautiful valley and in about six hours arrived at the foot of the Potala. Soon after we arrived some friends came by and invited me to go with them to hear the two chief assistant priors of Drepung speak in front of the courthouse. The prisoners serving sentences there had been transferred for the duration of Monlam to another jail, at the foot of the Potala. A crowd had gathered to watch the priors' retinue arrive on foot— first the kitchen help, then the junior assistants, and finally the assistant priors themselves. As they approached, moving very slowly, the crowd opened to make way, and walking in a circle, they took up positions before the courthouse door.

The first assistant prior spoke first. He was followed by the second. They said that the regular magistrates of the city were that day retiring from office for three weeks and would be replaced by the priors of Drepung. During this period the city magistrates would not be allowed to sentence prisoners, and as though to illustrate this statement, the public floggers came out of the main door of the courthouse and laid their whips in a heap before the two assistant priors. Standing behind the assistant priors all this while were twenty-one *geyogs*, brawny monks who had been appointed to assist the chief and assistant priors in the maintenance of law and order. They had been selected and appointed, upon application, from a class of monks at Drepung known as *dob-dobs*, who constituted a sort of sub-culture within the monasteries. Dob-dobs were not theological students, although some studied chanting and music. Some took care of theological students, doing their chores for them and so releasing them for study; but occasionally a dob-dob would himself graduate to theology, take degrees and, in later life, become even an abbot and good administrator. The majority, however, preferred work of a less sedentary sort, that would keep them outdoors and at physical tasks. Some were even given to petty fighting and so on. Dob-dobs wore robes differently from regular monks, and kept their hair longer, particularly the sidelocks. Some smeared their faces with black soot to make them look fierce, and wore red armbands over which a rosary, sometimes of rubies, was draped. Many dob-dobs also carried a big key that could be used as a formidable weapon, also swords carefully concealed. When serving as geyogs, however, dob-dobs carried staffs and wore long swords across their belts in full view.

On the first day of Monlam a great gift ceremony was to be held in the Jokhang, to which attendance was not obligatory, but my friends and I were eager to go. We found places in the balcony. The great building was packed full. After some time the members of the cabinet, each attended by seven servants, came walking very solemnly in and, having made the usual prostrations, sat where we could see them well. Below us, in the immense hall, monks were already seated—there must have been thousands present. After another long while the master of chanting and priors of Drepung appeared, coming down the central aisle, wearing their hats and walking slowly. The master of chanting took from the fold of his robe some flowers and, scattering these before the Lord Buddha's image, bowed his head and silently prayed. Then lifting his head, he walked to his throne at the end of the aisle and began to chant.

I have never heard a deeper and more beautiful voice in my whole life. He had been a dob-dob in the Kham originally, but after a few years' study, had become a superb musician. He then studied theology, and finally was appointed by the Thirteenth Dalai Lama to be master of chanting in Drepung. As I listened to him, enthralled, suddenly I became aware of a stir down below in the assembly hall, where five hundred tea servers had appeared bearing silver teapots. All the aristocratic families of Lhasa had loaned their own best servants for this occasion. They were mostly peasant lads, and had covered their mouths with white bands to keep their breath from the tea. I noticed that the monks seated on either side of the main aisle were all geshes and that most of them carried very large tea bowls. They were, moreover, the first to be served, which meant that the tea that they got was richly buttered. And since the tea servers coming up the aisle were continually pouring, what the monks in the back rows received contained less and less of the precious butter.

After all this a member of the priors' staff came solemnly down the aisle bearing on his shoulder the constitution of the Monlam wrapped in a heavy cloth of silk woven in the five symbolic colors of red, yellow, white, green, and blue. Another monk helped him unroll the document and display to all present its large red letters inscribed on yellow silk. This was a constitution composed by the Seventh Dalai Lama, and it was formally presented to the old prior of Drepung, who received it with great dignity and made a short speech about Monlam and the events that we were all going to experience.

My teacher, the second day, insisted that I should remain upstairs in our room memorizing four pages, which I tried to do. He felt that I was still too young and uninformed to derive any benefit from attending the main event of that day, which was the final examination of the lharampa geshe degree. However, downstairs in the house in which we were living, I did attend three little household ceremonies, one in the morning, one at noon, and one in the late afternoon. And in the course of the afternoon event, I happened to say to a couple of my teacher's classmates that although I had been at work upstairs for hours, I was finding it unusually difficult to learn those four assigned pages by heart. They told Konchog, and he reduced the quota to three.

In the evening on the culminating fifteenth day we celebrated the festival known as Offerings of the Fifteenth. Foreigners have called this the Butter Festival because of the butter sculptures exhibited all around the Barkor, the second circle of the city. Immense dough cakes, some thirty or forty feet high, set on wooden structures and covered with colored butter, were displayed as offerings. They were elaborately designed and covered with auspicious emblems. The two Gyudpa colleges, Muru and Shede, and many of the other monasteries both near and within Lhasa, as well as individual donors, monk officials, cabinet members, and the like, cooperated in having their offerings fashioned by professional artist monks; many of the butter images were extraordinarily well rendered and of no little aesthetic appeal. Most had required as long as two or three weeks to prepare. The butter ornaments had to be fashioned in icy water during February, some time before festival day, and they remained solid in the cold air. The government awarded prizes for the best. And in front of the most elaborate and tall of these offerings there were many smaller tormas, so that when the myriads of butter lamps were lit the city was turned into a fairyland.

That evening, the regent and high government officials would tour the Barkor to view the offerings, and the entire population of Lhasa would be strolling in the streets. No monks were permitted to participate, however, unless in connection with some assigned duty or for some specific reason. Dongye had a Nepalese friend with a shop in the section of the Barkor where the Gyudpa colleges had placed their pieces, and he asked this friend if he and I might view the scene from one of his windows. The building was three stories high, and we were invited to watch from the owner's own apartment on the second floor. We arrived before sunset and were conducted to an excellent place from which to view the vast display of butter lamps and the crowds who were then being held back by ropes from the center of the street.

When it grew dark the Dalai Lama's bodyguard marched to the sound of drums around the whole Barkor, followed by other squads of the Lhasa garrison, clearing the way for a procession of the regent. Thousands of butter lamps flickered all about like stars, and a full moon hung over the Lhasa roofs, illuminating the building fronts and casting deep shadows into the street. Presently, the procession appeared, headed by the prior of Drepung, holding incense sticks in his hands. The regent, who had been carried from his residence in a palanquin, had stepped down to walk the Barkor with the prime minister at his side, and he came now, slowly followed by members of his cabinet. We could not see him at first, but saw the soldiers beginning to salute and heard the officers shouting commands. Then he came into our view, a slender young man, and when he arrived before the offerings of the Gyudto he was shown to a seat where we could watch him receiving scarves presented formally to him by his lord chamberlain. He then stood up and passed along to the great tall offerings of the Gyudme monks which were also within our view.

And then something wonderful happened. Before those great tall images there appeared a little company of tiny moving figures, marionettes, and I recognized among them a little replica of the oracle of Nechung, moving his head up and down as if in trance. Another figure offered him a drink, and then a miniature prior of Drepung appeared in his ceremonial robes accompanied by a well-known personage of his retinue. I was enjoying all this secretly with Dongye, peeking out around the sides of the window curtains; for it was forbidden to watch from a house and especially from a floor above street level, above the regent's head. The monks manipulating the marionettes could not be seen and the little gestures in the soft light of the flickering lamps seemed to us wonderfully life-like.

In Tibet at that time there were not many such diversions as people in other countries enjoy. The Monlam festival was the most spectacular and exciting event of our lives. I had just turned fourteen (age is reckoned in Tibet, where everybody counts his years, not by the number of his birthdays, but by the number of New Years he has seen, so that the New Year festival is like a birthday party for everybody), and even by normal

Tibetan standards I had led an isolated life. This was the most thrilling thing I had ever seen.

The regent and his retinue, having passed now beyond our view, continued around the Barkor and back to the Jokhang; he stepped again into his palanquin to be returned to his residence, with the regiments of his guard before and behind. The ropes that shut off the side street and barred the public from the Barkor were now untied, and everybody surged into the circle to look more closely at the offerings, calling excitedly to one another.

Fortunately, I had that day met a friend who was living with the prior of Drepung, and I had asked him to speak to the prior and ask whether six or seven of us might have his permission to walk around the Barkor that evening. The request was granted, and the prior even sent a monk from Drepung to accompany us. Slowly we strolled along, stopping to study and admire all the wonders. The circle was so crowded that it was difficult to get through, but the people gradually made way for us, apparently assuming that we were out on some sort of assignment. For me, not a little of the wonder and instruction of the occasion lay in the fact that all these marvelous figures were destined to disappear before sunrise. The colleges that owned them would send their members out to take them back and their fragile lives would end. Two groups of villagers who had come into town for this full-moon celebration assembled, facing each other, and sang to each other all night long. And as we strolled homeward through those singing crowds I thought that Monlam had been all too brief. I had loved especially the marionettes and did not want to wait a whole year—a whole eon it seemed to me—to see them again. By morning, all the fairy charm had vanished, and not a sign of the festival images remained to be seen.

The concluding week would serve, like the declining light of the moon itself, to return us by stages from the mood of wonder of that magical night of Offerings on the Fifteenth. There would still be interesting events to observe, but nothing again of such marvelous fascination.

The first day thereafter a Chinese monk asked me to go shopping with him to help buy material for a new woolen robe. Stopping in the shops of Moslems and Nepalese, as well as of Tibetans, we walked around the no longer magical Barkor, until finally my friend saw something he liked in a Tibetan shop. We did not know how to judge whether it was of good or of bad quality, and when we asked the price, it seemed too high, though we had had no experience of prices either. So we paid the price that was asked and my friend carried the material out over his arm. We returned to my lodging and proudly showed the purchase to Dongye telling how much it had cost. He looked displeased. "Khyongla," he said, "you've been cheated. Why in the world didn't you ask the advice of someone who knows something?" I've spoiled you. With everything always arranged for you, you've never learned how to live." Then he said that he would go back with us and see if he could retrieve some of our money. But the merchant was very smart and told him he had not tried to sell us anything but had only told us the price, which we had paid without complaint; therefore, he could not see why he should now either take back the goods or return to us any of the money.

We left, defeated, and Dongye said to me, "Khyongla, I'm going to take you on a shopping tour and teach you how to bargain. You may know more than I do about religion, but in these practical matters, I believe I can teach you a thing or two." We went into a Moslem shop and Dongye told the shopkeeper that I wanted to buy a quantity of silk. The merchant was delighted and showed us a great many different rolls in all patterns and all colors. Finally, Dongye picked out a beautiful brocade and asked the price. When he heard it, he said that he was sorry, but couldn't afford it, and offered to pay half. The shopkeeper looked angry but came down a little. Dongye said he had decided not to buy anything at all, and taking me by the arm, walked out. We were already halfway down the street when the shopkeeper came running after, begging us to return, and the bargain was sealed very close to Dongye's original offer. I did not profit much from that lesson, however; even today, though I know that bargains exist, I do not know how to play the game, and when I have something of importance to buy, all that I know how to do is to enlist the help of a friend.

The final events of Monlam took place on the next to last and last days. The first was a terminal symbolic ceremony called *togyek* ("torma destruction"), when the two presiding abbots would set two huge tormas afire. The traditional meaning of this rite was to indicate that only through a union of the knowledges of emptiness and bliss can the delusions be dispelled of the Doctrine's enemies and of all those intending harm to other living creatures. It was to be a really spectacular affair, and at about ten in the morning, Dongye, my uncle, and I went to the Jokhang to observe it. The entire place in front of the temple was already crowded, but a center had been kept clear; above, the regent would be watching from a third-floor balcony. He was already up there in the Dalai Lama's chamber, where His Holiness's ceremonial robe was displayed on a throne maintained in his honor even though his incarnation had not yet been found; and when the curtains were pulled we could see clearly both the regent and the Dalai Lama's robe, also the members of the cabinet seated there on the balcony above the main portal of the Jokhang.

The ceremonies began. First, there came out of the temple a company of soldiers wearing ancient armored costumes and bearing shields, followed by a number of officials in old Tibetan and Mongolian outfits. These divided into two opposing groups and performed a mock battle. Next, the monks of the Namgyal Dratsang, the Dalai Lama's private college in the Potala, appeared from the main door of the temple, just as the monks of the Tantric college of Drepung emerged from another wing. These two processions met and strode side-by-side along the street, both companies of monks beating drums and clashing cymbals, while before both groups marched a muster of well-dressed laymen bearing ceremonial banners. While all this was going on a company of monks and laymen trundled two huge tormas, shaped like pyramids and each about nineteen feet high, to the place where they were to be sacrificed. They were colored red and their three sides were decorated with patterns of flame made of butter, while their pointed summits were garlanded with skulls made of white butter. Following these, the Gaden Tipa, head of the Gelugpa sect, came striding out of the temple accompanied by the new lharampas, who all turned and, facing the Dalai Lama's throne, took off their hats and bowed to both the regent and the robe of the Thirteenth Dalai Lama.

My friends and I then followed the crowd to the place where the tormas were to be burned. There a company of soldiers, using blank cartridges, shot off their ancient guns, and they aimed—or seemed to be aiming—precisely at the corner of the building where I was standing. The noise was deafening, and when all of us in that corner pressed together in fright and someone pushed, I fell and somebody fell on top of me. No one was hurt, but I was really frightened and ever since that moment have jumped whenever I have heard any sudden loud noise like the shot of a gun.

Having picked ourselves up and, laughing, dusted each other off, we all hurried to the site of the sacrifice and discovered there two big pyramid-shaped straw fires already burning. The abbots of the two colleges stepped forward and, with considerable assistance from a number of attendants, consigned the two huge tormas to the flames, where they crackled fiercely and burned. All the waiting beggars dashed forward to snatch pieces from the burning tormas to eat. Five hundred cavalrymen came riding and, at the same moment, a number of big guns were fired outward from the city toward the distant mountains. That was the end of the togyek fire-ceremony, and all that was left now of Monlam was to be one final event, the next morning.

Before breakfast I hurried out to join a number of friends in the Barkor, just in time to encounter there the procession of the Coming Buddha, Maitreya. The large silver image with its five-leafed crown was seated on a throne, not cross-legged but in the Western style, and was being drawn slowly along on wheels by a group of monks from the temple. Maitreya, we believe, is to be the next in line of those Thousand Buddhas who are to appear on earth during the period of this Kalpa. Gautama Buddha was the fourth in the line, Maitreya will be the fifth. We think of him as now waiting in the Tushita Heaven for his time to come; and when after many centuries the Doctrine of the Lord Buddha Gautama will have vanished like all things (like the spectacle of Monlam itself) from this earth, Maitreya will be born in India and the everlasting teaching of the way to be released from rebirth in sorrow will be renewed.

We hurried, when this symbolic procession had passed, to an area called Sunchos Rawa, by the west wing of the Jokhang, where the Gaden Tipa, following the example of Tsongkhapa, had been lecturing every morning of the festival on the Lord Buddha's previous lives. This morning he was not to lecture, and we climbed up close to the Dalai

Lama's throne which stood there high on a wide platform with three broad steps around the base. From these we could see out over the large crowd that had gathered; across from these, with an empty area between, there was another considerable crowd, several thousand in all. Then from each side we saw a villager step forward. The two men met in the center and each threw a handful of tsampa in the air. Next, they discarded their outer robes, faced each other, clapped their hands, and after a moment of silence moved in to wrestle. One was much taller and we expected him to win, but the other was the victor. Following that first bout, there were others. Then came the weight-lifting event, with four or five contestants, and after that the geyongs appeared to clear the street of the crowds who had been sitting on the ground watching. Those who did not move quickly got a whacking from the long sticks, and the noise of the sticks on their leather coats was like the beat of a drum.

After the streets were cleared, there was a foot race, followed by a horse race, and finally, as a grand conclusion, a mounted race with the riders in ancient Tibetan costumes. The crowds greeted these with enormous enthusiasm, shouting for them to whip up speed as they passed the regent's stand. The winners of that concluding event who had received scarves from the judges came riding back bearing wooden plaques that showed what number they had finished in the race. And that was the exciting end of my first Monlam.

The following year's Monlam was enhanced by the news that the regent had seen visions in the sacred lake indicating where the Dalai Lama's reincarnation was to be found and that search parties had set out to find him. The child was recognized in Amdo and brought to Lhasa in 1939. I joined the throngs of monks and laymen who went to greet the new Fourteenth Dalai Lama at the outskirts of Lhasa, and it was one of the great moments of my life when I first saw and then was touched in blessings by this solemn, dignified four-year-old who was to become Tibet's greatest scholar, teacher, and leader, and a continuing inspiration to all Tibetans.

9.

Intensive Studies

I cannot say that during my first two years in Central Tibet I was an enthusiastic student. Of course I did study and always tried my best to fulfill the daily requirements of my teacher, memorizing pages of scripture, and so on. But inwardly, it seems, I was resisting this daily discipline, and when I attended debating sessions in the chora of the college or in the courtyard of the khamtsen, I preferred to stray into a corner where the younger and less learned monks were gathered, to talk about more amusing things in the company of boys of my own age. Whenever one of the monk disciplinarians would unexpectedly arrive to observe the progress of the session, we youngsters would stand up and, changing the conversation to religious matters, pretend to debate with great intensity, using most energetically all the formal gestures we had learned. Thus it would appear to the disciplinarian that we were concentrating deeply on the subject he would hear us debating, and deceived by our pantomime he would go on his way. Actually, we found those debating sessions long and wearisome, for, after all, we were still very young.

Then one day my teacher suggested that I should attend a series of lectures that a famous incarnation named Khangser Rinpoche was going to be giving at Drepung. He said that although I would be unfamiliar with some of the subjects treated and might find the lectures difficult to follow, still it would be good for me to be in the presence of a lama of such sanctity. I was delighted to go, both because I had already heard a great deal about this particular teacher, and because the occasion would offer me a change of routine.

The morning of the opening lecture I went to Hardong khamtsen, where the talk was to be delivered, and found the lecture hall already filled with an audience of perhaps two thousand people. As Khangser Rinpoche entered the great assembly hall the leader of the choir began to chant the *Migtse Ma* hymn of Tsongkhapa, and everybody joined in. When he reached the center of the lecture hall where his throne was placed, he removed his shoes and, having flung over his shoulders the saffron-colored robe (called *choego*, the "religious robe") which is always worn on occasions of public teaching, he prostrated himself three times before the empty throne upon which he would himself soon be seated. I was surprised at this, but later learned that he was prostrating himself in reverence to his own guru and to the whole spiritual succession, from the Lord Buddha to the lama with whom he had first studied the text he would use in this teaching. He was praying that his exposition of this text might be of use to all those present toward their Enlightenment. Having concluded this act of reverence and submission to the teachings of the text that he was now about to elucidate, he ascended the high throne and began to recite some verses, and when finished gave a snap of his fingers.

I did not know what the verses were, nor to what purpose he was reciting them, but Konchog later told me that the Rinpoche had recited a celebrated text, the *Vajracchedika*, "Diamond Cutter Sutra," which deals with the realization that all concrete things are impermanent and comparable to stars, a delusory vision, the light of a lamp, the shining of dew, a bubble, a cloud, a flash of lightning, a dream. According to my teacher, the Rinpoche had begun with these verses to remind himself that all things, in particular teaching from a high throne and receiving the adulation of many students, are impermanent. His snap of the fingers was thus a sign that all things in all the worlds are as ephemeral as such a snap, and that on occasions such as that day one should therefore surrender all pride.

For the first few days I partly understood what he was saying, but as he went on it became more and more difficult for me to follow his meanings, as I was young and had not yet studied this part of the text. In front of me sat some other monks who were equally unfamiliar with the subject, and a couple of the youngest of these, perhaps not over thirteen years old, repeatedly disturbed me by wanting to play or ask questions. One day I became angry. "Stop all this," I said to them. "This is a lecture hall, not a playground." To which they retorted by making fun of me and imitating my cross expression. On my right there was sitting an older monk, a good friend of mine, who said to me: "Khyongla, you came here to learn tranquility and instead you have lost your temper. That is not good. Those lamas who are disturbing you are very young and they like to play, for it is their nature at that age. You should examine your own behavior." Then I realized that I was at fault and apologized to the youngsters, remembering too my own way of attending lectures not so very long before.

For one whole month the Rinpoche taught us every day from noon to six o'clock in the evening. He never depended on commentaries to his texts and always spoke with the spontaneity of a running brook. One day I asked Konchog whether it would be possible for me to become a learned scholar like that and he answered, "Of course, if you study as hard as Khangser Rinpoche did. Even Lord Buddha was no scholar at first, but he gained Enlightenment after much effort both in practice and in study." In other words, it was up to me. And for several evenings after the close of those lectures, I earnestly promised myself that I would study very hard from then on, praying that I might one day become a great scholar like the Rinpoche and preach to other scholars.

My next teacher at Drepung was Geshe Loyag Rinpoche, who taught me the *Prajnaparamita*, the "Perfection of Wisdom," from two commentaries, one by the great Indian scholar, Sinhabhadra, and the other by a well-known sixteenth-century Tibetan, Penchen Sodagk, who had been a tutor of the Third Dalai Lama. Those two texts combined consisted of about six hundred pages, and on Geshe Loyag's advice I memorized both completely, and in addition began to attend the daily debating sessions at Loseling College in Drepung.

After I had studied with him for some time, Geshe Loyag Rinpoche told me that he expected to leave soon for the Kham, since he had many students there who had invited him to pay them a visit. It would be best, he thought, for me to continue my studies with his chief disciple, Geshe Yeshe Loden, who was a well-known teacher at Loseling; and when I agreed, he took me to the geshe's room, presented me, and I was immediately accepted as a pupil. However, my new teacher told me that although he would be glad to help me in my studies, in order to fulfill the wishes of his own main teacher, he was extremely busy teaching his own hundreds of students. It would therefore be very difficult for him to teach me privately; I should write down whatever questions came up in the course of my readings, and bring these to him for discussion. He gave me a large assignment to read and to memorize from the works of Nagarjuna and his chief commentator Chandrakirti, together with all the commen-taries written by Tsongkhapa on the works of these two early Indian apostles of the Middle Path (*Madhyamika*). It took me over a year, but I finally succeeded in memorizing six hundred pages, seven books in all, of these Indian texts and Tibetan commentaries. First Geshe Yeshe Loden would explain the texts to me, word by word, then extend his explanations by correlating everything to the teaching of the Lord Buddha and to other commentaries written by the early Indian Buddhist scholars. Geshe Yeshe Loden, who was perhaps fifty years old, told me that he had studied in his lifetime under more than two hundred teachers, and that he had always tried to interpret everything according to the Lord Buddha's teaching. During my own life I have had more than seventy teachers, and among them twelve to whom I am particularly indebted, Geshe Yeshe Loden himself being one of those twelve.

Then, early one morning, there appeared in Drepung one of my family's servants from the Kham. He had come on foot from Lhasa to tell me that my father had just arrived there on business for our district. I was of course delighted with the unexpected news since it had been almost five years since we had parted. I had then been a boy of thirteen and was now growing into manhood, over seventeen years old.

Immediately I hurried to Geshe Yeshe Loden's house and begged to be allowed to go. And he said, "Khyongla, this is wonderful news. Go as soon as you can, and be of help to your father in whatever way you can. Children have always to repay a debt of kindness of their parents, for they brought you into this world, cared for you when you were a helpless infant, and gave you the opportunity to acquire learning. One of the principal religious requirements of a Buddhist is to treat his parents well." Then he added: "But if your father asks you to return immediately to your home town—in that case, I should not take his advice."

I found my father staying at an inn on the outskirts of the city, near the Lingkor, that special boulevard which people used to circumambulate the city to obtain merit. When I entered the room he was in he was talking with some friends. He rose and greeted me formally, calling me Rinpoche; then said to his friends, "This is my son, whom I have not seen for five years." They made a place for me at the table, arranging a high cushion for me to sit on.

We slept in the same room and that first night had much to talk about. The first thing he did when his friends had left was to hand me a letter from my mother, bringing her greeting and informing me that she was delighted I was studying so hard. She encouraged me to go on for the degree of lharampa, and said that she was hoping I would become as famous as the esteemed lamas, Khangser Rinpoche and Pabongka Rinpoche, whom Tibetans called respectively, the Sun and the Moon. None of us knew it then, but eleven years were to pass, from the day of my departure from my native village to that of my final metaphysical examination in the great Jokhang in Lhasa, before I would see my mother again. My mother for that occasion would undertake the long journey from the Kham and I would have the great joy of seeing her and having her present at the ceremony of my reception of the high lharampa degree.

In addition to my mother's letter, my father had brought letters and gifts from many friends and relatives in the Kham. Some begged me to return soon; others wrote that I should stay on and continue with my studies until I had become a great teacher and could instruct them when I returned. Letters in those days were an exciting rarity, for there was no regular postal service between the Kham and Central Tibet other than the government's system, used solely for official correspondence. My father and I, consequently, stayed awake very late that first night, telling each other about all the things of which we had never been able to write.

The next day my teacher Konchog arrived from Rato, having come especially to meet my father, and he gave a rather favorable report on the progress of my studies, which was a relief to me. He even said that he thought I would become in time a good lama. My father thanked him for having helped me, and said that during my first two years away he and the monks of my labrang had heard that I was not studying very hard. Both my parents and the members of the labrang had been worried about that, but the later news to reach them was that I had begun to apply myself seriously to the work—which made everyone very happy.

After Konchog had departed my father decided to test me out. "Won't you please," he asked, "discuss with me some topic you are now studying?" That would not be easy, since my father knew nothing of philosophy, which happened to be the subject I was then pursuing. He asked me to let him see the book I was then reading and to comment upon it, for he had noticed that I had arrived with a book wrapped in yellow brocade slung over my shoulder. I took up the book gladly, stripped off the cover, opened the long pages, read a few sentences from the "Clear Meaning of the Middle Way," and explained their meaning. While I do not think that my father understood very much of what he heard, he seemed greatly pleased with me. Actually, the meaning was not too clear to me either, but in my anxiety to impress my father I had rapidly improvised and said whatever came into my head, so that he should not think I was hesitant or unsure.

Two days later I paid a visit to the Gaden Ti Rinpoche—the highest official of the Yellow Hat sect and ninety-third successor to the throne of Tsongkhapa in Gaden Monastery. I introduced myself to the attendants at his door and, after a short wait, was ushered upstairs to his private apartments. Born in the Kham, he was now a man of about seventy with gray hair and a broad face. He received me kindly, and after tea had been served asked the object of my visit. I told him that, having come to Lhasa, I wished to study with him and that my teacher, Geshe Yeshe Loden, had suggested the plan. He inquired about the geshe's health and well-being, then passed his hand over his face, as if thinking very seriously about the request I had just made. Then he said, "But I don't know Buddhism very well, so how can I teach it to you. Certainly I don't know enough to say 'this is . . . this is not.' But perhaps we could get together and discuss and confer together on the subject of Buddhism, if that would be agreeable to you."

I was utterly astonished by this suggestion. What good fortune had come to me! But how could I possibly debate and discuss Buddhism with such a great scholar as the head of our Yellow Hat sect, who, further-more, was so old and wise—and I no more than seventeen. I could not find words to answer him and so bowed my head, as though in agreement.

Gaden Ti Rinpoche then asked what I was studying at the moment and when I told him that I was studying Nagarjuna's work on the Middle Path, he asked whether I thought I understood the subject very well. I answered that, as a matter of fact, I had found it difficult to understand at first, but since my teacher was a very learned man and had been so very kind to me, I now knew certain parts of the work rather well. The Rinpoche smiled and said that he was pleased to hear this, because he had had many students, but no one of them had ever informed him that he knew anything well. As for himself, he had studied Buddhism until his black hair had turned white, but he could not say that he knew very much. He would now try to test my knowledge.

He put to me a quick question. It was something I could answer immediately. He expanded his questions, and as they became deeper and darker, my answers became shallower and lighter. After a time, I could not give him a correct answer at all and became greatly confused. He suddenly changed to a different topic and though I tried to carry on the discussion, I could find no proper responses. The questions were very pointed and he was critical of every answer I gave. Then he said, "Before, you told me that you knew the subject rather well, and so I have been trying to make you realize that you have not really grasped its meanings." He paused and finally said to me, "Khyongla, it is true that you are intelligent, but you have not continually associated with great scholars. You have just fraternized with your own classmates and that is the reason you feel that you know these subjects well. As our proverb goes, 'In a small area, there is always a small leader.'"

By this time almost two hours had passed, and I was so uncomfortable that I kept wishing some visitor would come in and break up the session. I was perspiring as though I were sitting beside a hot stove. Nor was I very happy that when the Ti Rinpoche at last dismissed me, he invited me to come back the next day at the same hour.

I returned that next day with fear and trembling, and from then on, at the same dreadful hour almost every day of my three-week stay in Lhasa, I came to him and he put me through my paces. In short, I had become his private pupil. He used no book in his teachings but continued discussions of important subjects, one after another. The questions that he put to me were as sharp as swords. He compared my answers with those of various scholars on the subject, quoting from their commentaries, and he juxtaposed their opinions, to help me arrive at an informed interpretation of the truth of the matter. Moreover, he warned me that if I did not study from now on conscientiously, I would one day find myself in difficulties; when the day arrived for me to ascend a high throne and sit before many students, I would be able only to amuse them with stories and laughs instead of opening to them the true meaning of the blessed Doctrine of the Lord Buddha.

One day when I was walking back from the Ti Rinpoche's place to the inn, a young butcher leading a lamb ran after me and asked me to save the lamb's life. I was mystified by this strange request and said, "If you love that lamb so much, why do you want to kill her?" "It's because I don't have any money," he answered. "This is only a young lamb and I really don't want to kill her. Then I saw you and because of your manner of walking I said to myself, There goes a good pious monk who will save the lamb's life for me." I had to tell him that I had so little money I could not pay for the lamb, whereupon he looked at me very crossly and turned away, saying, "Such a monk!" I then looked down at my robe and at the religious book I was carrying over my left shoulder and thought to myself: If you don't help that lamb, you should be ashamed of yourself for wearing a monk's robe and studying religion. Why are you always praying for living creatures to become liberated from misery if you won't practice that doctrine when you are given a chance to do so? So I turned around and went back, calling to the man who was walking away. He came toward me again with his animal and I explained that what I had meant was that I had no money in my pocket. "But if you will come with me now to my place," I said, "I will get the money to pay for the lamb and it will be saved."

So he went along with me to the inn and, finding my father there, I told him what had happened. My father said it would give him great pleasure to save the lamb's life, and paid the boy. That evening he and I walked the lamb to Jokhang and the next morning we both circumambulated the Lingkor with the lamb; we believed that seeing holy images and making that trip around the sacred way was as worthwhile for animals as for human beings. We saw many other people likewise circumambulating with small dogs and sheep, turning their prayer wheels in their right hands as they led the animals with their left. A few days later we asked the keeper of the government park in which saved animals were harbored to accept the lamb. This government refuge was a small park situated in front of Drepung Monastery where over a thousand animals of all kinds were cared for. The Dalai Lama himself sent animals there, and all were maintained for the duration of their natural lives.

This little incident with the lamb brought me close to my father and I was happy in his company. He no longer treated me as a schoolboy but as a grown man and with the respect that he would have paid to any other incarnate monk. We had many intimate talks and he told me why he was paying this visit to Central Tibet at this time. He had come in the interest of our district, which he represented, and also to visit with me and to see how I was progressing in my studies. But there was another reason as well. That year he had become forty-four years old, and Tibetans believed this to be a dangerous age astrologically. The twenty-fourth and thirty-seventh years of a man's life also were thought to be critical times. So my father had come to make a pilgrimage to the holy places in Central Tibet and to visit some important monasteries where he wished to offer as many donations to monks as he could afford. He would begin by visiting the nearest monasteries to Lhasa, and since Drepung was the nearest of all, we should go there together.

We set out for Drepung on a beautiful spring morning. It was only five miles from Lhasa, and so we went on foot. The willow trees were putting out their soft, green, fuzzy leaves, and high above them towered the Potala, with its red and white walls like cut gems against the blue sky and its golden roofs shining like an immense crown in the sun. As we walked along we talked about our home and about how joyous it was to be in Lhasa with all its wonderful sights. We were very soon at the main gate of Drepung, and I brought my father first to my uncle's room.

When little Uncle Kunsang opened the door and saw his big younger brother standing there, he was astounded, for he had not heard of his trip. They embraced, and each told the other he didn't look a year older than when they had last met, when my father had visited Lhasa right after his marriage. They remained talking from sunset to midnight, exchanging news about our home village and friends, about the monks from our village who were studying in Drepung, and about their personal lives. Then my uncle brought my father to my room, where we talked for another hour, and it was almost morning before we lay down to sleep.

We remained in Drepung together a whole week, my father lodging with me in my room. Since I had to study every day, he went pretty much on his own way, paying visits to all the temples, shrines, and holy places in the monastery. There were some five hundred monks from our district in Drepung and among those my father had a number of good friends who invited him to dinner and would sometimes accompany him in his rambles around our monastic city. My father gave a donation of one coin to each of the whole community of monks, who numbered over ten thousand, and for the ceremony of donation the entire assembly was present along with the highest-ranking abbots and a number of government officials. Another day he donated two coins to each of the monks of my college, Loseling, this being—as already mentioned—the largest of the four at Drepung, with a membership of about seven thousand monks. Finally, at my khamtsen, my father offered a tea ceremony to all five hundred members, and during this event, which included prayers and chanting, each was served four cups of tea and received a donation of three coins.

At the end of our stay we left Drepung together, and he accompanied me to Rato. My father again lived with me in my room, where he met Konchog, who gave him many instructions on the use of his prayer book and on methods of meditation. Konchog answered willingly all the questions my father put to him, and since my father was not a philosopher but a practical man, his questions for the most part were related to observance of religious rituals and the correct procedures to follow in such matters. At the end of a week he left for the south, to visit the many famous pilgrimage places in that part of Tibet, and I remained behind in Rato, since I had now to participate in the daily debating sessions of my college.

There were a number of enthusiastic students in my class who liked to tease and badger the lazier ones. This was done not out of hostility but to stimulate and concentrate their interest in their work. Under their influence, I also began taunting, and when any gave a wrong answer or incorrect interpretation, I would join in the banter. One night a young monk who was highly intelligent but somewhat lax in his studies was called upon to answer questions and, one by one, my classmates and I put to him more and more difficult challenges. At first he answered correctly but finally could not justify one of his statements with a text, and used all the intellectual brilliance at his command to demonstrate the logic of his position, step by step. In doing this he assumed a haughty, superior manner toward us, and, resenting this, I intervened and said: "Now by your attitude you are disgracing the name of student." He turned on me with a contemptuous smile. "Well," he said, "we shall soon watch the way you disgrace the name of student when it comes your turn to answer questions."

On that occasion Konchog was participating in the session, but I was unaware of him there since he was seated behind me. The haughty monk at the end of the session bowed and thanked us, saying that he had received from the questions proposed to him in the debate many new ideas. And an hour later a student living with my teacher came to me and said that Konchog wanted me to come to him at once. I asked the reason, as it was already very late—almost one in the morning. He replied that he did not know. Then I asked, "Is Konchog ill?" And he answered, "No, not at all, but you better go and ask *him* these questions."

I ran in my bare feet to my teacher's room and entered very quietly. He was sitting waiting for me, and said: "Baiting that young monk was not a proper thing to do. To insult people deliberately at any time is wrong, and wrong especially in a debating session. It destroys their peace of mind and is, therefore, a sin." Luckily the monk I had taunted had withheld his anger, he said, but henceforth I should not try to disgrace any student because of ignorance. It was not my business to correct others, but the responsibility of each to attend to his own development. He said that he realized I had been influenced by my classmates, but I should not imitate everything others did. Then he added that to insult a person objectively and with a pure intention was in certain instances not forbidden, but that, he said, was a very difficult thing to do correctly, and required great purity on the part of the person doing it. He had noticed that I had insulted the monk with relish, for my own pleasure, and not out of loving kindness to give help. Konchog continued this discomforting lecture by telling me that whereas Tsongkhapa had written eighteen works on Buddhism, I would not find one single page with an insulting word directed at any person by name. And he summed up, finally, by telling me that I should try to meet that monk the next day and apologize for my behavior. I promised to do that and did the next day. The young monk replied that my insults had not disturbed him really, and from there on we became something like friends.

Konchog came to my room one day to say that a very great teacher, Pabongkha Rinpoche, was going to be giving a series of lectures at Sera Monastery on a very important Yellow Hat sect book called *Lamrim Chenmo*. The word *lamrim* refers in general to a special type of Gelugpa book dealing with techniques for experiencing the stages of the Path from its beginning to Supreme Enlightenment, providing expositions of both the indirect and the hidden content of Prajnaparamita teaching, as well as a brief introduction to the Tantric paths. The main topics are the Bodhicitta (motivation to achieve enlightenment for the benefit of all sentient beings, not for oneself) and the Six Perfections (*Paramitas*), the six basic virtues of generosity, morality, patience, energy, meditation, and insight.

There are two ways of producing Bodhicitta. One is in the practice of the so-called Sevenfold Cause and Effects Precepts, and the other is in changing one's attitude from selfishness to selflessness. In our teaching the Sevenfold Cause and Effects Precepts are: (1) to recognize one's mother in all sentient beings; (2) to think kindness toward all sentient beings; (3) to wish to return their kindness; (4) to cultivate loving kindness; (5) to cultivate the great compassion; (6) to resolve to help all sentient beings; (7) Bodhicitta itself, which is also the effect of the first six.

According to Buddhist thought, every sentient being has been our mother countless times, for we have been wandering in the world from an infinite past and have had in most of our lifetimes a mother. But in order really to know this, one must have become convinced through reasoning of the necessary existence of past lives, and that the mind in this life acts in continuance of a previous or prior mind. So it is that without hard study one is not likely to be convinced of Buddhist ideas—blind faith is not considered admirable. The first method of achieving Bodhicitta, then, is an extension of diligent study. The second method gives importance to a meditation on the delusory effects of selfishness and the benefits of self-negation, this being the main subject of the work called *Bodhicaryavatara,* "Entering the Path of Bohisattva Conduct."

In the lamrim, details are given of both methods of producing Bodhicitta, along with instructions for the combination of these two ways, in order to achieve a rapid and intensive experiencing of Bodhicitta. *Lamrim Chenmo* is the "Extensive Lamrim," and was composed by Tsongkhapa as a commentary on Atisha's book, *Bodhipathpradopa,* "The Lam of the Path of Enlightenment." Later he wrote an intermediate and abbreviated lamrim at the request of his disciples. And on the basis of these three lamrim, the Gelugpa lamas have written many commentaries, which also go by the name of lamrim.

Pabongkha Rinpoche had been born of an aristocratic family in Tsang Province, and was recognized as a reincarnation of the abbot of the monastic community of Pabongkha, which is located not far from Sera Monastery. He was an exceptionally learned and gifted scholar, and his interpretation of the Doctrine adhered to the meaning of the Lord Buddha's words exactly. He was short, broad-faced, and of rather heavy build, but when he opened his mouth to speak, his words had such clarity and sweetness that no one could help being moved. When he led the chanting his mellifluous voice would have charmed even a snake, and his large audiences listened as under a spell.

He gave his first lecture of the series before an audience of about four thousand people in the large assembly hall of Med College, and for three months that summer the series continued, every day from noon to six. During that summer session several traders and at least two high government officials found their lives transformed by his eloquence: they forsook their jobs to study religion and to give themselves to meditation. One very high government official, whose title was Ta Lama, resigned his position and followed the Rinpoche thereafter wherever he went. It was said of the official that when Tibet had been at war with China he was sent off to the front as an officer, but ran away without fighting. People called him, therefore, Wa Lama, *Wa* meaning "fox."

The Rinpoche was accustomed to illustrate his teaching by means of concrete examples and personal stories, with abundant references to the teaching of the Lord Buddha and to the commentaries of ancient scholars and saints. Whenever he noticed that his audience was becoming tired or restless, he would tell a comical story to rouse them and get a laugh. Once, for example, he told that when on a long journey in the far north of Tibet, he had refused in sub-zero weather to wear a fur-lined jacket with sleeves simply because in Tibet sleeves belonged to the dress of laymen and were therefore not suitable for monks. His bare arms, however, had not frozen, he said, and he held them up before us saying, "They were brown before that trip and, as you may see, they are still brown." To illustrate his point that study is of the greatest benefit to all, he said that if a man studying in Lhasa were to return to his home in the Kham or Amdo and on the road plundered by thieves of everything he had, still they could not take away his knowledge: knowledge gained through study could never be lost or stolen except through its owner's own deliberate forgetfulness.

Every day in his lectures the Rinpoche repeated his major theme, which was also that of the Lord Buddha: "Life is impermanent. On the day of your death you must part with your family, friends, fame, and fortune. Your reputation will no longer be of use to you on that day." And then he would outline the Path. He showed us that from the moment we enter upon it until our achievement of Enlightenment, the Path is continuous, and only step by step do we progress upon it, keeping ever the goal in mind and daily exerting ourselves to the best of our ability. "Let us begin, therefore," the Rinpoche reminded us, "by correcting right now, right here in this room, our attitudes in listening to his Doctrine, and become thereby already more aware of its meaning."

From that time on I began to think less of competing in my lessons, like a schoolboy, and gave myself more honestly to the task of understanding deeply what it was I was learning.

10.

I Am Ordained a Gelong

When I was twenty, my teacher Konchog decided that it was time for me to take ordination as a gelong. This is the highest form of ordination for a monk, given only to those who are twenty or older. Up to that time I had been a getsul or novice; and the question now arose as to who should ordain me.

Everyone, of course, would have chosen to be ordained by the Dalai Lama himself, but at that time His Holiness was only nine years old and he had not yet been himself ordained as a gelong. The rule was that no monk could administer the rite until at least five years and usually ten years after his own ordination as a gelong. Every candidate was allowed to select a qualified lama of his own choice, preferably one whom he admired and felt drawn to; my own first choice was Pabongkha Rinpoche who, I learned, would be in Lhasa at the time I was to be ordained. When he arrived and I visited him to present my request, he replied by asking me to wait a few days, since some of the other monks had also asked for ordination and it could all be done in one ceremony. That was in the first month of 1943, during Monlam, when Lhasa again was in its carnival mood, crowded with visitors and monks from every part of Tibet.

When I arrived at the Rinpoche's residence on the date set, I was immediately conducted upstairs to a large room where I found many other young monks already waiting, most of them wearing new robes for the occasion. All together we were sixty. After an interval, the Rinpoche's first assistant entered, and after greeting us all, began to check our names against a list, making sure that each had everything required, including the two types of saffron-colored robes. The first, known as a *chugu*, could be worn by all ordained monks when attending lectures and ceremonies, and in some monasteries it was required dress. The second, the *namgyer*, was for gelongs, who wore it over their chugu at special ceremonies. A third item required of each of us was a kind of rug, a *dingwa*, which was to be spread over our cushions at ceremonies and lectures. When this check-up had been completed we were ushered into a luxurious reception room, where Pabongka Rinpoche himself was seated on a throne before a large shrine of the Lord Buddha, a book on a stand which described the correct procedure for ordination, and an iron alms bowl filled with dried apricots, walnuts, and sweet candies. His four assistants were seated in a row in front of him, off to one side, and the candidates would pass in front of them when approaching the Rinpoche's throne.

The assistants were middle-aged, pious, and tranquil-looking gelongs, none of whom I knew; and of the four, three would have special functions to serve in the ceremony. The most involved assistant would be the *lelob*, performer of the main ordination ritual. The second, known as *sangte tonpa*, "he who secretly inquires of everything and reveals," would determine whether we were actually qualified for ordination according to the requirements of the Vinaya. And the third, *dugo wa*, "time teller," would register the precise time at which the ordination occurred. These four, plus the Rinpoche, made up the number of five gelongs required for an ordination, the Rinpoche himself playing the role of *khenpo*, "chief performer in a ritual releasing candidates from the vortex of rebirths." *Khenpo* is a word used generally in reference to the abbot of a monastery, but in the context of an ordination it refers to the initiating lama.

When initiations of this kind were held in Central India ten gelongs were required. In remote countries like Tibet, Buddha, it appears, himself instituted two distinct ways of ordination. The first and earlier, now known as *nonchog*, "earlier ritual," was an ordination for only six years, administered with a less formal ritual by the Lord Buddha himself immediately after he had achieved Supreme Enlightenment. Thereafter the way required was that now known as *dachog*, "present ritual," and it was this that was to be the way of our Tibetan rite.

A few minutes after we had all taken our places in the reception room the Rinpoche stood up from his throne, made three prostrations to his assistants, and said, "Please listen, gelongs!" Addressing each assistant then by his monk name, he asked if he was ready to perform his function as lelob, sangte tonpa, or dugo wa; and on receiving the sign of silent assent from each, he went on next to ask if he was ready to perform the gelong ordination for Nawang Losang and so on. He did not give my name as Khyongla, but as Nawang Losang, part of the monastic name that had been given me in my getsul ordination. I was not the oldest of the candidates, but had the title of incarnation, and therefore the Rinpoche, counting me as the chief candidate, mentioned my name. The assistants again remained silent, which again indicated their acceptance—this way of indicating assent by remaining silent being a Buddhist tradition based on the fact that whenever the Lord Buddha himself was invited anywhere he indicated his acceptance in this way.

At the request of the Rinpoche we all prostrated ourselves three times to the image of the Lord Buddha, three times to the Rinpoche, and three times to each of his assistants. At the end of each set of prostrations, the gelong so reverenced scattered barley over our heads and prayed for our prospective gelongship. When our times came, we candidates went up to the Rinpoche in groups of three. We had on our usual monk's robes, carrying the two saffron-colored robes, chugu and namgyer, over our left shoulders. The Rinpoche and we, together, held out the edges of these robes and he blessed them with a ritual formula that we had to repeat three times after him. Rather nervous, I found it difficult to repeat the words correctly, as did my friends, but the Rinpoche was patient enough, repeating the formula several times. Then each of us with him, together, picked up and held first an alms bowl (*lhung zed*), then a dingwa, and then a strainer, while he explained the use and purpose of each. The alms bowl was for begging food. (In some monasteries it was required of monks to have one, but I never saw any monk eating from such an alms bowl in Tibet.) In 1960, however, when I had escaped from Tibet and was in Kalimpong, I saw begging Theravada (Hinayana) monks in the streets, holding out the alms bowl, and I admired their way of begging according to the Vinaya. The dingwa, a small woolen rug, was used to cover the ordinary cushions when you sat down. The strainer we used mainly to remove insects from water, so that we should not accidentally kill them when making use of the water. And when all these things had been explained to us, the Rinpoche's assistants helped us to put on the two saffron-colored robes.

About twenty minutes later the sangte tonpa rose from his place and asked us to accompany him out of the room. One of the candidates, thinking the ordination already finished, whispered to me that it had not taken very long. I had heard something about ordinations from my teacher Konchog, but was not sure of the details, and could not give him an answer. We soon found, however, that that was not to be the end. In an adjoining chamber the sangte tonpa closely questioned each one of us to find out if we were actually qualified for ordination. His questions were taken from the *Vinaya Sutra* and were of such kind as: "Are you a male?" "Are you at least twenty years old?" "Do your parents object to your becoming a monk?" And then, further, "You have not killed your parents?" "You do not have any such disease as leprosy?" and so on.

When this questioning was finished, the sangte tonpa returned without us to the reception hall, and the monk who was beside me whispered that he had never heard of anyone who had killed his parents, and that he thought some of the questions ridiculous. I said nothing, but just smiled at him. I did not mind the strange questions because I had heard similar ones when I took my getsul vows; and Konchog, furthermore, had told me that every single word of an ordination had to follow the Vinaya text.

Shortly after, the sangte tonpa returned to lead us all back into the assembly hall before the Rinpoche and the sangha (represented by the four assistants). There the lelob repeated the questions already asked by the sangte tonpa, and we all responded in unison as we had separately in the other room. The lelob then gave us a lecture on the proper attitude we should have toward the ordination as gelongs. The formula was recited in low tones three times to each group, and during the third part of the third recitation the lelob lifted his right hand and snapped his fingers, indicating that the three he was then addressing had obtained their gelong vows. The recitation was to be heard only by the group there before him, the other candidates having to sit with their hands covering their ears.

When all sixty had been ordained by threes in this way, the dugo wa went outside to measure the sun's shadow so he could determine the precise time for the conclusion ceremony for the ordinations. The idea behind this was that gelongs who have been ordained at the same time as we would not be required to prostrate themselves and proffer formal respect to us. On the other hand, respect was to be given and prostrations made to gelongs who had been ordained at earlier times. The difference of even a few minutes would be significant. When the dugo wa, having performed his task outside, returned to the room, he announced clearly the year, the season, the date, and so on, of the ordination just completed, and asked us to respect all gelongs senior to ourselves, telling us also that it would be proper for us to accept the respect of junior gelongs and getsuls. Then he read to us the Vinaya precepts concerning the conduct of a gelong, what was proper and what forbidden—although he read clearly and slowly, I was unfamiliar with the Vinaya and did not follow him very well. At the end, each of us was presented with a three-inch clay image of the Lord Buddha, to be carried always as a reminder of the Lord Buddha's kindness and his teaching.

Later that day some of us went to pray in the great Jokhang. I asked there for guidance in my studies and in the practice of religion, so that like Pabongkha Rinpoche, I might learn to help people by teaching, writing, and discussion.

Next day Konchog had a long and serious talk with me, saying that now that I was an ordained gelong it was of the utmost importance for me to begin a thorough study of the Vinaya. Otherwise I would not know what was acceptable for a gelong and what not, and thus out of ignorance would commit many sins every day. Since my studies of the Middle Path were not concluded, I immediately took his advice and transferred to a class in Vinaya. I studied Vinaya mainly at Drepung with Yeshe Loden, who taught me word by word from the book, which I memorized. Then Konchog one day asked me to take up the teaching of some of his students, since it was arduous for him, he said, to have so many. I replied that if he thought me qualified, I would try to do my best, and he sent me six engaged in the study of Pramāna.

During that winter I went again to Jang, as I did thereafter every year until I received my degree of lharampa, and while I was there some of my other teachers and friends sent me students from Drepung, Sera, and Gaden. Many of these were intellectually very keen, so that I had to study hard to serve them. They put questions to me to which I could sometimes give proper answers immediately; but there were times also when I would tell them that I would have to look up the answers, or that I would ask my own teacher. Occasionally when I gave a reply of which I was not quite certain, I would state clearly that it was only a conjecture on my part. From that time on I was kept busy from morning until night, for my students alternated in coming to me privately for consultation, and I had my own studying to do besides.

After working on the Vinaya for two years, I began the study of *Abhidharmakosha*, "metaphysics," and again worked mainly with Yeshe Loden at Drepung. I memorized the entire *Abhidharmakosha* of the early Indian scholar, Vasubandhu. Although I had reviewed some six or seven times the other important books studied with Yeshe Loden, I went through the *Abhidharmakosha* with him only once, since he said that I was now advanced in my studies and did not have to be taught word by word.

In Rato, before receiving the degree of geshe, one had to take the degree of *kachu*, which required one to be able to recite and interpret the meaning of ten important books of the Buddhist canon. Actually, in my time, however, the kachu had lost much of its scholarly luster and had become chiefly a gift ceremony. In fact, when I was at Rato a monk untrained in theology could hire a deputy to take his place in the debating session and pass the examination by reciting one book by heart. The kachu gift ceremony was more expensive, however, than the one that had marked my admission to the monastery as a monk, though much less expensive than that which would have to follow my final examination for geshe. The gift ceremonies occupied three days: the first day, I held one for the members of my khamtsen, and recited, during the ceremonies, texts that I had learned by heart. The next day I did the same for about four hundred monks. And on the third day, banquets were held for the staff both of my khamtsen and of the college.

It was also required of all monks from Rato that before receiving the geshe degree they should participate at Drepung in a session of that special method of debate, already described, known as tsog lang. Rato as a rule sent either one or two monks to that annual tsog lang. One day our abbot summoned me and a colleague to his room to inform us that it was we who had been appointed to go to Drepung for that dangerous event. He told us that the subject to be discussed was going to be Pramāna, and I knew that even though I had been studying logic in Rato for some time now, and had gone every year to Jang for the seminar there in this subject, tradition required me to prepare myself for this particularly challenging task by weeks of intensive study and review. For my sake and my colleague's our khamtsen announced Pramāna as the regular topic of discussion for its next series of debating sessions. It was nearing the seventh month (August) when we felt ourselves ready, and prepared to set off for Drepung.

Early that critical morning I presented myself at the daily assembly. The hall at Drepung was the largest in Tibet and could accommodate over ten thousand, which was the usual number of monks in residence there. Lama Shunglepa stood on top of the front gate clapping white sandalwood sticks together to call us all to the meeting. Commencing very softly and rising gradually in crescendo, the sound was resonant, and we monks, gathering very promptly, entered the hall. My opponent, a learned scholar named Losang Gawa, was there before me and a monk beside me whispered when we saw him: "Be on your guard or you won't be able to keep your end up."

First came the chanting, shortened for this occasion, and when the moment arrived for us to commence our duel, my opponent and I stood together at the door and prostrated ourselves three times to the assembly. We then walked up the center aisle between the long rows of monks until we reached the altar, standing before the life-sized image of Jamyong Chose, the founder of Drepung, who had been one of the chief disciples of Tsongkhapa. We each presented a scarf to this image, after which we turned to Lama Shunglepa, who was seated before the shrine at the head of all the rows of monks. The older monks were seated on one side of each row; the younger, on the other. The lama recited a verse from the Pramā-na, which we repeated after him and then took our places—I, in the center of the main aisle, my opponent, behind the first row of monks.

Losang Gawa began the discussion by quoting from the Pramāna a verse referring to the Lord Buddha's Enlightenment, looked at me, and asked me to interpret it. The meaning was not clear to me, but I took a

chance and guessed the answer. The guess was wrong and he said so. I
felt that this was not the ideal way to begin. He went on challenging, and
I responding, until Lama Shunglepa in a deep solemn voice halted us, and
it was my turn to pose the questions. I began by quoting a verse dealing
with the non-Buddhist Ishvara doctrine, which holds that everything was
created by a personal god. My opponent responded, and our discussion
ranged over various points of difference between Ishvara doctrine and the
teaching of Mahayana Buddhism, until Lama Shunglepa's deep voice
again called "Stop!" We turned and, facing the image of Jamyong Chose,
prayed for peace. After that I recited some verses and finished the
discussion by intoning "*Dhi!*" in a high voice. We both then returned to
our cushions, which had been kept for us in the row of monks, and the
ceremony concluded with a short chant.

When I was back again in my room many friends came to see me, to
congratulate me and bring me presents. Lama Shunglepa came in and
said, "Well, I thought at first you were going to disgrace yourself before
all, but you escaped splendidly." Since in the tsog lang we considered our
opponent to be a friend, the following day I was invited to pay a visit to
Losang Gawa. Still a poor monk at that time, he had arranged a festive
meal in the room of a rich friend, a student monk from his college. Next
day I returned the hospitality by inviting him to a festive meal in my room,
to which there were also invited many of my friends and teachers from
Drepung. All those visits, meetings, and discussions of that debating
session were very fruitful to me. The scholars discussed the differing
viewpoints of the great Indian and Tibetan Buddhist teachers and their
points of disagreement in interpreting the Lord Buddha's words. And I
was fresh from all the main texts and topics, having just been hard at work
for weeks on an intensive review of Abhidharma and Vinaya.

One day soon after that some monks from Rato arrived with the sad
news of the sudden death of our abbot, Losang Phuntsog, who had
occupied the abbotical throne for little more than two years. A few days
later another monk arrived and informed me that the college had
announced in the assembly hall that it would be necessary to choose
immediately a new abbot. Those monks already in the Vinaya class were
to write their choice on slips of paper, which then were to be placed on a

dish covered with barley and wheat grains. The slips would be counted out aloud at the meeting of the college council—and as it turned out when all the writing and counting was done, Konchog had received the greatest number of votes. The names of the first five candidates were forwarded to the regent in Lhasa, and Konchog Gyatso was appointed abbot of Rato.

My good teacher at that time had retreated to a hermitage near Lhasa. Rato sent a delegation to apprise him of the vote and the regent's decision, and to invite him to return to take up his duties in the monastery as abbot. I too had received a letter from my friends and students asking me to return to Rato immediately, and when I did so I learned that my teacher too had just arrived.

I went to his room to greet and congratulate him. My last sight of him had been two months before, when I had made a trip from Drepung to visit him in his hermitage at Chuzang, and had found him very happy there in his retirement. I now surmised that the honor just bestowed on him probably did not accord very well with his personal desires. And indeed, he told me that he had wanted to refuse. But the fact that his teacher, the Regent Tagdag, had urged him to accept the abbotship for the sake of the monastery had caused him to put aside his desire for retirement and return. He had been hoping to withdraw completely from the administrative work and all such externalizing activities, in order to spend the remainder of his life in seclusion, practicing religion. He conceded that anyone who had reached the *highest* level of spiritual development—such as, for example, the Dalai Lama or the Panchen Rinpoche—would find no conflict between activities in the outer world and his inner spiritual life. But a beginner on the Path—which was what he considered himself to be—is best served in the effort to reach his spiritual goal by retiring from the world, concentrating on meditation and spiritual exercises, until strong enough to overcome in his own mind the apparent duality of the world and his inner self, thus achieving at last the realization that *Samsara* and *Shunyata*—the "Things of this World" and the "Void of Non-Being"—are one and the same reality. But since Konchog could not refuse his teacher's advice, he left his hermitage and was installed as abbot of Rato. My teacher had lost forever his hermitage, and, as abbot, he could not longer be my private teacher.

11.

My Final Examination
in the Sutras

The examination for the Gelugpa geshe degree, or Master of General Buddhist Studies, had several forms. They were known as *lharampa, tsogrampa, kachen, lingse, doram* or *pigram, choete sepo,* and *robjamb.* The lharampa examination was taken before the entire congregation of the three great monasteries when they gathered annually for the Monlam festival in Lhasa the tsogrampa was also taken in Lhasa, during Tsogchod festival, and the other degrees in the candidate's own monastery. A candidate could not choose the degree form he personally desired; the abbot of his college made this decision, based on his scholarly attainments. Every abbot examined his own candidates, and if any were chosen for the lharampa or tsogrampa, their names were forwarded to the government and they had then to undergo before the Dalai Lama's assistants a preliminary examination of two or three days. Anyone failing in this was sent back to his college to be examined there for one or another of the lesser degrees. However, it remained at the discretion of the abbot whether a returned candidate, after a season of further study, might have his name proposed another year.

There were many reasons why the lharampa degree was regarded as the most important. To most monks it was desirable because it represented the highest scholarship and the final examination for it took place in the great Jokhang Temple in Lhasa, before Jowo Rinpoche, the most revered image of the Lord Buddha in the country. Moreover, the Monlam festival drew the largest congregation of scholar-monks in the world, including those from the "Three Pillars" as well as many from other parts of Tibet; and all Gelugpa monasteries preferred to choose as abbots monks who had taken this degree. The abbots of Sera, Drepung, and Gaden were usually chosen from the highest-placed lharampa geshes, and it was a rare thing to find in any of those major monasteries an abbot without this

126

degree—except in the Tantric colleges of Sera and Drepung, where no degrees were granted and there were consequently no geshes. One further reason for the importance of the lharampa was that it was a prerequisite for a degree in Tantric Buddhism from the Gyudpa colleges, and this, in turn, was a prerequisite to becoming Gaden Ti Rinpoche, head of the whole Gelugpa hierarchy.

A high-ranking scholar would occasionally choose, however, to take a lower geshe degree, and while this was exceptional, there were sometimes good reasons for it; for instance, if a monk wished to return to his home monastery, or if his saintliness was great and he preferred spending his life in seclusion to giving additional time to studies for a degree. Sometimes the Dalai Lama would summon such a monk back to Central Tibet and appoint him abbot of one of the major monasteries. This could happen in the case of a monk from a remote area, such as Amdo or Mongolia, which were controlled by the Chinese.

One day in 1945 an attendant to our abbot of Rato (when the abbot was still Losang Phuntsog) came to my room to announce that he wished to see me next morning at ten. When I arrived I was informed, after a gracious reception, that since I was now qualified in my studies I could take the geshe degree two or three years sooner than originally planned. The abbot said that he had even thought of suggesting my name earlier, but had not done so because Konchog felt that I should continue in my studies. Now, however, it had been decided to propose my name for the degree in 1947, only two years away. The abbot urged me to keep studying hard until that time, and to teach my students, meanwhile, as well as I could. From that day on I was excused from all ceremonies and assemblies except debating sessions. Even my meals were served to me in my room so that I might devote full time to my studies.

Throughout the spring of 1945 I was called upon frequently in the debating sessions both of my college and of my khamtsen, always on the answering side. I was expected to attend such sessions regularly and to prepare myself particularly for the answering of questions. Between semesters, sessions were held every night in the courtyard of the khamtsen, one night of debating alternating with two of reciting. All those not taking degrees were expected to attend the debating, and all who had been in the monastery less than fifteen years were obliged to participate in the reciting.

My room, as I have said, overlooked the courtyard. The debates would usually start around seven, when it was getting dark; and when I would hear the presiding monk clap his hands very loudly, each time twice, I would know that I was being summoned. Ready and only waiting for the call, I would immediately go down in to the court, where two hundred monks or so would be seated in long rows. Bearing burning incense sticks as an offering to the "Three Jewels," I would pass through the monks to the respondent's throne at the other end of the court. As I proceeded the presiding monk would clap his hands, ever more rapidly and loudly to summon all who had not yet arrived. When he stopped, I would mount in silence the three steps and, turning to face the assembly, pay homage to the images visible through our chapel doors. Removing my yellow hat, I would place it against my forehead for a moment and pray that the discussion to follow might reduce our ignorance and be of value in our practice of religion. I would then turn and sit down, and the debate would begin.

A monk would stand up, quote a verse from the Vinaya and, demanding that I elucidate it, clap his hands. The assembled monks would start chanting loudly, "Give the answer!" and I would try to respond at once. Meanwhile the prior of the khamtsen would be going through the monks' rooms upstairs with a big lamp. We could see him moving form room to room, checking to see whether any of his charges had failed to respond to the summons. He would then come down into the courtyard to check upon those present, urging those whom he suspected of not being very diligent to rise and take part in the debate. I remember one young monk who, having asked his question, could not follow it up, and the prior scolded him publicly, enumerating his faults in detail. "You failed twice before and now can't even formulate a proper question. You are lazy and lax," he said, then struck him with a stick. We felt great pity for that young man, shamed before us all, but were not allowed to intervene and kept silent.

Presently the prior would retire to the assembly hall to pray and, after half an hour, come back to see how things were going, finally departing for his room, after which the monks could either remain for further debate or go to study in their rooms. Many would remain and be so greatly interested that our debates lasted sometimes to sunrise. Only when we heard the cocks crow would we stop, and I, as the one answering, could not leave as long as the challenging continued. But I do not recall ever having felt tired or hungry during those sessions. I had to concentrate my whole mind on the questions put to me, and the hours went by very fast. Others would come or go as they pleased, but I would be on duty there all night.

After Monlam, 1946, I went to study at Drepung, and when three and a half months had passed, the abbot of my college, Loseling, sent a messenger to inform me that in two days I would be invited to the Norbulingka, the Dalai Lama's summer palace, for my preliminary lharampa examination. I recalled the words of Dongye spoken many years before, when we had been riding past those garden walls on my way to enter Rato, that I should one day see what lay behind them, the lovely Jewel Park of gardens, fish ponds, running brooks, and flowering trees; where the birds nest and sing all day, and tame deer wander on the lawns.

On the night I arrived at Norbulingka, I stayed in a guest room, graciously offered to me by the superintendent. It was a cloudless summer night, the end of June, and from the window of our room I could see the stars brilliantly shining in the dark void of the sky. Suddenly I heard the deep resonant voices of the Dalai Lama's bodyguards chanting in the night the praises of the Goddess Tara: hundreds of men's voices resounding in the peaceful air. I thought to myself that Tibet was truly a country of religion, where even the soldiers sang the praises of our goddess.

About seven the next morning I proceeded to the regent's palace, where the other candidates were already assembling. Some had spent the night nearby; others, coming from Lhasa, had gotten up before dawn; and we all waited at the palace entrance, where the body guards before it stood at attention. Two *tsenhabs* appeared from within, assistants in the young Dalai Lama's theological education, and the elder read from a sheet of paper the names of the waiting candidates. Since the Dalai Lama in his studies had no companions with whom to debate, it was one of the duties of these tsenhabs to engage him in a debate. When his studies were concluded, they would remain in office in Lhasa to oversee all examinations, not only for the degrees of lharampa and tsogrampa, but also for abbotical posts in Drepung, Sera, Gaden, and Gyudme.

The number of our company was eighteen, and when all our names had been called, we were admitted to the palace and conducted to the assembly hall, to be seated there in rows on cushions. Across the aisle from us sat our four examiners: the two tsenhabs who had met us at the palace gate, and the two present occupants of the roles and thrones of Tsongkhapa's leading disciples, Kredup and Gyeltseb, both among the highest-ranking scholars of Tibet. According to tradition, sixteen candidates were to be selected, corresponding to the original Arhats appointed by the Buddha to carry on his Doctrine. However, the government had the power to increase this number on occasion, and so this year there were eighteen, including three Mongolians and four incarnate lamas. We took seats according to the rank of our monasteries, in the order of Drepung, Sera, and Gaden; and since Gomang College was the oldest in Drepung, its candidates were the first in the front row. Loseling was next, as the largest college in Drepung, and the others followed.

The first candidate from Gomang was a very handsome Mongolian with a small mustache. When he had taken his seat flanked by the examiners, a colleague of his from Gomang rose and put to him the first question. Challenges then followed from fourteen of the others present, from Drepung, Sera, Gaden, and Rato (i.e., myself), challenges touching the five obligatory branches of study in all these monasteries. To each candidate fifteen questions were to be addressed, three in each of the five branches: Pramāna (logic and dialectics), Madhyamika (the "Middle Path"), Prajnaparamita (the "Perfection of Wisdom" sutras), Abhidharma (metaphysics), and Vinaya (the monastic discipline). The handsome Mongolian was not impressive in his responses in Pramāna and Vinaya, but made up for this with his knowledge of the Perfection of Wisdom, Middle Path, and metaphysics.

There was a break at noon for lunch, and when the examiners rose and left we candidates were served in the assembly hall itself, a simple meal of dumpling-broth and tea, after which we all strolled outdoors and rested on the lawn. There we could hear the peacocks' cries behind the inner yellow wall of the Dalai Lama's palace. A young deer came to look us over and scampered away. The garden was beautiful in its summer green, and I particularly remember a great bed of sunflowers, like a mass of gold against the clear blue sky. The willows grew luxuriously, trailing their pale green branches in the grass, and fruit trees bloomed against a background of juniper. But as lovely as it all was, I could not enjoy it, since I was too preoccupied with wondering what questions I would have to face. I was all nerves and tension, and realized when I looked around at my colleagues that they, too, were in a similar state.

Only the four members from Gomang College were examined that first day, but the next morning the ordeal began for us of Loseling, and I was the fourth to be called. The first question put to me was from the candidate from Sera. It concerned the Perfection of Wisdom, and though I had studied the subject intensely, I found it difficult to answer. The matter was being discussed on a deeper level than I had anticipated, requiring answers hinging on my own interpretations of the subject, and as the cross-examination continued I faced many challenges of this kind. On the whole, however, I felt that my average in the five subjects was not going to be bad.

After four and a half days the examination ended, but we would not know the results until after Monlam, when the two tsenshabs would submit their report to the regent (the Dalai Lama being only eleven at the time), who would then make appropriate adjustments according both to his personal knowledge of a candidate's qualifications and to information from other scholars. Uneasy and anxious to find out how I might have done, I returned in haste to Lhasa to give to three of my teachers a full account of the questions I had been asked, my responses, and the questions that I had myself put to the others. They seemed pleased enough to discuss these matters with me, and I gained from them new insights, but no real assurance that I had passed the examination. I returned, therefore, to Rato; and as soon as I reached my room an urgent message came from the abbot (who was now Konchog) inviting me up immediately. The moment I entered his room he asked whether I had good or bad news to tell. I replied that I had tried my best, and gave him a full account. He responded that he felt that it had gone pretty well, and told me not to worry, but to keep right on with my studies until the final examination, which would be much more important. So I remained in Rato for two more months, hard at my books every day.

About that time travelers from the Kham to Lhasa on pilgrimage brought me a letter, and I learned that my mother and Dongye were coming to be present at the gift ceremony for my geshe degree (my father's duties kept him at home). I had not seen my mother for eleven years and was immensely exited by this news, now realizing fully how much I had missed her. A few weeks later, one of the students living in my kitchen came running to announce that my mother and Dongye had arrived with a caravan, and were now just entering the monastery gate. I ran out and down the stairs to meet her as she came in. Some of our monks were already helping with the mules and baggage, and Dongye followed them into the courtyard. We do not have the custom in Tibet of kissing our parents, as in the West. She addressed me formally as Rinpoche, but had tears of joy in her eyes as I put my arms around her. I sent a monk to ask our prior's permission to bring her into my apartment, for though it was not allowed to bring a woman into the khamtsen, I was sure there would be no objection, and was already conducting both her and Dongye upstairs. We had a long intimate conversation, and I was given all the latest news. They had brought many letters and gifts from my friends and teachers in the Kham, as well as reports of life at home and in the labrang.

I arranged for my mother to stay with a family not far from the monastery, and brought her to them before dark. Dongye stayed in my guest room, and that evening I was kept busy reading all the letters and opening the presents I had received. My mother had brought me an especially precious gift, a large *zi* stone from her favorite necklace, a beautiful black-and-brown stone with white stripes and circles, or "eyes," as we called them, which Tibetans considered more desirable even than coral. (Coral was generally the most valued stone in Tibet; turquoise and amber were also favored.) Zis were valued according to the number of eyes they contained, and this one, having nine, was exceptionally fine. We later sold it for a good price, which helped to finance the gift ceremony that was traditionally held before taking the formal examination for the lharampa.

Dongye rested for his first ten days with us, then met together with my students, all of whom had volunteered to help with the ceremony. His first suggestion was that we should offer silk banners for the pillars and beams in the assembly halls of both the khamtsen and the college, and when everyone had agreed to this, he went to Lhasa and bought yards and yards of Benares silk in many colors. Then he invited three Lhasan tailors to come to Rato to cut and sew the banners, and in addition some of our tailor monks were drafted to help out.

The morning of that important day, at around eight, directly after the first morning ceremony, I came to the courtyard where the Abbot Konchog was already seated on a throne of stone set against the college wall. The monks had assembled and were chanting the praises of the eight renowned Indian scholars known as the Six Ornaments and Two Principles of This World. The writings of these eight formed the basis of the greater part of the curriculum in the monasteries, and I had studied and memorized many of their texts. I entered during the chanting, and when the chant concluded took my place on a smaller throne in front of the abbot's, where I began immediately to chant in praise of my teachers, the tutelary deities, Buddhas, Bodhisattvas, and protective deities. When I had finished, another monk stood up, who, walking back and forth in the aisle, chanted the history of the transmission of the Lord Buddha's Doctrine of Tibet, and then started to put questions to me, which he limited to Pramāna, as all the others during that morning session. I was tested during the afternoon in the Prajnaparamita and Madhyamika, and that evening in Abhidharma and Vinaya. The first two sessions lasted an hour each; the evening session, about three. During a tea ceremony shortly before noon that day, we celebrated the presentation of gifts to the abbot.

Some thirty people attended, including my mother and Dongye, as well as my guests and classmates. I led the procession, bearing an image of the Lord Buddha; behind me a classmate carried a book of scripture; and behind him a third brought a chorten. One by one we came down the aisle to pass before the abbot's throne and present to him our gifts. Then followed our classmates, each responsible for one gift: tea bricks, yak skins full of butter, different parts of a new robe, and so on. As was customary, all these had been purchased for this occasion from the abbot himself, so that in our ceremony we were simply returning to him things that was already his.

The fourth ceremony of that day took place about noon and the assembly hall was so crowded that the latecomers overflowed into the courtyard. There must have been fifteen hundred monks, the guests I had especially invited, the Abbot Konchog and some of my teachers, friends from both Drepung, and a few Moslem and Nepalese friends. I was not required, as donor, to participate in this ceremony, and so could sit in the gallery among my guests. There was a throne for me there, as the incarnation donor, another for Konchog as abbot of Rato, and from our places we could look down and watch everything going on. I was pleased to see how handsome our new banners and pillar decorations looked with all their brilliant colors, and I told Dongye it seemed to me the monks were enjoying their tea ceremony enormously. It was served twice, along with rice porridge seasoned with generous chunks of yak meat and dried fruits. Konchog, too, was greatly pleased and declared himself delighted with the whole occasion. We distributed twice as much money that day as at the time of my admission ceremony at Rato, and the following day, in the khamtsen, we offered even more gifts than had been distributed in the college.

A great reception was held in the khamtsen assembly hall the afternoon of that second day. Thrones again had been prepared for us. Friends, relatives, and all the monks from my khamtsen came up to congratulate me, bringing gifts, and it required about an hour for the two or three hundred present to perform this ceremony. The following afternoon I gave a banquet for two hundred, again in the khamtsen assembly hall, and later on that day, another party for my classmates—and finally my last great gift ceremony concluded.

I was to the first monk of my class to take the lharampa examination because, as an incarnation, I had the privilege of being advanced rapidly in my studies. Incarnations gained their degrees normally in six or seven years, but because of Konchog's advice I had prolonged my studies to eleven. Regular monks, on the other hand, were chosen for the examination by their abbots mainly by seniority, and some had to wait as many as twenty years for their degree—but, as a result of this, they were frequently better educated than incarnations. However, there were never in Tibet any barriers, such as social standing, lack of property, or nationality, to keep a monk from progressing in his scholarship. All that was required were personal ability and arduous study to bring one to the top. Indeed, only a few incarnations ever rose to become the abbots of Drepung, Sera, Gaden, or Gyudpa colleges: most of the great leaders were from the regular ranks. On the other hand, an incarnation had an advantage in that if he chose to return to his own labrang, he would be recognized as the head of his monastery if he was in possession of one, though not necessarily its abbot. In some cases the functions of monastery head and abbot were combined, but in others the religious authority of the incarnation and administrative authority of the abbot were kept apart.

After my examination and gift ceremony at Jang, I returned to Rato and serious study. Shortly before the New Year and Monlam, I paid a visit to a nearby hermitage, where the Lama Lhotul Rinpoche was in retirement, and asked him to pray for me in my final examination. He looked at me hard and responded: "This one day should not be thought important in your life. If you win a great reputation by answering questions, that will be no use to you whatsoever when you die. What counts is to go on studying to the close of this life and to grow in knowledge, so that in the end you may become a Buddha."

I was ashamed. I had brought the lama an unintelligent request, and I have never forgotten his words.

On the second day of the New Year, all was ready, and I rode to Lhasa. I had already rented a room there with a religious family near the Jokhang, and the following day went to the Potala to join the other seventeen candidates for our interview with the Dalai Lama (now twelve years old) and the regent. We had to wait about two hours for two tall ornamental poles to be set up on the grounds below, which are put there every year; while nervously waiting we strolled about the chapels, trying to interest ourselves in all the wall paintings there of the life story of the great Fifth Dalai Lama. Finally, we entered the assembly hall, where His Holiness and the regent were sitting on chairs in Western fashion. One by one, we went up before them and, prostrating ourselves, received their blessings. The occasion was surprisingly informal, with only a few masters of ceremonies, and master of the table. Our interview was brief, and from there we went to the residence of the Gaden Tipa (the same with whom I had once studied and whose questions had so humbled me) to learn from him the precise dates of our separate examinations. The examinations were to begin of the fifth day of the New Year. Those who had fared best in the preliminaries would be examined on the eleventh, twelfth, thirteenth, and fourteenth. My own date I found listed as the twelfth.

The huge assembly hall of the Jokhang was filled to capacity with monks for the opening ceremony of Monlam, which took place late that afternoon. We eighteen, on the high dais to the left of the Dalai Lama's throne, sat facing the multitude; and I, for one, was deeply thrilled to be at last on that great platform which I had regarded with awe the first day I came to Lhasa many years before. The beautiful chanting began and since on that first day there would be only a tea service, I felt free to watch with full attention all that was going on.

Next morning, before sun-up, we were again in that hall. It was still completely dark and the prior's assistants moved about the temple with flares of butter-saturated cotton wrapped around straw. We were not to use flashlights, but since they made life that much easier, I had brought one along to guide my steps on the way.

This initial day of the examination was momentous for us candidates, and, as usual, it commenced with chanting and a service of tea. Throughout the two weeks of the ordeal there were always two abbots from Drepung sitting near the candidate under fire. Only those of lesser distinction would be examined the first few days, but later on, when the better scholars were called up, more monks from the monasteries round about came to listen, and from the eleven to the fourteenth, when the best were on display, interest would be running high and the temple packed.

From early morning to about ten at night we were all duty-bound to remain in the assembly hall with only short interludes of rest—brief intermissions after each of the main ceremonies of morning, noon, and late afternoon, when we were allowed to return to our rooms. The time, however, passed quickly, for there were many interesting discussions.

Moreover, it was helpful to those of us who were going to be called up later to hear how the earlier candidates answered challenges and to consider how we might have replied in their places. Sometimes one would get stuck for an answer simply because he was nervous; another would impress us by his phenomenal memory as he quoted appropriate texts. Occasionally a surprising reply would be given that would seem marvelously fit and logical until later, when one thought about it, when it would not make such very good sense.

On the eleventh day, just preceding my examination, I was allowed to leave before the evening session. When that commenced and the first question had been asked, I removed my hat, bowed to the abbot sitting next to the candidate, took my leave, and going back to my rooms, found a number of friends there awaiting me. They had brought some scarves and liquid butter in tall copper flagons, and together we all went with these to the main temple to pray.

Since this was the time of year when almost everybody in Lhasa was visiting the main temples, the ancient building was crowded, but we as lharampa candidates were let through and went immediately to pay our respects to the images of the Lord Buddha and Chenresig. My own silent prayer was that the next day our discussions should be fruitful not for myself alone, but for all living beings, helping to destroy ignorance and to bring the light of knowledge to all. Then, on our way back home, we stopped off at the residence of the Abbot Konchog, who said to me, very seriously: "It may happen in tomorrow's discussion that you may feel that your opponent has insulted you. Do not insult him in return, no matter what he may have said. Secondly, you need not answer a question if you have not understood its meaning. And thirdly, if you do not know the answer you should immediately say so." He added that he was coming himself to see how well I fared.

The next, my greatest, day, I rose about 2 A.M., said my morning prayers, and left my lodging for Jokhang. Again, the streets were dark and the stars still shining, but there were many monks already making their way to the temple. The assembly hall quickly filled; the ceremony began; and after a short time, I left the dais, going down the aisle to sit far back, before a pillar. Monks were crowded into every available inch of space, perhaps twenty thousand gathered under that one great roof. The chanting stopped and I rose, holding my hat before me. I was extremely nervous, but the training I had received for so many years sustained me. Reciting loudly ten verses selected from various texts, I concluded with a prayer to the line of spiritual succession from the Lord Buddha Gautama to my own chief teachers. And at the end of each verse, in sign of respect, I would touch my hat to my forehead.

When that morning ceremony had ended I proceeded, according to custom, from the assembly hall to the Sungchos Rawa, the courtyard where Tsongkhapa in the fifteenth century had delivered his daily lectures and the Dalai Lamas and Gaden Tipas, the head abbots of Gelugpa had all continued the tradition. His Holiness's throne was set very high there with broad steps leading up to it—the same steps from which I had watched the concluding events of Monlam, twelve years before. Again I mounted them, but this time in a very different spirit, took my seat on the right side of the dais with the other candidates at right angles to me, and sat facing all the monks. There were not many monks present at the beginning but more were steadily arriving and when the time came for the questioning, there were a number from the big "Three Pillar" monasteries (Loseling of Drepung excepted, since I was a member of that college) who rose, one after another, to test me on my knowledge of Pramāna, but suddenly, our sharp exchanges were interrupted by the sounding of a conch.

The crowds that had gathered in the street were being shooed aside by the assistant priors of Drepung. Dob-dobs cleared a path down which a major assistant of the prior came, bearing an incense stick, followed by a group of monks. All of this was but a prelude to the appearance of the old Gaden Tipa himself, who was coming to deliver his daily lecture form the platform on which we were all seated. He leaned on the arm of an attendant monk, with another behind him holding an orange silk parasol over his head. Although he looked older than when I had first visited him in Lhasa, thinner and with hair completely white, he still walked with dignity and assurance. He entered the courtyard and we all, rising, bowed down to him as he climbed to his throne. There was a permanent throne platform for the Dalai Lama. When the Dalai Lama was not there, the Gaden Tipa took his position on another throne placed before it. When he had taken his seat there, we again bowed.

On the first broad step below the Gaden Tipa's throne were the cushions for the incarnations of previous regents; on the next below, those of certain other important incarnations together with the abbots of Gaden Sera, Drepung, Gyudto, and Gyudme; and on the lowest step, the third, those of the geshe candidates, namely ourselves. We sat facing the Gaden Tipa, as he delivered a lecture on one of the earlier incarnations of the Buddha, the famous story told in the *Jakatas* of his encounter with a starving tigress that was about to eat her own cubs. When the Buddha saw this, he felt such compassion that he offered his own body, and was consumed. The Gaden Tipa was an excellent speaker and this talk, I am sure, was fascinating. However, I was so preoccupied with my own imminent ordeal that I heard scarcely a sentence, or even a word. When he had finished, the monks chanted and the old Gaden Tipa stepped down carefully from his throne and left the scene. The entire assembly then moved to the interior of the temple, and twice we had tea, porridge, and money distributions—these were enormous affairs, for there were over a hundred donors sitting in the gallery. It was only after all that that the second part of my examination began.

My dingwa—the large piece of cloth that we used either as a mat or as a cushion covering—was placed on the floor in the center of the immense hall, and I sat facing the main door of the central temple of Tibet. Directly above my head was the large white banner, symbolic of the Tushita heaven, that always hung from the ceiling during Monlam. The first to challenge my seat on that spot was a Sera monk from Amdo, who stood up to ask me to explain the importance of Compassion (*Karuna*) in the achievement of Buddhahood. "How," he asked, "is it important in the beginning stages, in the middle stages, and in the final stage of the progress to Buddhahood?"

I replied: "Great compassion is of the utmost importance in the beginning since without it, no one is a Bodhisattva. Compassion is like a seed. Without seeds one cannot grow a crop. Without compassion no one can begin to grow to Enlightenment.

"Great compassion is of supreme importance also in the middle stages; for without it, the practice of the Six Perfections (generosity, morality, patience, energy, meditation, and insight) is impossible; whereas, without the practice of these, a Bodhisattva cannot become a Buddha.

"And thirdly, great compassion is no less important in the final stages, since without it a Buddha would not, without thought of reward or reputation, teach to all the Doctrine he had mastered."

My opponent was a keen scholar and his discussion was absorbing, but he had not pursued it long before another monk pushed him aside and posed a question of his own. Then others stood up and interjected further questions, for when a lively argument got going, interest was aroused and everybody wanted to participate. The younger monks in their eagerness even shoved each other, but in a friendly, harmless way; and whenever an especially well-known scholar rose, respect was shown him by giving way and letting him come forward. Sometimes the little tussles could be turned to advantage by the respondent if he happened at the time to be in difficulty with some question: the intervention of those pushing forward to ask new questions—often even grabbing his robe and tugging to get attention—might convincingly distract him, and then he could get off the hook, listening with real pleasure to the suggestion of a new theme.

A dozen or more monks, in the course of that session, had risen to examine me on the Prajnaparamita and Madhyamika, before the Gaden Tipa again appeared and interrupted the examination. He prostrated himself full-length three times before the image of Jowo Rinpoche, and ascending his throne, sat facing the image. The prayers and chanting were resumed, reciting this time, the story of Tsongkhapa's life, with the deep bass voice of the master of chanting filling the assembly hall. His open manner, his handsome face, and the way he wore his robe were perfect, and I took great pleasure both in hearing and in seeing him. The high voices of the younger monks and novices made a perfect contrast to his deep solo. After some time, the Gaden Tipa himself chanted from a famous book by Tsongkhapa and prayed that in the next life we should all be born in the Sweet Paradise, *Sukhavati,* where the Buddha Amitabha presides.

My third and final period of examination, the most important of all, began around five in the afternoon. The two tsenshabs who had monitored our preliminary session were now in the gallery; and sitting all around me on the floor were the geshes from the Gyudto and Gyudme colleges, with their two abbots watching to evaluate their performances. And it was they, the geshes of those two great schools, who began the questioning. When they had finished, both they and their abbots retired and any monk then remaining in the hall was thereafter permitted to challenge.

These final discussions lasted long, for no pushing was now tolerated. One who was later to be the abbot of Gyudme asked a question about the Vinaya to which I could not recall any answer, and so I said that I did not know and asked him to continue with another question. He, however, insisted that I should answer the question posed and so I had to guess. All during that day my own students and teachers were present, as well as my mother and a number of relatives. By ten, when it was over, I felt immensely relieved. I had found it difficult to answer quite a number of the questions, but had the feeling that I had performed, on the whole, rather well.

Next morning over a hundred of my teachers and friends arrived before noon to congratulate me. When Konchog came in he said, "Now that you have obtained your degree, you must not think you have finished your studies. This is only a beginning. You must go on now in such a way as to achieve Buddhahood."

My mother, who was in the room all the while, was very happy, she told me privately, and greatly relieved. She had listened all day but from my answers could not tell how things were going. Sometimes, when I had paused to think before responding, she had become stiff with tension for fear that I might not be able to reply. And Dongye, too, had been there through it all. "I have worked for you many years," he said; "and have now seen my dearest wish fulfilled. So, even if I die soon, I shall not regret anything I have done, for I have seen the results of your study and am deeply pleased."

On the twenty-fourth day of Monlam the ceremony of Torgyag was celebrated with its two huge tormas set afire. After this we candidates came back into the Jokhang to hear the results of the examination. The Dalai Lama did not attend this reception but was represented by the regent. The abbots of Sera, Drepung, and Gaden, the prior of Drepung, and their assistants all were present. There were in all, perhaps over a hundred.

The door of the Dalai Lama's great reception chamber was thrown open but behind it was a screen so we could not see in. A monk appeared before the screen and read a long letter telling of the importance of the geshe in the Buddhist monastic order and then read out the names of those candidates who had received scholastic honors.

First he called the name of the monk from Sera, who was already a mature man and well-known scholar. Responding and entering the reception room, he passed beyond the screen and out of sight. Three more names were called, and then I heard my own name. It was a shock that set my nerves tingling, but I hurriedly composed myself and, following the required procedure, entered the room. It was a large, square room with an open ceiling, the light coming in through high windows. Against the far wall stood the Dalai Lama's throne of a dark carved wood, his silken robes spread upon its cushions. To its right sat the regent, Tagdag Rinpoche, on a throne facing the eastern wall. And the cushions for the new lharampa geshes were placed directly opposite him on the floor.

Before taking my place beside the first monk, who was already seated, I made my obeisance to the Dalai Lama's throne and stood respectfully before the regent. The monk who had taken first honors had received a full monk's robe and twelve tea bricks wrapped in a yak skin. He was sitting with the robe draped on his shoulders with the tea bricks out in front of him. I sat down on the cushion beside him. An assistant of the regent's chamberlain threw a robe over my shoulders, and placed before me a packet of tea half the size of that of the Sera scholar. There were about seven assistants moving about, taking care of all these arrangements. And then after me, one by one, the next three candidates arrived, who were also awarded honors. All received gifts, each proportionately smaller than the last, so that the eighth received but a portion of a monk's robe and a single brick of tea. Those remaining, who now numbered seven, entered the chamber in a group, made their obeisances, and sat down. Tea and droma were served, after which one of the Dalai Lama's guardians came in with heavily padded shoulders and commanded in a loud voice: "Stand up." We all did so and, prostrating ourselves, thanked the government for the gifts we had received, gathered up our presents, and left the room.

12.

I Begin My Tantric Studies

I was relaxing in my room after Monlam, with a pleasant sense of accomplishment, when my mother and Dongye entered.

"Now that you have received your degree with high scholastic honors," she said happily, "I know it was worthwhile to have borne such a son, and now you will be coming home with us. Your father, all our relatives, and all the people of Dayab are looking forward to seeing you after so many years."

She was wonderfully excited, and I did not find it easy to say what I knew had now to be said. I responded with a question. "Do you not think it would perhaps be better for me to remain here one year more, to study Tantric Buddhism at Gyudto?"

"But there are some very great lamas in our own district," she replied. "You might study with one of them. And you could then teach what you have been learning here."

Dongye, in the middle, assumed a neutral position. "I am satisfied," he said quietly, "with what you have accomplished. By succeeding so well you have fulfilled my dearest wish. And so I should prefer to leave all decisions about your future up to you, who are the best judge of what you require for your further development."

I must confess that at the time I was not really very enthusiastic about entering Gyudto. All I knew was that I had still a great deal to learn, and so felt that I simply had to go on. Both Gyudto and Gyudme, our two leading Tantric colleges, were notorious for their extremely strict discipline. Their rules of conduct were even stiffer that those of the "Three Pillar" monasteries. I was young, energetic, and for years had studied long and hard to succeed in what I had just accomplished. I dreamed of seeing the world, especially India, the Buddhist Holy Land. Was I then strong enough in character, and willing enough in spirit, to take on unresentfully a new, different, and probably very difficult course of studies under the most rigorous supervision?—a discipline so strict that were I to break for any reason any of the rules of the Gyudto, the authorities could expel me without a hearing? And if anything like that should occur, it would stain my record forever. Eager as I was to learn about Tantric Buddhism, I was uneasy about submitting to the harsh drill of those two colleges, and so had toyed, from time to time, with the idea of going on with Tantric studies privately, under some lama in Lhasa. For, homesick though I might feel at times, I was not yet ready to return to the Kham. Lhasa was the highest center of Buddhist teaching in the world, and it was clear to me that I should remain there for another while at least, among the many great teachers living in the neighborhood of that fabulous city. These sentiments and thoughts crowded through my mind as I tried to reply to my mother's plea.

"I feel, Mother," I said finally, "that the proper thing for me to do is to ask Konchog's advice and guidance in this crucial matter."

She agreed. In fact, both she and Dongye seemed pleased with the idea. Together, we went to call on my trusted friend, who happened to be stopping nearby in an official residence.

Admitted to his rooms, we found him sitting on the terrace in the sun. He looked up, and when he saw me exclaimed with a large smile, "A new geshe as big as a mountain has come to pay me a visit." He rose and invited us inside to sit down, motioning us to cushions by the window. After a glance at each of us, having himself sat down, he turned to us and said: "I feel sure that you now intend to go on with your studies in Gyudto. As one of the greatest institutes for Tantric studies in the world, that is surely the place you have in mind."

Taken aback, I hesitated, and stalling for time replied clumsily that I had thought I might study Tantric Buddhism privately. In fact, I said, I had come to ask his recommendation of the best lama with whom to do that.

He seemed to consider the point. "Yes," he replied thoughtfully, "in theory that would be possible. Many before you have done so. But such a course would take you much longer than a season of work at Gyudto and finally not be as thorough. Furthermore, people are going to respect you more if you have a Gyudto degree, and that for a teacher is important. Your students will pay attention to everything you have to say, and your words will have more authority. But finally," he conceded, "this will have to be your own decision. Some, after gaining their geshe degree, return directly to their own monasteries and either teach or devote themselves there to meditation. Others, retiring to hermitages, concentrate exclusively on religious practice. Many return to their homes to work and teach among the people. The majority, however, would choose to go on to higher Buddhist studies, and what that means is intensive study of the Tantras."

All three of us knew that this was a wise and compassionate lama speaking, one devoted to his students, always considerate of their characters and needs when giving advice, and never swayed by self-interest or thought of worldly concerns. My mother, although sorely disappointed in her personal wish to have me home again, readily agreed with him, as did Dongye; and as for myself, I knew intuitively that his advice was sound.

In Tibet we have always considered it extremely important to obey religious teachers. However, if one were to ask a student to perform some act that was either beyond his capacity or morally wrong, obedience would not be required. In such a case the pupil might excuse himself, but never despise the teacher; nor should he feel contempt even toward one who had suggested an evil course. We had the same reverence for our teachers as for our parents.

In Tibet, there were many Tantric colleges, but of these the most highly regarded were Gyudto and Gyudme in Lhasa, which together were known as the *Gyudpa;—Gyud* is our word for *Tantra* and *Gyudpa*, the specialized study of a *Gyud*—a Tantric text—and practice of its contents. We used to say of the two Gyudpas that they were so glorious, they were like the sun and moon in the sky. Gyudme, the older, had been founded by one of the chief disciples of Tsongkhapa, Sherab Senge, in 1433, five years after his master's death. It was in my time an institution of about five hundred monks. Gyudto had been founded in 1474 by a disciple of Sherab Senge, Kunga Thondub, and had at first only thirty-two members. When I began my studies at Gyudto there were nine hundred or more, residing in five khamtsens. The government had designated the Ramoche Temple in Lhasa as its headquarters.

Having recognized the wisdom of my beloved abbot's advice, I decided to enter Gyudto College. This required a sponsor; for although I now was a geshe, I was nevertheless going to have to start all over again, at the bottom, and be introduced by a member of the school of my choice. Actually, I had a number of Gyudto friends in Lhasa, and it was one of these, a genial, highly respected monk named Chödan, who very kindly offered to present me. It was his offer that finally helped me to decide.

As a geshe, I would be excused from a difficult series of oral examinations to gain entrance to the monastery. However, geshes were not excused from the hard monastic rules which required our renunciation of every luxury and the assumption of a far more frugal style of life than that of any of the other monasteries of Tibet. In Rato, I had been allowed (as an incarnation) to wear robes of a better fabric than those of the regular monks. Many of my waistcoats had been imported silk or brocade. But in the Gyudpa no one could wear anything imported, nor even the better woolens of Tibet. Everything had to be of domestic manufacture and as simple as could be. In fact, I owned nothing appropriate for a Gyudpa monk, and had to order new robes to be made. For this I had to ask my sponsor for assistance. He brought me some coarse Tibetan woolen cloth and we carried this to a tailor—in Tibet there were no ready-made clothes of any kind, and consequently one had always either to take one's cloth to a tailor or to bring the tailor to one's home. I could not differ in any way from the other monks in dress, or alter a single detail of the costume prescribed in the rules. And, of course, I would have to give up my precious pocket watch.

However, I had not yet been accepted. No one enters a Gyudpa college immediately. It was going to be necessary, first, for my sponsor to obtain permission for my entry from the prior of my khamtsen—the Dagpa khamtsen—at Gyudto, and for this he was going to have to arrange for three formal consultations on three successive weeks. These were soon attended to, and following a trip to Rato to tidy up my affairs, I entered the monastery.

On the first morning of my Gyudto life, I got up early and put on my coarse new robe. I would now have to learn to carry a number of required objects in its folds: a small case called a *shoka li* for one or two books, made of bamboo neatly covered with a white cloth, to be used also as a reading stand; a black bowl, like the one the Lord Buddha used for collecting alms; a big, unpainted wooden cup in a blue sack for broth and buttered tea; a white tsampa bag; my dingwa; and my saffron-colored chugu. Arrayed and equipped in this unaccustomed style, I walked to the Ramoche Temple where my sponsor was already waiting. He introduced me to the prior of my khamtsen, who, in turn, conducted me to the abbot—not failing to remind me at the door to his apartment to remove my shoes.

The abbot, seated on his cushion, was a man of about fifty, handsome, tall, and with a silky moustache. He had been formerly at Drepung and I had seen and known him there, but this was to be our first formal meeting. I prostrated myself three times before him and knelt as he leaned to touch his forehead to mine. "The whole reason," he said, following this greeting, "for becoming a member of Gyudto is to study Tantric Buddhism. You must study hard and abide by all our rules. Perhaps, at first, you will find the life difficult, for we keep a very strict discipline. But just remember: there is nothing difficult once you become used to it."

I rose, bowed, and retiring from the room, was brought next to the Lama Unze, chief disciplinarian of the college and second in command. He would become the abbot in three years, and the present abbot would then retire. His rooms were high beneath the golden temple roof, and when I entered, again performing prostrations, he leaned forward touching his forehead to mine but had nothing at all to say. Originally a nomad from the northernmost part of Tibet, he was a powerful, heavyset man with strongly Mongolian features, imperturbable and taciturn. He simply looked at me, said "Thank you!" and retreating, I left the room.

With these two interviews behind me I was physically as well as emotionally relieved, for my new robe was scratching my skin. Used to a fine silk undervest, I was finding the wool against the flesh a torture. The hair shirt of penance of the early Christian saints evidently was to be, for the period of my career at Gyudto at least, my basic article of costume.

Pinching and shaking the rough cloth here and there, to lift it from my skin, I hurried alone to the chora, which I found to be a large garden shaded by willow trees, with deep holes in it everywhere, dug by monks using the area for study and meditation. They would creep into these in the wintertime, setting stones about the edges, to protect themselves from the cold and to achieve some sort of privacy. It was said in banter that Gyudto monks were the only people on earth who went into holes in the ground *before* death. When I arrived all the holes were empty. The monks were in the assembly hall for the morning ceremony. I sat down to consider my case.

Presently a monk came in who proved to be from my own district in the Kham. Greeting me, he sat beside me, asked who I was, and, when I told him, warned seriously: "Incarnate lamas in other monasteries enjoy a lot of privileges, but not here, not in Gyudto. Here we are all on the same level. So I suggest that for the first year, at least, you had better attend all our ceremonies. Pretty tiresome you may find this; but here it is best to mind the rules, or you'll be punished and disgraced."

"Have you ever been disgraced?" I asked.

"Yes," he answered, "more than once. And the offense was always the same: failing to recite from some text verbatim at an oral examination. The punishment, also, was the same: to lug ten sand bags from the riverbank into the chora. Do you know how heavy such bags are? And there were always a lot of the younger monks, making fun of me, all the way."

He went on, next, to explain to me why he thought Gyudto a better Tantric college than Gyudme; and I, though wondering why the two should not be judged equally good, kept nodding as though in agreement, which seemed to give him satisfaction. Then, suddenly, all the other monks came streaming out of the assembly hall. I noticed they were all barefoot, and guessing that this would be a rest period of about a quarter of an hour, I looked for my watch and remembered I had given it up.

My companion rose. So did I. And the monk who was to be my instructor in the rules approached, told me who he was, and announced that he would go with me to the next session. From the college roof a gong sounded and the monks put on their yellow hats. They began filing into the courtyard that opened out from the chora, and I as the latest among them followed with my guide at the end. We then stood in the courtyard waiting for the prior to appear, and when he did he signalled us with gestures of his right hand to proceed into the Ramoche assembly hall—the chanting master first, then the elder monks, and finally all the rest.

Compared to that of the Jokhang, the assembly hall of the Ramoche Temple was small, holding hardly more that six hundred, and since not everyone could find room there, some were directed to a chamber upstairs. As we took our places, the prior kept walking up and down the aisles with a very serious look on his face. I cannot recall ever having seen him smile while performing his official duties. He was always quick to criticize anyone caught doing anything wrong, but never gave even a word of praise to anyone doing something right. However, most of the monks, I learned, held him in very high regard as an excellent disciplinarian and earnest, forthright monk.

With my instructor at my side I took my seat in the back row, third aisle from the left. He was to teach me everything I would have to know about the rules and regulations, and though young, not yet a geshe, he had already been a member of the college for eight years. When we were all seated, the chief chanting master made a circular gesture with his right hand and began the chant in a very deep voice. Gradually everyone joined in, and soon the whole assembly hall was reverberating with the deep, resonant sound of men's voices in a service of great dignity. The keeper of the hall and his aides presently passed out drums and cymbals to the monks in the first two rows, and these then accompanied the chanting, with the chanting master conducting. One unfortunate player gave his drum an extra beat and at once the prior descended upon him as though to thrash him.

I leaned toward my instructor. "Isn't he terribly short-tempered!"

"Not really," he whispered back. "All our priors, when on duty, are like that."

"But why so harsh? Why not more lenient?"

"If he were soft, he would be let go when his term was up without a word. But if he serves well, this way, to the end, he will be given a gift and praise in appreciation."

A very young novice came by serving tea, and before I noticed what he was doing, he had filled my large wooden cup to the brim; since this held as much as five ordinary cupfuls, I could not possibly drink it all down in time to go on with the ceremony. Alarmed, I broke out all over in a sweat, my face becoming suddenly as wet as though I had been hatless in the rain. Gulping as much as I could, I looked around for someone to help out and found, fortunately, that the monks directly in front of me would be willing enough. The ceremony, resuming, lasted another hour; since there were to be no more such chants that day, I started back to my borrowed apartment with another monk.

We had not gone far, however, when our abbot appeared in the street before us with his attendants. My companion quickly called to me, "Run! Run! Run fast!" Since I was wearing at the time an uncomfortable pair of new shoes and could not run at all, I ducked into the courtyard of an aristocratic home, tore the shoes off, and hurried on barefoot to my room. For it was a curious custom of the Gyudpa colleges, not known to any other in Tibet, that its monks should not meet their leaders face to face in the streets. Endangered students would take refuge down a side street or in some doorway, and when the monks of other monasteries saw us saving ourselves in this way from our own advancing abbot, they would mock the whole bizarre custom—by bending over to show us their robed rear ends.

When I had brought myself safely to my room, my young Gyudto instructor came in to let me know that except on special occasions I should have to sleep with the other monks in the assembly hall. In the fifteenth century, when the college had been founded, not all its members had had rooms, and so they lived, ate, studied, and attended ceremonies together; in the course of time this custom became an established Gyudto tradition. Furthermore, every new member was on probation during his first three days, and if at the end of that time his deportment and character—which the leaders of the college had been observing—were thought not to have been satisfactory, he would be then and there dismissed. Every monk of less than nine years' membership had to be present at all four of the daily ceremonies; only those who had been members longer were allowed, now and then, to skip a session or two. Geshes newly admitted were expected to attend faithfully for the first few days, observing strictly all the rules; if their conduct proved satisfactory, however, their status would then be automatically advanced to that of one who had been a member for three years.

At about five that the afternoon, therefore, I walked dutifully back to the chora, where the evening chant was to be held. The monks were already assembling to sing the Gyud of the *Guhyasamaja-tantra*, "Tantra of the Secret [or Concealed] Assembly." When the service ended and the sound of the stone gong let us know that it was time to retire we all moved into the assembly hall to sleep in a space that was much to small for so many.

First the older monks took their places, stretching out on their right sides, heads resting on their right hands, in what is known as the lion posture. This is the pose the Lord Buddha assumed when he passed away. The older monks lay this way, full-length, but the younger ones had generally to pull up their knees, there was so little room remaining. I arranged my cup and tsampa bag as a pillow, covered with my saffron-colored chugu robe, and with my other robe still on me, lay down like the rest on my right side in the position required of all believers according to the Buddhist teaching. I found, however, that like the rest I had to pull my knees up to my chest.

When we were all there in our places, the prior with a small butter lamp in hand came checking to see that our postures were correct. He passed slowly by, went to the altar with an incense stick, prayed there a few minutes, and himself retired.

I could not sleep. Presently my legs began to feel cramped. I was afraid to move for fear of disturbing those around me, and whispered to the monk at my side that I was wide awake and afraid that at the ceremony next morning I might fall asleep. He murmured softly, "Don't worry! I'll nudge you when the prior comes." And at last, mercifully, I fell asleep.

At three the stone gong sounded: softly at first, then louder. We stirred, unfolded, and went out into the yard for a breath of air before returning to the hall, where at dawn the chanting began. After tea had been served, the chanting resumed and I fell asleep almost immediately. At Gyudto our chanting was very slow, perhaps four or five times slower than at other monasteries, so that we might meditate as we chanted, experiencing every word, not only vocally but internally, for its inmost meaning. Having been given vocal training with a special type of breathing, many were able to sound all the notes of a tonic chord simultaneously. It was the most solemn, sonorous music of Tibet; and while I slept to its sound, the prior came by, stopping before me with his little light. The monk at my right, however, had moved closer to give me a gentle nudge. I woke and received no punishment—the prior may well have observed our little trick. He could show leniency (as I later observed) to newcomers.

After my first three days, the same prior—as chief disciplinarian of my khamtsen—invited the leaders of the whole college for a meeting to be held in the assembly hall directly after the morning ceremony. The buttered tea for this critical occasion had been prepared for me by friends from tea that had been brought for me from home. I was not to participate in the meeting, but stood at the door with my sponsor and watched as the prior, when the proper moment came, addressed himself to the Lama Unze and abbot: "Are we permitted to admit Khyongla into Gyudto? May he take his place, now, with the other geshes?" Since the answers to both questions were affirmative, I was recognized from that time forward as a Gyudto member of three years' standing, could use the main door of the chora, and might enjoy in recognition of my status many special privileges.

I now had to formally invite the prior, my sponsor, and my instructor in the rules into my apartment that noon for a collation and to serve, as was our custom on such occasions, those dumplings filled with chopped meat known as *momos*, that are a favorite of most Tibetans. The momos as well as the service had been arranged for by a student of mine from Rato and a very helpful Gyudto friend, so that all was ready when the prior appeared. I was a little fearful of his presence, having seen how severe he could be. Many of the younger monks were not fond of him at all, regarding him as very much too harsh and calling him, behind his back, the Old Bear, for his little black beard. And since it was he who stood between all the monks under his charge and the higher officials of the college, it was no wonder that he should have become the butt of student criticism and jokes. We had to obtain permission for anything we might want, or even require, beyond the regulations. Should I fall sick, for example, and so be unable to attend a ceremony, I should have to ask some friend who was not a geshe to let him know, and he, as prior of my khamtsen, would then ask the Lama Unze, abbot, and prior of the college (the leading triumvirate of the monastery) to permit my absence. What I found, however, was that this same stern personage could be relaxed, friendly, and outgoing when he came to my apartment as a guest. He was in fact a close friend, as I learned, of my sponsor, the two having worked together for years, creating mandalas and tormas for the Tantric ceremonies of the college.

When the meal ended and my guests had returned to their duties, I was free to spend the rest of the day as I wished. I spent it with my mother and Dongye, who would soon be leaving. None of us had any idea how long it would be before we saw each other again. My mother would be expecting me home when I passed my final examination, but we did not know when that would be. She felt very sad, she said, returning without me. However, she had gone to the Ramoche Temple to listen to our chanting and had been immensely impressed by the service. She confessed that she had not understood a word, the chanting was so slow and different in form from any she had ever heard. But she had been deeply moved and felt proud that her son had become a member of this religious order.

That was our last long visit in Lhasa. We sat chatting over tea, took supper together, and I wrote some letters to friends for her to take back with her to the Kham. Her baggage was already packed, and two days later, she and Dongye departed. But I was on duty at the time, compelled to attend the daily ceremonies, and could snatch only the briefest final moment for a cruelly short farewell. Deeply downcast, my saddened heart during the following days yearned eastward, and I wished that I had left with them on their long journey home.

13.

Gyudto

Although the main Gyudto residence was in Lhasa, in the Ramoche Temple, it was customary for the younger monks to be taken on tours to certain other centers, regarded as important because the founder, Kunga Thondub, had visited them with his followers. In most of these Gyudto had its own buildings. For this first year of my membership the places scheduled to be visited were Chuda, Gaden, Sera, Yerpa, and the Potala, in that order, with then a second visit to Gaden, a visit to Drepung, and a final session at Chormo Lung.

It was in the middle of the third month (April) of our year, only a few days after my admission, that we were all set out for Chuda, two days' journey to the east. Gyudpa monks were not allowed under any circumstances to ride either mules or horses; since I had never before made such a long journey on foot, I was seriously worried, and received permission to leave two days ahead of the rest, with one of my students from Rato as a companion. We had, of course, to carry our own provisions. I took only my alms bowl and my book-frame full of texts, while my sturdy student packed all the rest: our dried meat, butter, broiled eggs, cakes, tea, and changes of robes.

It took us three and a half days to reach Chuda, which turned out to be a poor village of a few families. The monastery buildings were located in the village itself, each of the five khamtsens having a small house of its own with a local family to take care of it. Between sessions these villagers had the places to themselves. Even during sessions they were hardly inconvenienced, since the monks, having to sleep in the assembly hall, could occupy the houses only during the day. Actually the khamtsens had no real assembly halls in Chuda; a number of the buildings had large rooms and it was in there that our general meetings were held.

Around noon on the day after we arrived we all strolled to the main Gyudto building, the largest in the village. We waited in the portico with the other monks then gathering for the prior of the college to arrive. When he appeared he announced that our session was to begin that day and continue for six weeks. The usual seating had been changed, and I learned that my place was now to be to the right, not left, of the altar—such changes, common in Buddhist monastery life, are in keeping with our teaching on nonattachment. In fact, every gesture, every detail of our lives was symbolic of some belief. The hall selected for the assembly was large enough to hold four to five hundred, and since not all nine hundred of our monks were present, there was plenty of room for us all. During the course of the opening ceremony, however, I learned that I had brought along some uninvited guests, namely, fleas, from our night before, when I'd stayed in the home of a farmer. These gave to the long ceremony a special interest; and when it was over I went scratching to my khamtsen, where rooms had been assigned to us geshes for study by day. Every night, of course, we slept in the assembly hall.

The first topic of interest during the period of our stay in Chuda was to be the *Guhyasamaja-tantra*, which was one of three fundamental Tantric texts taught in both colleges of the Gyudpa. The second was *Samvara Tantra*, the "Covering [Concealing, Enclosing, or Enveloping] Tantra"; these two were devoted to the disciplines, respectively, of the *Rupakaya* ("apparent" or "phenomenal" aspect of Buddhahood) and the *Dharmakaya* ("causal" or "essential" aspect).

All the forms that we behold around us in this world, it was explained to us in these lectures, are generated from the Clear Light, through insight comprehending the void, or, to use the image of marriage, out of the union of insight penetrating the void. Such unions are of two kinds: one, where insight is obscured by emotivity (attraction, repulsion, and the like), and so bound to experiences of gain and loss, pleasure and pain, birth, death, and rebirth; the second, cleared of emotivity, and so released from engagement in the above states. The first is "impure insight," the second, "pure"; and the forms of life, the phenomenal or "formal" bodies produced of these two orders of insight, are themselves, accordingly, "impure" and "pure," bound and unbound. It is important for the Tantric student to arrive at an understanding of this principle. The Formal Body (Rupakaya) generated of "pure insight" (*Vijnāna*) is not a product of self-bounded thought, perception, understanding, and impulse. It is therefore said to be "non-self-originated," and displays the characteristics, not of suffering, but of illumination. Only insight cleared absolutely of emotivity can lead us to liberation from suffering (nirvana). Not even prayer and meditation addressed for years and years to the greatest and most merciful of gods will disengage the devotee from his bondage to the world. Indeed, Tibetan Buddhist historians tell of people who through all their lives recited faithfully the sutra of their chosen god, only in their next life to be reborn as demons.

For two weeks, we listened to our abbot lecture each day, and during the entire six weeks we were there, we slept each night in the assembly hall. Our meals during this time were the simplest fare, though we did not have to cook for ourselves. The hours passed quickly as the days grew hotter, and soon the time came to move on to Gaden. Once again, we walked the distance and, after a hot journey through the countryside, we caught our first glimpse of Gaden. The many shade trees around the monastery were green, in the full flower of summer, and as we looked straight up to the white monastic city, we could see many narrow streets and stairways leading upward. The main buildings were clustered about a great white assembly hall with a roof of shining gold, and beside this there was a much smaller, older hall—very precious, since it held, as we knew—the golden chorten, or mausoleum, of Tsongkhapa. And to the left of this, in a still smaller yellow building, was the apartment in which he had lived and written many of the works we had studied.

Tsongkhapa in his early years had been always on the move, invited to lecture in many parts of Tibet; but his disciples, as he gained them, began urging him to settle in one place. Many old monasteries were offered him as well as land on which to build a new one. He could come to no decision, however, until in his fifty-third year when establishing the Monlam festival in Lhasa. He paid a visit to Jowo Rinpoche, and presenting many offerings, praying for guidance, he performed a divination which led him to believe that a certain mountain in the Lhasa valley would be the best location for his following. He went to visit it, found it perfect, and established his base there, which he named Gaden, "Joyous Place." It was soon one of the most important monasteries in all Tibet, as the main seat of the Gelugpa sect, and although not as large as either Drepung or Sera, it was situated so prominently on the side and summit of its high peak that it seemed in its very situation to proclaim itself the "Central Point."

During the period of our session at Gaden, every Geshe who was not a lharampa or tsongrampa had to come up for a grueling all-night examination on the sutras. Curiously, however, each could have a "helper" at his side to see him through, and two monks from Sera Monastery asked me to play this part for them. I welcomed the opportunity, for it was thought good luck to participate in exercises of this kind in such a place as Gaden. There would be a certain risk involved, for if the monks present at the examinations were not interested in our answers and left before the drums sounded at dawn, we should all be disgraced and might even lose our membership in Gyudto. But since it was only a few months since I had taken my own lharampa examination and everything I had studied was still fresh in my mind, I was not anxious. Both of the monks I was to help were considerably older than I. One—Chuphel by name—had sat near me in the assembly hall in Lhasa and was a close friend. Dark-skinned, short, and with a heavy underlip, he was not particularly attractive. The monks had nicknamed him Baby and joked about his appearance, but he knew how to take all this with humor. The other was not such a close friend, but he had a pleasant personality and I liked him.

My first all-night session was Chuphel's, and although my friend could himself have given many of the answers, he remained absolutely silent all night long. I had to assume the whole responsibility. Many of the geshes and all the theological students of Jangtse College were there, six hundred or so, I would say. And to my discomfort, toward morning the audience began thinning out. Moreover, there were a number of times when I found the questions of the older and best geshes very difficult indeed. I was relieved to hear the drums and to see the dawn light that released me. Two nights later, when I performed the same task for my other friend, I again had a real sense of relief at the end. When the session at Gaden ended, a small group of us leaving in the morning hiked down into the valley by the river, where we met a company of wood-sellers. They had hired themselves a coracle to carry their cargo to Lhasa. We bargained with them to take us aboard, and when they had packed in all their wood, climbed on top. The current was swift and we made good time—but everyone of us became miserably seasick in that wildly rocking craft and, one by one, threw up breakfast. Then we all fell asleep. When we opened our eyes, there was Lhasa before us.

We were free the next four days to enjoy a holiday between terms, and it was during that time that a great piece of luck came our way: the offer of an apartment close by the Ramoche Temple. A Gyudto friend of mine from Dayab had been selected by divination to be one of the monastery's treasurers and so moved into the temple. He was to be one of a committee of five, each representing one of our khamtsens, and since by custom these were to live as well as to work together, his own apartment in one of the two Gyudto residence buildings would be empty for the five years of his service. He offered it to me, and I was delighted, though I should have liked very much to have remained in my own place in the center of the city near the Jokhang and the shopping sections, the two Gyudto buildings only four blocks from the temple, and all my friends and advisors thought it definitely best for me to be close to the college. I should have to return every night to the assembly hall to sleep, but might occasionally be allowed free time when I could cook in my apartment and even, every now and then, stay overnight.

Those were my first attempts to cook and although I had frequently watched my aides in Rato making fires with dung and rhododendron branches, I now learned that I should have watched more closely. My first adventure filled the room with smoke, bringing tears to my eyes and my neighbor to the rescue, who, having smelled the smoke, came running and remained at my side to help. Laughing, he taught me to arrange the bricks of dung in a pyramid; to let the air circulate; to insert the rhododendron sticks as kindling into the openings; and finally, how and when to light the flames. When he left, I put tea into water to boil and when I thought it ready, poured what I had brewed into the tea churn, adding the butter and soda. But when I shook the churn the butter and tea sloshed out all over the place so that I had to call him back. The man, fortunately, was a saint. I couldn't even make tea! And when I shopped for meat or vegetables I was inevitably overcharged; for Tibetan shops were not like American, where the prices are fixed and clearly marked. As I had already learned—or, rather, as I thought I had learned from Dongye, many years before—every purchase was a catch-as-catch-can transaction between a buyer and a seller, with no referee. As I did not know how to bargain, it turned out that every time I showed a purchase I had made to my neighbor, he told me I had been charged too much.

One day, one of my sponsor's students who was still a very small boy came to pay me a visit, and we decided to make momos. It was customary in the monastery for the doors of the rooms to be left open and for friends to enter and leave without ceremony. But if a door was closed, they would come back later. My little friend and I decided to shut the door, not wanting to be ridiculed for our cooking, and set to work to steam our dumplings and fill them with chopped meat. We labored for about four hours and produced some real surprises: some momos as dry as nuts, others as though in a soup. After these adventures in private living, I at last realized how kind and considerate my servants and helpers had been to me all these years—how much patience and skill had been theirs in making my life what it had been. Although in lectures I had often heard it told how kind to us the world is—servants are kind, parents are kind, friends are kind, and the like—until I had had this bit of experience in doing things for myself, I had no idea of the real meaning of those words.

On the fourteenth day of the seventh month, we Gyudto monks trooped off to Yerpa, some miles to the northeast. Yerpa was situated high on a tranquil mountain, surrounded by junipers and rhododendrons, and the birds kept up a sweet choir all day. Its buildings mounted in tiers up the cliffs to the summit, where there were many caves for meditation, some containing shrines. And here again, as in the other monasteries, Gyudto had its own buildings: one large one with an assembly hall, and five smaller, for the five khamtsens. The place was illustrious in Tibetan history, since many of the early Indian missionaries had stayed and taught there for long periods—among others, Padmasambhava and Atisha—

attracting many disciples. However, there were now no more than thirty monks in permanent residence.

Now according to the Vinaya, three of the most important ceremonies of the monastic life are *Sojong, Yarnay,* and *Gagye.* The first, a ceremony of confession, is to be celebrated twice monthly; and this was to be our first ceremony at Yerpa. The presiding abbot on such an occasion recites aloud from the *Pratimoksha Sutra* ("Manual of Absolution") where the whole list of 253 rules set down by the Lord Buddha is recorded, to which every gelong must conform. Usually an abbot would recite only certain sections of this enumeration; however, once a year—and this, usually, during the summer session—he was required to go through the entire text from memory. Since it is a document some eighty pages long, he would always go rushing through it quickly; even so, it required three hours. And during the course of such a recitation he would pause after each list of regulations of a certain type to ask, three times, whether with respect to that particular type of regulation everybody present was innocent. And always, everybody would remain silent. In fact, I have never heard anybody admit, on any of these occasions, to a transgression of any kind. I must conclude that monks either do not sin, or else keep quiet about it.

Yarnay, the second great ceremony, was established for the seasons of the Indian summer rains by the Lord Buddha, when he would retire with his monks to a quiet place for study and meditation, and to repair the house of the monks. There were in Tibet two seasons for Yarnay, an earlier and later. In most monasteries the celebration would commence on the fifteenth day of the sixth month, but traditionally the two Gyudpas, Gyudme and Gyudto, would start theirs on the fifteenth of the seventh month. The observance is made up of two parts: a preparation, and the ceremony itself.

Our abbot, upon concluding the Sojong, proceeded directly to the preparation of a Yarnay by appointing the Lama Unze, prior, and a leading geshe as his assistants, in a ritual ceremony called the Nomination of Those Who Offer the Residence and Cushion to the Sangha. When these three had then made prostrations, they rose and stood facing the Sangha, while the Lama Unze recited the rules of Yarnay from memory, concluding by requesting all those able to practice these rules to participate.

Next, the Lama Unze, prior, and appointed geshe ran up and down the aisles with wooden trays containing hundreds of wooden sticks, and every gelong took one. These were collected and counted and marked the number of gelongs who would be participating in Yarnay. Sticks then were passed for the getsuls, and counted, after which the Lama Unze read out to the assembly the number of gelongs and the number of getsuls present, each group responding in unison affirmatively when the number of its participants was announced. The assistants next went around holding a lock and key in hand, first touching each monk's hand with these, asking that he use the Sangha's building properly, and then touching the monk's cushion, asking that he use it according to the regulations of Yarnay. The Lama Unze then announced that no one was to use the Sangha's cushions without first covering them with his dingwa, nor should a soiled or improper dingwa ever be used.

Next morning we were roused about 2 A.M. for the ceremony itself, the first stage of which required us to go up in groups of no more than three, and repeat before one of the "leaders" the whole statement of rules, with the added declaration, "I am now to participate in Yarnay and to observe its special rules." We had also to name the government of Tibet as patron of the ceremony, the walking place in which the rituals were to be celebrated, the Sangha's cook who would be feeding us, and those friends of ours who, in case of illness, would be our nurses. All this required about three hours. When it was completed and we had our morning tea before dawn, the Lama Unze made a long speech to us about our duties in general as monks and the special duties that would be ours during the period of our stay in Yerpa. He was a nomad's son from the northern grazing lands who interlaced his speech with the sayings of his people, and whenever he angrily raised his voice the accent became stronger. Directly in front of me a monk sat who on one of these occasions turned and whispered in disgust: "He talks like a filthy nomad in sheepskins selling his beasts to be slaughtered." I could hardly believe my ears, and for a moment sat looking at him in shock. For that a monk, a respected scholar from Sera who performed meticulously all the duties of his post (and who later, in fact, became an abbot, highly esteemed), should express such contempt, not only for another monk, but for a whole species of mankind, was something contrary to the entire spirit and teaching of our Buddhist training. It took me hours to wipe this incident from my mind.

My teacher Konchog had once told me that while in Yerpa I should seize the occasion to learn something of the art of fashioning mandalas— or, as we say in Tibetan, *khyilkor*. The Sanskrit *mandala* is a many-faceted term meaning "circle, disk, or circumference," but also, "enclosure," and, in relation to religious designs, the "house or enclosure of a tutelary deity." Tibetan mandalas, I had already learned, are of three kinds: those painted on boards or on cloth, those of powdered colors on flat surfaces, and those of three-dimensional form. We were to have six one-week sessions during the period of our stay at Yerpa for the study and fashioning of mandalas. Those specializing in the study would of course spend many more such weeks through the years, but we who were simply to acquire an elementary understanding were expected to learn what we could in these six.

Each khamtsen in the monastery had its own set of special earth-platforms for the study and practice of this art, which had been made by digging shallow excavations, packing down the earth in them, and then covering this hard base with a clay that could be worked and polished to a surface firm and smooth enough to be drawn upon. There were many smaller panels of this kind for practice, but each khamtsen had also a larger one under a tent for examinations, twelve to fifteen feet in diameter, with a path around it for easy viewing.

When a number of us asked one of the monks specializing in the art to be our teacher, he had us first repair and refresh a couple of the practice frames. We cleared the debris, patched the rough spots with fresh clay, smoothed the surfaces, and then set to work to plot mandalas according to the principles of the *Vajramala Tantra* ("Thunderbolt-rosary"). Our instructor first drew the basic outline of our model, measuring it out with a long string while reciting aloud the relevant textual passages, we then drew our lines over his, repeating the same passages. When we had finished, he would study and correct the work. Though assigned only a few lines each day, yet progressing little by little, we soon found that we had fashioned accurate mandalas of all three of the chief tutelaries of the Gelugpa sect, which are Sangdhus (Sanskrit, *Guhyasamaja*), Dechog (*Chakrasamvara*), and Jigjed (*Vajrabhairava*). The three mandalas had almost identical framing-forms, but inside differed considerably in their patterns, colors, and symbols. Occasionally, for comparison, we would draw sections of all three on the same platform. The work at first was difficult, but our instructor was very patient, pointing out in detail our mistakes. And when he found that we had learned these first three mandalas well, he went on to instruct us in many more.

We learned, for example, the mandalas of the four types of fire offering: the peaceful, developing, empowering, and wrathful. The "peaceful" is an offering made to overcome impediments to the realization of freedom and enlightenment and the center of its mandala is circular and colored white. The "developing" fire rite develops merit, longer life, success in study, and the like. The center of its mandala is square and colored yellow. "Empowering" ceremonies attack the influences and defilements of delusion with a mandala that has a red lunate form in the center. And for the "wrathful" fire offering, to undo the effects of evil thoughts against sentient beings and the teachings of the Lord Buddha, the center is a triangle of black. Upon each of these symbolic centers, three-dimensional figures of wood or of dung are placed, each corresponding to the center on which it stands. For example, the figure standing on the circle, would be a cylinder, and that on the square, a cube. A long stick with a tuft of cotton on the end, saturated with butter, is ignited during the ceremony and the symbolic figure set afire. Then the person performing the ceremony pours into the flames melted butter from a long-handled, shallow ladle of cast iron (*ganglug*), which has an opening at the end from which the butter flows.

When we had all learned well the outlines of our mandalas, we next learned to visualize the colors in their places—not actually to paint these in, but to memorize their future positions and to visualize them there. In Gyudto we had seen our chodyogpa monks set up wooden platforms for special ceremonies and prepare on these large, colorful mandalas of finely powdered colored stones, always fashioning them to follow exactly the

Tantric rules. So did we try in our own attempts. Nothing in either the lines or the colors was to be altered in any way.

During our second month at Yerpa we had a special, one-week intensive session on mandalas, starting each day after the morning ceremony and working on until night—interrupted only for the daily chants, and occasionally excused even from these. At the close of that week each of the five khamtsens had to prepare on a large earthen platform a mandala of one of the three great tutelary deities. The khamtsen buildings were not far apart, and in the open space beside each a tent was erected for three platforms with a judging throne for the abbot.

When he arrived on the final afternoon, he passed hurriedly from one tent to another, not lingering long in any since he not only had to examine five mandalas, but also we geshes, standing to one side of his throne, were expected to explain the figures, while on the other side, the chodyogpas who had made them were responsible for their accuracy.

When the abbot came into our tent he assumed his seat, and we all lined up in our places. He turned his head this way and that, looking sharply down at each display, and our hearts stood still when we saw his eyes become fixed on a detail in ours of the tutelary Vajrabhairava. He had detected a mistake in the measurements of the wall of the pictured palace: a figure of five bands of color. In ours the red was a little too wide. Lifting his eyes to us, he asked sternly: "Who drew the lines of that wall incorrectly, not in accordance with the teachings of the Lord Buddha? Perhaps you think you know more than the Lord Buddha about mandalas; or possibly you thought to invent some new teaching of your own?" There was nothing we could say. Bending our heads, we just stood there in shame. "If you make another mistake like that," he said to the chodyogpas, "I shall definitely dismiss you from the Gyudto." Then he turned no less sternly to us geshes and began examining us on the various theories of Indian scholars concerning the mandala before us. We found some of his questions difficult, and he kept at us with these, repeating them without mercy. "What is the meaning of this form?" "What is the measurement of this mandala from the center to the rim?" When we made a mistake he would snap at us: "And so what have you been doing here in Yerpa? Sleeping? Eating? Is that why you have had no time to work?"

But if the answer was correct he gave no sign of approval. Finally, he got up and left, and in came the Lama Unze, to sit upon the same judging throne and go through the whole thing again. It was a real ordeal.

Next was a three-day session of chanting for the Dongdewa monks and we geshes during those days were absolved from attending ceremonies. This gave us time to study our texts and discuss them. It also gave us an opportunity to express our appreciation to our abbot, Lama Unze, chanting master, and prior, for all that they had done for us. They were much too busy to be brought together for a single grand event, however, so we served a luncheon to each in his own apartment. The meals were prepared in one of the larger college rooms and then brought separately to our guests. Above all we respected our abbot, who, though direct and forceful in his criticism, was a gentle, saintly man. Much the same could be said of the Lama Unze, at whom we poked fun for his northern nomadic accent, but whom we all really greatly liked. The master of chanting was a young monk from the Kham with a melodious, powerful voice, whose chanting was an inspiration. But the prior was an ugly type, and our service to him did not carry all the warmth of our hearts.

He was new to Yerpa, where the priors customarily served only four months apiece each year. Like myself, he had come from the Kham, and was about fifty, but he was always critical and irritable, with an overhanging underlip and bad teeth. During ceremonies, on more than one occasion, he criticized in a most improper way the junior master of chanting whose voice, unfortunately, was not very strong. For example, one day at the morning assembly, the prior accused him first of chanting too fast, then complained that he was slow, and finally that he never chanted as he should. "The junior master with that feeble rhythm of his voice," he shouted, "won't finish this chant before sun-up over the mountain." And then suddenly, jumping up with a short, heavy stick that he carried, he struck the young monk with all his strength as many as thirty times, calling out as he did so to the wrathful aspect of our college's protective deities: "Eat his flesh! Drink up his blood! Consume his heart!"

I was not too far away and thought the young man would surely not be able to go on; but, seated with his head bowed, he began again very softly. I felt for him great pity, and also felt pity for the prior. I had never seen such anger in any person before in my life. And I was not surprised when, a month later, at the end of the prior's term of office, the Lama Unze made a speech to the college censuring his unseemly behavior. The abbot had already reproved the man privately, and during the course of his brief term his conduct had somewhat improved—but not much. He remained to the end the victim of his own temper.

Our summer session was brought to a close with Gagye, the third most important ceremony of our Buddhist monasteries. In India the rainy season of Yarnay would have lasted for three months; we, however, could conclude the ceremonial term after forty-five days. We had begun on the fifteenth day of the seventh month and so could finish at the end of the eighth month.

We got up very early, as we had for opening Yarnay, and held, first, a brief version of the regular morning tea ceremony. To my surprise I had had no difficulty waking up at that hour at all—I was so eager to get back to my own apartment in Lhasa. The whole period at Yerpa had been austere and difficult for us all, rising early every morning and attending ceremonies all day, existing on very simple food, being watched over by inspectors whenever we went. Moreover, that prior had been very cruel and we had all been afraid. Throughout the season of Yarnay we had not been allowed to divide among ourselves and enjoy individually any of the foods and goods provided by the Sangha; nor had we been permitted to criticize each other. Gagye would reopen the customs of dividing property and criticizing of each other. It was a ceremony that in its preparation and in many parts resembled the Sojong. We had again to make prostrations in the four directions, however, not as in the Sojong, in the direction of the abbot. While making these we had to say, "Please forgive me for any offense I may have committed during Yarnay."

After this ceremony, we set out in the dark before dawn to walk to Lhasa, glad to be returning to what, given the perspective of Yerpa, seemed our luxurious life back at Gyudto.

Following our return to Lhasa, we made our visits to the places next scheduled in our tour—Potala, Gaden, Drepung, and finally Chormo Lung. The rest of the year passed quickly, and since I like all the other junior monks, had lived according to the rules, I was granted as a geshe the privileges of a member of fifteen years' standing. It would no longer be required of me to attend the ceremonies in the assembly hall; the visit to Chormo Lung had been the last of my tours of duty; and I was now to be allowed to spend time comfortably in my room, devoting myself to study. This naturally made a very great difference in my life.

But shortly following this agreeable turn in my fortune, a series of ominous, greatly distressing events took place in the city and round about by which I, like many others, was deeply disturbed. My first inkling of what was happening came the late afternoon of April 17, 1947, when a woman who sold food and miscellaneous articles in the street near our residence hall told me as I passed that a company of government officers and soldiers had gone to Zede Monastery, in the northwest quarter of the city, and sealed off Rating Rinpoche's labrang. Rating Rinpoche, the former regent, had his main residence two days' journey to the north of Lhasa, in Rating, but whenever he came into the city he stayed at Zede. The woman said she had learned from her husband that the government had sent two members of the cabinet out to Rating, along with another company of soldiers, to bring the Rinpoche himself to Lhasa.

At first I could not believe such terrifying news and said sharply to the woman, "Do not repeat such rumors. This simply cannot be true." She only turned her face away, muttering that there was no reason for her to repeat lies. During the next couple of hours many others told me the same tale—some had even seen the Rinpoche's residence in Rating being sealed off by the officers. I was stunned, having no idea why our government should have taken such an action. I had never met the Rinpoche in person, but greatly honored and admired him for his discovery of our present reincarnation of the Dalai Lama, and I was now concerned for his safety. When next day he was conducted back to Lhasa, under arrest, the monks of Chye College at Sera tried unsuccessfully to rescue him. Completely surrounded by soldiers, he was taken to a prison in the eastern wing of the Potala that was reserved—like the Tower of London—for high-ranking officials. For the Rinpoche had been caught, as I now heard, in some kind of conspiracy. The chief conspirator, it appeared, had been a certain Nyungne Lama, who had committed suicide before he could be apprehended; but the rest—Khardo Rinpoche, and the chief administrator of the Rating Labrang, Rating Rinpoche's younger brother—had been seized and now were in jail.

Many of the previous incarnations both of Nyungne Lama and of Khardo Rinpoche had been celebrated for their learning and for great services to the Gelugpa sect. It was therefore all the more shocking to see them dishonored. The Chye monks, in violent reaction, rose in revolt against the government, for Rating Rinpoche was not only the leading member of their college, but also its most influential patron. And so it happened that, a few days later, when on my way to the Ramoche for a ceremony, I saw Tibetan government soldiers setting up guns on the temple roof. For several days thereafter, these guns fired towards Sera, without actually hitting the buildings—the firing was mostly a show of power to convince the monks to surrender. Each day a cluster of old people and middle-aged ladies would gather about our Gyudto buildings, crying aloud while watching all this and looking anxiously over at Sera.

I could only reflect that when I had arrived as a newcomer to Lhasa and Rating had been regent, everybody in the city had tried to become his friend, so that even his mulekeeper and housecleaners had hangers-on; but now even his closest friends were careful not to let their friendship be known. The Lord Buddha's basic teaching is that nothing is everlasting— happiness, unhappiness, positions, reputation, property. All is impermanent. All things pass. And such cruel events as this, along with all that soon was to follow, had now given us Tibetans stunning evidence of that truth. By the time ten days had passed, the government had rounded up all those responsible for the plot. They were paraded past our college, and on the way from my apartment I saw the soldiers and officials marching them to prison with their hands bound. Some I recognized, whom I had known as friends, and it distressed me to see them now. Indeed, everybody in the city was distressed. In our country, government and religion had always been inseparable, yet here were government troops bombarding a monastery instead of defending it, and the monks there taking up arms against the government. It was terribly upsetting and difficult to understand.

Little by little, we learned what had happened. In its official account of the episode, the government said that Rating Rinpoche's staff members had conspired to kill the reigning regent, my friend and teacher, Tagdag. They had sent emissaries to Chiang Kai-shek for help in overthrowing him, but Rating had himself found them out and charged them to use no violence. An attempt nevertheless was made to present Tagdag with a bomb disguised as a gift, which, however, was discovered before he received it. In the meantime the Tibetan ambassador in Nanking, getting wind of the revolt, informed Tagdag, who took immediate steps to apprehend the conspirators and rebellious monks. No death sentences were issued, but the two principal conspirators, Khardo Rinpoche and Rating's younger brother, were condemned to life imprisonment. The National Assembly decided they should be blinded, but Tagdag objected and modified the sentence. Two separate houses were put up for them within the camp of the Dalai Lama's bodyguard, and in those they were to be confined. However, three years later, when the young Dalai Lama assumed his throne in 1950, they and all others were released, by His Holiness's command.

Though I initially felt that Rating was honest and had been unjustly accused, on considering all the facts, I came to believe that his guilt lay in not maintaining his authority with his subordinates. That he was irresponsible is well-documented in letters he wrote to the principal conspirators. He was at first opposed to their plan to overthrow the government, and told them so. But later, after much pressure, he relented and wrote to them that they should do as they pleased.

Rating Rinpoche died in prison on May 5, as I learned two days later from my next-door neighbor, who declared that he believed the rinpoche had been killed by one of the wardens. There were two such government wardens, one a monk, the other a layman; and my neighbor thought the layman must have done the killing to avenge his father, who had lost his government post when Rating came into office. On the other hand, the information given out by government sources was that because of the strain he had suffered, the rinpoche had been taken ill and died of a fever.

I was young at the time and in no position to know the facts, but rumors of Rating's murder remained widespread throughout Lhasa. It was only years later that I had the chance to ask the very doctor who had attended him. He was the leading physician of Lhasa and at one time had been my teacher; we had remained close friends, and I have no reason to doubt his word. What he told me was that in the midst of a National Assembly meeting, he had suddenly been called to examine Rating in the prison, had found him seriously ill, and had recommended a certain medicine. This then was brought to the assembly, where he tested it by swallowing some in full view of the members and then proceeded to the prison room. He administered the remedy to Rating but it was not sufficient to effect a cure. He believed, he said, that the rinpoche's death had been caused by his very great mental distress, and that the rumors of his murder were untrue.

Not long after the passions of this ugly affair had subsided, our prior's assistant came running early one morning to my room, breathing heavily. He had raced the half-mile from the Ramoche Temple, and up the flight of stairs to my floor to tell me that the abbot had sent him, post haste, to let all the lharampa geshes now preparing for Tantric degrees know that in two days they were to present themselves at the regent's palace in the Norbulingka for the crucial preliminary examination. The messenger was a monk of about my own age with whom I had had many friendly conversations during my year at Gyudto, and he had come to me first, he declared, so that I might set to work immediately in preparation. I had often teased him about his nose, which was always running (a not uncommon feature in Tibet), and after he had told me of the sudden alert, I said, "Please blow your nose and sit down." He shook his head. "Rinpoche, you may kid me as you like, but what I've told you is important. You'd better set to work right away."

Luckily, I had been expecting this news and had been preparing for it right along, but now that it had come, I was scared. I had been studying Tantric subjects no longer than a year, whereas some of the others who would be taking the test had been at it for two or three. Moreover, the Gyudpa system was unique in that its preliminary examination was more important than the final. When a preliminary was announced, some ten to fifteen lharampa geshes would be chosen to participate, and of these only the top two would be eligible for the final of that year. The others would come up for their finals, two at a time, in succeeding years, according to their rankings in the preliminary. And it would be only after all had passed that a preliminary would again be held; which is to say, after about five to eight years. Since only two became eligible each year, there were no additional honors to be awarded beyond that of being examined; and unless one took and passed the examination, one would not be eligible to become the Lama Unze and, finally, abbot of the Gyudpa.

On the appointed day, therefore, only two days after our reception of the news, sixteen of us started walking to the Norbulingka at dawn. We were to arrive at the regent's door before seven, and to be conducted to the same assembly hall in which, two years before, I had sat for the lharampa examination. In fact, I found that even the four examiners were now the same. Although their questions would be designed primarily to test our knowledge of the Tantras, they would also retest us in knowledge of the Sutras; for without the Sutras no one can understand the deeper meanings of the Tantras. The subject of our learning was as large, therefore, as the ocean, and my knowledge as small as a drop on a blade of grass. But as luck would have it, the questions put to me were only about the texts and topics I had studied, and I left the place marvelously relieved, with a feeling of having done rather well.

It would be several weeks, though, before the results were announced. Customarily, the highest honors were given to the reincarnations of regents, regardless of their scholarship, and since Tsomonling Rinpoche, who had been one of our sixteen, was the reincarnation of a regent, everybody assumed that he would surely be ranked first. Which left the second place in doubt and, of course, all of the next fourteen as well. During the period of our waiting I heard rumors that I had ranked in every place from the sixteenth to the first. All I hoped for was to be in one of the top four. At last, our abbot received the announcement and we learned that Tsomonling Rinpoche had, indeed, placed first, and I second. I was overjoyed especially since this was to be my last chance for academic honors—the final session would be the last examination I should ever have to face. After so many years of study for honors of this kind, it was a great relief for me to realize that I should henceforth be working only for myself, to improve my knowledge and understanding, which, after all, were the only important goals.

I had frequently visited the abbot of Gyudto following his acceptance of me as a private pupil, and one day shortly after the announcement of these results he asked whether I had felt proud on receiving in 1947 fifth highest honors in the Sutras, and now again second place in the preliminary Tantric testing. It was difficult to reply, for actually I did feel proud, but wanted to deny it. Since one is not permitted to lie, especially to one's religious teacher, I said nothing and politely stuck out my tongue—a Tibetan sign of respect. The abbot said: "Perhaps you are feeling a *little* proud. You are young. But in the Land of Snow there have been so many scholars that there is no reason for you to be proud. And even if you were the best scholar in Tibet," he added, "you could never achieve Enlightenment only by knowing *about* the Path." You must now begin to try to have experiences of the Path."

The date for the final examination was set for the autumn of that year, and to prepare for it I went to work intensively with all my major teachers—including Ling Rinpoche, who had now become the Dalai Lama's senior tutor. I memorized some sixty pages, concentrating particularly on Kunga Thondub's commentary on the *Guhyasamaja Tantra*. My teacher Konchog, who was still the abbot of Rato, came one day to Lhasa to test my knowledge of this text and assure himself that I had learned it thoroughly; after all my years of study with him, that was the last test he ever gave me.

The final event itself took place in December, in our assembly hall, and was an ordeal of seven days. The first day I had to provide a gift ceremony which means giving butter tea to monks as well as money and other offerings. The monks chanted, starting this ceremony, then I had to recite from memory page after page of my Tantric texts, continuing even while tea and rice porridge were twice served to all the monks. I was allowed only one brief pause, and could neither eat nor drink, such being the rigorous rule. And had I forgotten or confused a single line, I should have been automatically expelled.

At the beginning I frequently cleared my throat, for my voice is poor and I had to speak out loudly. My friends told me later that that had made them apprehensive, thinking I might be unsure. But I came through all right, completing some sixty pages, and when the long recitation ended, the Lama Unze questioned me. We then retired to the courtyard where two geshes tested me further; and that evening and for the next six days all the rest of the geshes in the college took their turns. Some days there would be three testing sessions, morning, noon, and evening; others, only one. Those in the evening were the longest, going on for about four hours. Occasionally I had difficulties, but most of the time, little trouble. When all was finished and my examination passed, Konchog, who chanced to be in Lhasa at the time, came to the college to congratulate me. It touched me deeply to see him. He was happy, he said, to have been the teacher of a better scholar than himself—which was a compliment more generous than truthful: for compared to his knowledge, mine was like a firefly's light to the sun. With all my heart I thanked him for his unstinting care as my teacher, my guide, and my friend of the past eleven years.

14.

Extracurricular Studies

Having completed my last examination, I asked permission to absent myself from the regular ceremonies for a year, to attend lectures outside the college and devote myself to uninterrupted study. Such a leave was called The Year Permission and could be granted to senior monks thought to have a good reason for requesting it. I was but twenty-five at the time and, having been only two years in the Gyudto, not yet a senior monk. However, lharampa geshes of any age who had passed their finals in Tantric studies were regarded officially as senior monks and might be allowed to absent themselves. During such a year one could forfeit as much as half the support normally received; for on great feast days the contributions both in goods and in money from the college and from donors were unusually generous. Moreover, what the college supplied its monks in attendance was barely sufficient for their basic needs, and for many such a forfeiture would be a real deprivation. However, I had my own labrang in the Kham and could depend on support from there.

One day I learned that one of the tsenshabs, or assistants of the Dalai Lama in his studies, was about to deliver a month of lectures at Zede, the seat of the late regent, Rating, who had died the previous year in prison. I had heard a great deal about the qualifications of this lama, Trijang Rinpoche by name. He was, in fact, one of the best-known and most popular lecturers on Buddhism in the country. The talks were to be on lamrim, the "Account of the Stages of the Path," composed by the Second Panchen Rinpoche; and at the end of the week I proceeded to Zede for my first visit to that famous monastery. Some three thousand people had already arrived, mostly monks from the nearby monasteries, and I joined them with high expectations. I had studied many lamrim when working with Pabongkha

Rinpoche, who (as I now learned) had been Trijang Rinpoche's principal teacher. But at that time I had been hardly nineteen, having just begun my studies of Nagarjuna's *Madhyamika*, and what I had understood of these difficult works had been little more than ten percent of the chapters.

Trijang Rinpoche, when lecturing, used a method of instruction known as *nyam tee*, "teaching from experience," which I had not encountered before, and which opened to me a fresh approach to the understanding of texts. Sitting high on his teaching throne before his auditors, the Rinpoche held a book in hand to which, however, he seldom referred. He lectured, rather, from his own experience of the Stages of the Way, advising us to meditate at the end of each day of listening not only on the teachings heard, but also on our own thoughts concerning them. A teacher using this method of instruction interprets and explains, instead of reading his text word for word, and the student then must meditate, not on the text exactly, but on what he has heard of the master's own experience. I found, however, that at the end of each long day of concentrated listening it was all but impossible for me to meditate. The five hours of lecturing would end each day at six, and to try then to recall everything the Rinpoche had said was not only difficult, but fatiguing. I frequently fell asleep before the end of my meditation, not to wake until the next day. Nevertheless, I did learn from these lectures something of the method of nyam tee.

My next ritual study was of the Fire Sacrifice, to which I was introduced when I heard that a geshe with a great reputation for saintliness, Geshe Samdub Rinpoche, was about to lecture on the subject in the home of a distinguished Lhasa aristocrat. In the elegant home in which the sessions were to be held I found a company of ten, mostly well-known scholars. The first thing one noticed about the white-haired Rinpoche, already seated before them, was his extraordinary eyebrows—extremely long and strangely turned upward. Some believed they had turned upward that way only after his practice of *Nyenchen*—an extensive recitation sometimes lasting a few years—because of the great spiritual powers he then achieved.

When I entered the room and began to make my formal prostrations, he said, "No, no! Don't do that! It's not necessary!" So I stopped and, without further ado, sat down. Whereupon he rebuked me sharply, saying, "Look at Khyongla! A well-known scholar-geshe! Yet he doesn't know how to attend a lecture, how to approach a guru, or how to listen to what he is told." I rose, completed my three prostrations, again sat down, and the lecture began.

Samdub Rinpoche had a very strong Amdo accent and spoke so softly that I at first found him difficult to follow. Presently, however, I became absorbed in his lecture which dealt with the symbolism of the four forms of the Fire Sacrifices.

While attending these lectures I became acquainted with a scholar from the great Tashe Khyil Monastery in Amdo, Junger Rinpoche by name, whose circle of friends was to play, thereafter, an important role in my life. He one day invited me to his rooms, which were in a building belonging to the Dalai Lama's court chamberlain, Thubten Woden of the Phala family. The mansion had been partly burned down during the Chinese invasion of 1910, but rebuilt on a much larger scale, three stories high, with an enormous courtyard in the center. I happened to be looking for an apartment at the time, and when I spoke of the beauty of the building, the Rinpoche remarked that there was a vacancy. Hearing of my interest, he introduced me to Thubten Woden's steward and before the week was out, I was installed in a pleasant efficiency apartment in the compound of one of the finest family residences in Lhasa—the residence, moreover, of one of the most pious and generous-hearted, as well as distinguished, families of Tibet.

Thubten Woden's younger brother, commander of the Dalai Lama's bodyguard, was a member of the old Nyingmapa sect, known commonly as the Red Hats, while Thubten Woden himself was of the Yellow Hats, the Gelugpa. Yet there was perfect harmony between them, and both Nyingmapa and Gelugpa lamas, monks, and court officials were frequent visitors in the Phala home. I soon became acquainted with Thubten Woden himself, the elder Phala, and a friendship developed that has lasted to this day.

Gradually I become a close friend, also, of my neighbor, Junger Rinpoche, for we had many interests in common, lived in adjoining apartments, and frequently exchanged visits. He had begun the study of poetry in Amdo, when he was abbot of Tashe Khyil; and when he told me, one day, that he wished now to resume the study and would like it if I joined him, I recalled that before coming to Lhasa, I had been advised by Tsering Choephel, my dear childhood teacher in the Kham, that when I had received my degrees in philosophy and metaphysics, I should take up the study of poetry and Sanskrit. So we agreed to do the work together, and asked the senior tutor of the Dalai Lama, Ling Rinpoche, to teach us these subjects.

We completed our study of poetry but not Sanskrit for not only were Ling Rinpoche's duties becoming ever more demanding, but I, shortly after we had started on this study, left Tibet for a visit to Bhutan.

A good friend of mine, a learned incarnate lama from Rato, had been living for some three years in Bhutan as teacher of Ang-Gyan, the aged sister of the late King Urgyen Wangchuk. Knowing that I had long hoped to make a pilgrimage to India, he wrote to me in the summer of 1952, suggesting that if I left soon and went by way of Bhutan, he would ask Ang-Gyan to send an interpreter along with me. Another advantage of that route, he pointed out, would be that I could visit on the way Milarepa's famous tower, called Se Khar Guthog, which that great saint built not far from the Bhutanese border. The suggestion struck me as a great idea, and I immediately wrote to tell him so. A few months later he returned to Lhasa, and a few months after that there came a formal invitation from Ang-Gyan, who even sent along mules for my journey.

The elder brother of Ang-Gyan, the late King Urgyen Wangchuk, had risen suddenly to undisputed power in the country when his spiritual ruling superior, known as the incarnate Shabdung Rinpoche, was assassinated in 1885. So my first experience beyond the borders of my native land was as a guest in the household of a royal family.

I was still a member, of course, of Gyudto, and, since I was a lharampa geshe of scholarly rank, had just been automatically named as a candidate for the position of Lama Unze of my college. I had, therefore, to ask permission of the government to leave Tibet. I turned for a letter of consent to one of the Dalai Lama's tsenshabs, which I received and then submitted to the Gyud leaders.

Ang-Gyan had sent two of her servants and three business agents commissioned to sell rice and paper in Lhasa and then to accompany me to Bhutan. As a Gyudpa monk, not permitted to ride, I had to walk out of the city while the rest of the party rode. Once outside, however, I was free to mount the gray mule that had been sent for me, and to ride the rest of the way. We were counting on seventeen days to reach the border of Bhutan, and, after twelve days of hard riding over high passes, we came to the village of Do Wo Lung, where Milarepa's Tower stands. Its name, Se Khar Guthog, means the "Tower of Nine Stories, Built for the Son."

Milarepa, who was a powerful youth, had been ordered by his teacher Marpa to build with his own hands a tower of stone as a gift for Marpa's son. The grueling, utterly frustrating task had been assigned to him as a penance, to wipe out through hardship the bad karma he had acquired through practicing magic. The tower is now nearly a thousand years old, and I had long wanted to see it, since it is the most celebrated relic of our most illustrious saint. I knew well the biography composed by Rechung, his disciple, and had long been familiar with the stories of his life, illustrated in thangkas, and recounted in the folk tradition.

Milarepa's father had died when he was an infant, and relatives had appropriated the inheritance, leaving the widow and child destitute. In revenge, Milarepa's mother sent him to a sorcerer to study the black arts. When he had become proficient in these, he had, on a festal occasion brought the roof down by magic upon the heads of most of his guilty relatives. Later, repenting that sin, he set forth to find a religious guru, discovered Marpa, and under his direction spent years wiping out his karma, meditating in caves, and suffering deprivations, until Enlightenment was achieved. Disciples then came flocking to him from all sides. He was a member of the Kagyudpa sect, which was founded by his teacher about the year 1050; but all of Tibet, all the people of Tibet—no matter what sect— have revered him as one who in a single lifetime attained Enlightenment. His story is one to encourage us all to believe that no matter how black our sins may be, salvation is possible here and now, if we repent and enter the Path.

I wanted to visit, besides the tower, a number of other holy sites where the saint had studied and served his harsh master Marpa, so we remained in Do Wo Lung for two days. When I had satisfied myself at last, I rejoined my friends, who had tarried in the village, and, setting out again, we rode through mountains for two days, climbing even higher, until we finally crossed a snowcapped ridge, the south side of which belonged to Bhutan.

The country was now very heavily forested, and the road no more than a rut threading up and down jagged peaks and ridges. We passed people bearing on their backs loads of logs held by a broad headband, a method of carrying I had never seen before. We also passed traders riding yaks, which were thought to be safer than mules where the snows were heavy in rocky ravines. Shortly before nightfall, we entered a village where most of the inhabitants were retainers of Ang-Gyan's estate, and we were received with a warm and very friendly welcome.

The next day, having passed the night in a substantial peasant's house, we set out early and in short time arrived at a place called Wangdu Choeling, which was the principal residence of the younger of the two queens of Bhutan. For the present king, the son of the great Urgyen Wangchuk, had two consorts, between whose separate palaces he and his court alternated in residence. As it chanced, at the time of my arrival, the royal family was in the palace of the elder of the two queens, some two days' journey away, but Ang-Gyan was present to receive us, and as we approached the large wooden palace we saw one of her retainers waiting. He had brought rice, sausages, and buttered tea, which the cook at her hermitage had prepared.

Having thus refreshed ourselves, we lingered only to inspect the large wooden palace briefly from outside, and remounting, passed across a little wooden bridge that brought us to Ang-Gyan's nearby hermitage. The late king, her brother, had given her in his lifetime large properties and many peasants, so that, when young, she had been a rich heiress. The palace we had just seen had at that time belonged to her, but when her brother died and his son assumed the throne, much of her property went to the second, younger queen, and so returned to the crown. Moreover, her own son, who did not enjoy his subordinate role in the little court, went off to Lhasa and was ordained a monk by the Thirteenth Dalai Lama. He died shortly thereafter, and his mother, retiring, built this little place in which to live out her old age.

Surrounded by fields of chili peppers, this was a retreat of two wooden houses on a hill, well hidden behind a high wall of bamboo. We rode into the compound and, dismounting, I was directed by a servant to the upper house. Before the house there were standing, to receive me, a white-haired lady beside an elderly man, both holding scarves. No one introduced us, but I recognized the lady as Ang-Gyan; and when we had exchanged our scarves, she brought me upstairs to her guest room. This was a fully furnished chapel, containing a single elevated couch, to which she motioned me. I hesitated, but she insisted; and when I had sat down, she sank to the floor beside me.

I was somewhat taken aback, for I had never liked sitting on cushions when there was anyone on the floor—and certainly no member of a high-ranking family in Lhasa would ever have thought of sitting on the floor that way. But there we were. Ang-Gyan told me of her pleasure at my arrival and inquired about our trip. She asked also about her teacher, my friend, who had now, I replied, left Lhasa for a visit to the Kham. Then she told me that she had frequently visited Lhasa, and had even had the privilege of receiving the "Long Life" initiation from the Thirteenth Dalai Lama. When I asked her age, she declared she was eighty-three.

It was not thought impolite in Tibet to ask a lady her age. In fact, when meeting strangers we often ask their age. That was a way of opening conversations, like mentioning the weather. We had, furthermore, great respect for old age, and there were some who liked to boast about how old they were. Ang-Gyan, in spite of her years, and aside from the fact that when sitting down or getting up she required some assistance, was still very active, with a good memory and a lively intelligent mind. After half an hour's conversation, she got up, and on the arm of one of the servants, returned to her own apartment in the neighboring house.

Soon servants appeared with the main meal of steamed rice and hot plates of various sorts of pork, but no eating utensils. I told their leader that since I was unacquainted with the Bhutanese way of eating, I should be grateful if he would start first. He ate with his fingers—so I did too. When the meal was over, he told me that if there was anything I required, I should not hesitate to let him know.

Early my first morning, I was served a rice broth with hot chutney, and a few hours later, buttered tea; and while I was enjoying the drink, the servant explained that although the tea of Bhutan was the same as that served in Lhasa, the manner of preparation was very different. The Bhutanese did not have our sort of hollowed-out wooden tea-maker, but churned their drink by inserting a fan into the bowl, holding its handle between the palms, and then rubbing their hands together to rotate it. Ang-Gyan came in when I had finished my tea and presented me with a gold-lined ivory bowl set on a base of solid gold. I was amazed. The beautiful gift contained a handful of rice, in keeping with the Tibetan custom of not presenting an empty vessel to a lama, for Milarepa, it is said, once presented an empty bronze bowl to Marpa, who struck it, and when it gave forth a ringing sound, predicted that although his pupil would acquire great knowledge, he would suffer all his life from poverty. The prophecy came true, and Tibetans ever since have believed that to give an empty vessel to a lama brings bad luck to the giver. On returning to Rato, I gave this elegant bowl to Konchog, as the first and finest gift I had received in Bhutan.

Ang-Gyan's style of conversation was unusual and amusing. Her mind hopped from one topic to another rapidly, and she would break off at times to recite mantras on her rosary. So that she might, at one moment, be repeating the Mani; the next, rebuking an erring servant; and with the next breath commenting on some theme of the conversation, all without a pause. The old man whom I had seen with her at the time of my arrival had gone home a few days later, and his place beside her had been taken by another, who had been to Lhasa and thought of himself as a mathematician.

Life at the hermitage was odd in many ways. Thousands of pigeons, for example, had their nests in a little house that Ang-Gyan had had built for them nearby, and every day they would come flying to her room where she would feed them corn. She also kept some twenty-five or thirty Lhasa Apso dogs, each of which had a name and would come when called. There was a woman whose sole duty it was to attend to these little pets. Ang-Gyan once told me that she felt great sympathy for animals, but not so much for her servants, who were always taking advantage of her age. She was, in any case, wonderfully hospitable to her numerous visitors, most of whom were monks and nuns, Tibetan as well as Bhutanese. There were usually at least two or three of them at the hermitage, often more.

I was becoming impatient to get on with my intended pilgrimage to India, but to my severe disappointment, Ang-Gyan became suddenly ill a few weeks after my arrival, and I postponed my departure to pray for her and to hold ceremonies on her behalf. I had arrived in Bhutan in November, and I was still there in February when my hostess asked me to give a general lecture on Buddhism to an audience of about two hundred Bhutanese and Tibetans from the neighborhood.

I was, of course, delighted to comply; but the occasion turned into something more elaborate than I had planned. Ang-Gyan, all her friends, and even her servants, insisted that I should wear for the occasion the new robes that I had brought with me from Tibet, and since I did not have a yellow hat they made me one. I protested, but they were unrelenting; and although I knew that it was wrong to show off in such a manner, I finally gave in. Whereupon, as though that were not enough, when I stepped out to walk to the courtyard where the lecture was to be held, two musicians began playing flutes. I was so embarrassed that although it was actually only a short way, it seemed to me miles long. When I gave my second lecture I saw to it that nothing of this kind occurred, making it very clear to all that I did not want a repetition of that experience.

Shortly after the New Year, the king's younger queen, Pema Dechen, arrived in Wangdu Choeling with her court. One day she visited the hermitage to pay her respects to Ang-Gyan. From my window I could watch her as she came riding on a mule, with all her servants on foot. Some hours later a servant came to my room to announce her desire to meet me, and I went over at once to Ang-Gyan's house. The young queen was beautiful and charming, and after many polite exchanges of scarves and formal greetings, I was invited to sit down and tell of my journey from Lhasa and impressions of Bhutan. A few days later her children came for a visit with their great-aunt—two little daughters and a son—and again I was invited over. They were very young and seemed extraordinarily cheerful, laughing and gaily chatting with the old lady. I thought them delightful, but later learned that the reason for all the amusement had been my own partially bald head.

Then one fine day the king arrived for a stay of several months, and I was advised to pay my respects as soon as possible. Ang-Gyan and the young queen arranged for the audience, and when the day arrived, I was formally escorted to the large wooden palace and into a waiting room full of servants sitting cross-legged on the floor, most of them barefoot and all equipped with very long swords. One got up when I entered and began giving me instructions in the etiquette to be observed when meeting a Bhutanese king. Another made a list of all the gifts that I was bearing, which included a box of Tibetan tea, four Tibetan woolen blankets, and a scarf. The attendant who was to conduct me to the king went a little ahead, and before introducing me, looked in to make sure that His Majesty would have his eyes directed toward us when I entered. He was found reading an Indian newspaper, and I was therefore not allowed to appear until the servant had caught his eye. This, I learned, was an act of great respect for the king, so that he should not be surprised by suddenly finding a visitor in his room. He was comfortably seated on a great cushion, a round-faced, heavy-set, serious-looking man of average height, about fifty years old, and after we had exchanged our scarves and greetings, he asked me to sit down before him on a square mat by a small table. He was wearing a short *chuba*, or lay-person's robe, over a shirt, and a colorful Bhutanese cloth covered his knees. I noticed that he had a sword stuck in his belt with an ivory handle that jutted prominently from his side, and, as I looked around, I saw that many guns hung on the walls.

The king had been told that I was originally from the Kham and so spoke to me in the Khampa dialect, inquiring about my stay in Lhasa and religious studies there. From time to time people came in to pay their respects, prostrating themselves, offering scarves, and immediately departing. A servant approached to serve tea from a silver kettle, and every time he poured for the king, music was played on a flute. His Majesty's cup was of wood, beautifully lined with gold, smaller than the bowls we had in Tibet. On the low table before me a cup of china was placed, and, following Bhutanese etiquette, I held the cup in my hands, waiting for the king to drink first. But when he saw what I was doing, he told me to put the cup down and drink at my ease.

The king had heard that I was planning to make a pilgrimage to India, and offered to furnish interpreters for the trip. I had decided, however, to return to Tibet, my hostess's illness having so delayed me. The hot season would soon be beginning, and I did not want to be in India at that time. Moreover, I was becoming impatient to get back to my neglected studies. I thanked the king, and he then suddenly asked whether I liked swords, to which I replied that I was not interested in weapons. (One of Ang-Gyan's servants said to me later that I had been greatly mistaken to tell the king I was not interested in swords. Had I told him that I was, he would have presented me with a very nice one indeed.) Again the servant approached and poured for each a second cup, but since the king did not touch his, I did not drink mine. I rose, and as I took my leave, he told me graciously that I should not hesitate to ask him for any help or advice I might require while in Bhutan.

During the greater part of the fourth month of our Tibetan calendar (May), Ang-Gyan had about twenty monks at the hermitage for a festive reading of the Kanjur. They recited, day by day, in unison, the whole text of 108 books, and when they had concluded, I joined them for a two-day fast. We had many serious discussions of Buddhist doctrine during the period of their stay, for these were not Gelugpa, but Nyingmapa and Kagyudpa monks, both of which sects are strong in Bhutan, where Kagyudpa is the national religion. There were also many prominent Bhutanese laymen who came to attend the festival and discuss religion with the monks. Some of these asked me, too, for instruction and interpretations. We also talked of other matters, and I found that everybody had great respect for their king and his two queens—or, at least, everybody who had talked to me. But after all, since I was a guest of the royal family, it would hardly have been likely that anyone unhappy with his lot would have chosen me as one in whom to confide.

When the reading of the Kanjur had ended, therefore, and the whole company had departed, preparations began to be made for my return journey to Tibet. First, I should have to pay a farewell visit to the king in his other palace, since he had meanwhile returned to the elder queen, and for this Ang-Gyan made arrangements. A company of her servants escorted me on the two-day ride, and we arrived at the palace late the second afternoon. I was taken to a richly furnished guest room for the night. In the morning I was brought, first, to see the elder queen, who showed me all the beautiful images she had had made. I was sincerely impressed. Then I was conducted to the king, and when I bade him farewell, he presented me with gifts of rice, money, and Bhutanese cloth, suggesting very kindly that he would look forward to seeing me again when he visited Lhasa.

And so, with all that accomplished, I returned by the same mountainous way to Ang-Gyan's hermitage and a few days later left for Tibet. As we rode away and I turned for a last glance, I noticed that a servant of Ang-Gyan was on the roof waving a white scarf.

My trip to Bhutan was, however, to be only the first of several excursions to explore the world outside my native country. While I was in Bhutan the king had very kindly offered to provide me with an escort to India and to arrange my visits to the holy places, most of which were not far from Bhutan. I had of course been greatly tempted. Ever since childhood I had dreamed of visiting those sites where the Lord Buddha had lived and taught in his earthly career. However, I had to keep my promise to return for the Gyudto summer session at Yerpa, and, having done so, I was now as far from my goal as ever. While a student at Rato, I had been unable to take the trip since our teachers there considered study to be more important than pilgrimages, and student monks were required first to pass their geshe examinations. I had passed mine, but then had gone directly into Gyudto, to be confronted there with a whole new set of studies and limitations. More than a year passed before I gained my Tantra degree; another year, before my return from Bhutan. Now that I was back, what I wanted most in the world to do was to prepare myself properly and thoroughly for the experience so long delayed.

I commenced with a complete review of the teachings of the Lord Buddha, which took me another two years; for although the thirteen volumes of the Vinaya are relatively easy to follow with understanding, Tantric texts and certain sections of the *Prajnaparamita* sutras are subtle and extremely difficult. Certain parts seemed to me clear; others, however, I failed to grasp. Resorting to prayer, I asked for greater clarity of mind so that in time I should not only grasp their sense, but also learn to apply their wisdom in my life.

Finally, I felt ready for my pilgrimage and began the cold trip by mule across the mountains to India. We arrived after two weeks' travel at the first Indian outpost. It was there that I saw my first telephone, watching an Indian officer talk into a little black mouthpiece, holding another black object to his ear. But this was no more than the first stage of my entry into a universe of wonders and surprise. From Kalimpong the road descends to the Indian plain, which I was not to view from the back of a mule. Together with my young attendant, I stepped into an automobile and was driven at breakneck speed downhill to Siliguri, where the airport is located. For breakfast we had had fresh oranges and strong buttered tea, and on that serpentine road I became carsick. In fact I was so dizzy that I saw nothing of the scenery at all as we passed along at what seemed to me an incredible pace. The car took us directly to the airport, where a friend had reserved seats for us on the Calcutta plane, and when I saw what we now were to step into I said to my companion, "If anything happens, how do we get out?" He had not been sick and, in fact, had been having a very good time. He answered indifferently, "Oh, one can have an accident anywhere, in a car, a train, or just walking along a road."

I was still suffering from dizziness, and when we had climbed aboard asked my young friend to take the window seat. Closing my eyes, I tried to relax as we left the ground. Curiously, the plane was much less disturbing to me than the automobile had been, but I was still pretty sick, and, after a while, became a little annoyed with my buoyant companion, who clearly enjoyed the flight and offered me no sympathy at all.

In two hours we landed in Calcutta, and at the airport to greet me was a Nepalese merchant whom I had known in Lhasa, where he had once had a shop in the Barkor, selling Nepalese and Indian wares. He had invited me to his home; I again found myself in a car. As we moved through crowded, noisy streets, I was amazed by the number of people and of cars and buses, and thought Calcutta surely was a great metropolis. (Years later, however, after living in New York, I returned and found that in the interval Calcutta had become much smaller.) But it was sticky-hot, and before we finally drew up in front of the building in which my host had his apartment, I had again become miserably carsick. When they got me inside, my only thought was to lie down.

Next day the family took me on a sightseeing tour. At one place they stopped the car and we all got out to visit some monument; I felt suddenly very weak and could hardly stand. I was still wearing my

Tibetan robes, and a crowd of curious young Indian boys, surrounding me, started chattering in a language I had never heard before. In utter confusion I felt myself fainting. I do not remember how my friends ever got me back to their place and into bed, but they found that I had a very high fever. For several days I was confined to the house, and my very kind hostess, the merchant's wife, served me only soft foods and juices. The moment I started feeling better, I began asking for Coca-Cola and ice cream, but no one would let me have either. It took me a week to get back on my feet; and as soon as I was thought fit for the trip, my host and hostess drove me over the busy Howrah Bridge, across the river Hooghly, to board an Indian train for the ten-hour journey to Bodh Gaya.

This was my first experience of a train, and I found it, to my pleasant surprise, more comfortable than a car. I watched with lively interest as we glided over the tawny plain of endless India, with its innumerable small villages, and saw at stations the masses of people waiting, then excitedly crowding onto the cars. When we got out at Gaya, we hired a rickshaw to take us to the sacred site of the bodhi tree, some seven miles further on, where, as soon as we arrived, a crowd of ragged children swarmed around us begging. A couple of Tibetans, whom we had met on the train and who had joined us, stopped me when I started handing out coins. The ragamuffins, they said, were calling us lice-eaters. Yet one could feel only the greatest pity for them, with their scrawny little bodies barely covered by a few soiled rags.

I and my companion had been invited to stay in a Tibetan monastery in Bodh Gaya, and, with that as my home base, I went each day to visit and pray at the most sacred spots in India—the temple of Bodh Gaya, the bodhi tree where the Buddha obtained Enlightenment, and Nalanda, once the most renowned university of Mahayana Buddhism. From there I took the train to Benares and then to Kushiagara, where the Lord Buddha departed from this world. Then, heading north, I made a final stop at Lumbini, just over the border in Nepal, where the Lord Buddha was born. I and my companions then proceeded to Kalimpong, and following the same rugged road by which we had come to India, returned to Lhasa with a greatly enhanced appreciation of the Doctrine and tradition by which we lived.

About a year after my return from India, I embarked on another expedition, this time to Nepal, to found a Gelugpa monastery. Our khamtsen had long been friendly with a Nepalese merchant whose shop was in the Barkor, and I had also become well acquainted with three Nepalese monks in Lhasa. When a Nepalese monk named Suba, who had formerly been an officer in the Nepalese army, gained support of donors in Katmandu to help found a monastery there, at Konchog's urging I agreed to go to help. I had been hoping to conclude my studies and return to the Kham to visit my labrang and my home, but since Konchog insisted that this mission was of importance for our religion, as well as for Rato, I had no choice but to accept.

But my task was not to be an easy one. Some of the Nepalese who wished to study with me were of the Nyingmapa sect, and some were of the Gelugpa, and they could not agree about the rules under which the monastery was to be run. I tried to explain to them that it was not important to decide right away what sect the monastery was to be, saying, "First you must build the building and after that, you can decide. Every sect holds that its own way is the best. You must yourselves study the differences and *then* make up your minds." I talked at some length to them, outlining the differences between the two sects, and emphasizing that sound instruction and thorough understanding must precede any enlightenment. But since I spoke no Nepalese and had to communicate through an interpreter, I found it extremely difficult to make my points in these talks and so came to realize how important for the work I had undertaken knowledge of the Nepalese tongue would be. I tried to learn a few phrases, but when no one understood my pronunciation, I gave up and continued to rely on an interpreter. Suba encouraged me to learn both English and Nepalese, and today I know that one of the greatest mistakes of my life was not to have studied English at that time.

The original plan had been for me to stay until the monastery was built and to act as its abbot, but as the months wore on and the land for the monastery had not been purchased, it became clear that it would be two or three years before the building would be completed. I wished to return to Lhasa before winter to assume my duties as prior at Gyudto, and I had begun to feel a bit homesick, longing to be back with my teacher and friends. I had a strange feeling that if I did not continue with my studies now, a time might not be far away when there would be no studies at all. I had heard that the Communist Chinese, who were already well into our country, were against our Buddhist religion and doing everything they could to uproot it.

We finally agreed on a date for the formal inauguration of our monastery, the fourth day of the sixth Tibetan month, the anniversary of the Lord Buddha's "First Sermons" in the Deer Park of Benares, and soon after that, I returned home to Rato.

15.

My Term as Prior at Gyudto

When I arrived at Rato, I hurried first to see Konchog, who greeted me with great affection. He had been dreaming of me lately, he said, and so had been expecting to hear from me soon. On seeing me off, he had asked me to buy a pocket watch for him in Nepal, and when I now presented him with one he was greatly pleased, not only that I had found him a fine gold timepiece, but more especially that I had remembered his wish. I was extremely happy to be back with him. He asked for a full account of my experiences, and when I had finished the long story, he sat in thought for a while, then said: "In early times the Nepalese came bringing Buddhism to us; now you have gone to Nepal and brought Buddhism to them." He admonished me, however, for not having taken the time when I had had the opportunity to learn English. "The Chinese," Konchog said very gravely, "are taking over our country. We do not know what the future holds. We may have to leave our homeland and flee to some foreign land where no one will ever have heard a word of Tibetan. English, I have been told, is the most useful international tongue. Had you begun its study in Nepal you could have continued with it here. For it well may be that you will one day have to use English in some country where you will be of no use without it. Do you remember the case of the Indian saint Maitripa? He was even more famous in India than Atisha, but when he came to Tibet and his interpreter died, he was left helpless in a strange land, unable to speak a word. Since not one of the simple people he met recognized him as the great scholar he was, he was forced for a while to hire himself out as a shepherd. I hope," said Konchog with a wry smile, "that you will never have to be a shepherd."

I did not take my teacher's warning very seriously at the time. Many of our texts had prophesied that the union of Tantric and Sutric Buddhism, as we knew it in Tibet, would endure for another four hundred years; and since I thought the union could exist no place else in the world, I was confident that the rest of my life would be spent in my native land. For a short while after my teacher's admonition, I considered the possibility of starting the study of English. But it would have been hard to find a teacher, and the Chinese, furthermore, would surely not have been happy to hear of a Tibetan monk learning English. So I dropped the whole idea, partly out of laziness, but mainly because I was confident of the future of the Lord Buddha's Doctrine in Tibet. Moreover—as it seemed to me—even if bad times were ahead for us, my choice would surely be to remain with the Dalai Lama and my teachers, sharing their hardships and not taking flight to start a new life alone in some foreign land. I have frequently had reason, since that time, to recall my wise and good friend Konchog's words. They echoed in my mind with particular force when I was stamping prices on merchandise in a big New York department store—which might well be said to be about the Western equivalent to being a shepherd in Tibet.

My Nepalese friends in Katmandu had presented me with a gift of money when I left, which I divided now in two parts. The first I gave to Rato in a gift ceremony for my khamtsen and college; and when that was done I moved to Lhasa, where I lived again in the Phala mansion. My long journey had been exhausting, and since very few of my friends knew, as yet, that I returned, I had a chance for a few days' rest.

Then, on the eighth day of our eleventh month (December) of 1953, I was summoned to my duties at Gyudto as prior for the winter session. Proceeding immediately to the Ramoche, I presented myself to both the abbot and the Lama Unze. My interview with the first was surprisingly brief. After graciously greeting me, the new abbot merely said that I was to maintain the strictest discipline and, with a nod, let me know the visit was over. With the Lama Unze I had a pleasant chat over buttered tea, during which he gave me even fewer instructions than the abbot. With those formalities attended to, I returned at peace to my rooms in Phala's house, for I was to be exempted from ceremonies until my formal inauguration. While walking from the temple home, I was spotted by an approaching group of Gyudto monks, who, the moment they saw me, turned and fled, though I was not yet officially their prior. My new career had already unofficially begun, and I was now to experience the comedy of our lives from the other side.

In most Tibetan monasteries every college has its prior. Thus in Drepung, where there were four colleges, there were four priors. When the colleges met or functioned together in what was called a Tsogchen, however, these priors had no power. There were two other priors known as *Shelongo*, appointed by the government, who supervised the gathering as a whole; and they ranked higher than the individual priors who had been selected by their own abbots and were not, as a rule, theological students. Neither were they often geshes. In the "big three" monasteries they could be identified by their attire, the upper part of their robe being a bright red with broad, heavily-padded shoulders. They carried a heavy staff at assemblies and its thudding on the stone floor could be heard as they passed up and down the aisles. The Shelongo carried heavier, very much more elaborate staffs, often of beautiful craftsmanship, encased in iron sheaths ornamented with intricate designs.

In our two Tantric colleges, on the other hand, the priors wore regular monk's dress, and at Gyudto a new prior was appointed every four months, one of whom during the year had to be a geshe lharampa. Non-geshes appointed to the office had to have been members almost twenty years, but the geshe was automatically appointed on the basis of his rank gained at the time of his examination. The highest Gyudpa officials were, of course, the abbots and lama unzes. One would serve first as lama unze, and then, automatically, as abbot, the term of each of these offices being three years.

My own inauguration took place in the Ramoche, the morning of the thirteenth day of our eleventh Tibetan month, 1953, and my official duties began immediately.

One of my main duties as prior was enforcing the rules of the monastery and administering punishment. Holding a butter lamp to help me see in the darkness of the assembly hall, I would walk up and down the aisles during ceremonies to see if there were anyone who was not chanting or had fallen back to sleep. Spotting a sleeper, I would scuff my shoes on the stone floor to signal his neighbors to wake him; but if I found the same fellow again asleep, I would stand before him with the lamp held close to his face until he awoke. Should I catch him so every morning, I had the right to use my little whip on him; but since I did not enjoy that sort of thing, I worked out a psychological method that I found served well enough. Assuming a severe expression, I would stand in front of the culprit, brandishing the whip, staring fiercely into his eyes, as if I were having a hard time controlling myself. Because of these dramatics I gained the reputation of a passionate defender of the regulations. Alone in my room, I would have to laugh, recalling on this or that occasion, how well the ruse had worked.

My friends had warned me that if I were not strict from the very start I would lose everybody's respect and never regain control. I took this to heart, and so, was prepared when the first real test came on my second and third nights. These happened to be special nights, with all members of the college, including its senior monks, required to sleep in the assembly hall. Since about nine hundred were present, the floor was so overcrowded that some were forced into the corridor which encircled the interior and ran all the way to the altar, where it was separated only by a silk curtain from the shrine. At night, no one was to make a sound. If a monk who found that he could not sleep sat up to meditate or recite prayers, he had to do this in perfect silence. Yet, on the first of these two nights, half an hour after everyone had gone to sleep and I was just about drifting off, I heard voices and even laughter coming from behind the silk curtain. I got up, strode to the altar, pulled the curtain aside, and discovered a little company of young monks chatting, laughing, and having a fine time. I gave them a severe scolding, yet the next night the performance was repeated, even noisier than before, and this time I realized I would have to make my authority stand. I strode down the aisle into the chapel, and, pulling the curtain aside, entered the ambulatory, whip in hand. With what I hoped were blazing eyes, I looked around and, noticing a big pile of cushions stacked against the curved wall, walked over to these and began beating the stack with my little whip, counting loudly with slow deliberation more than one hundred resounding strokes. Since monks were not allowed to look when a prior was administering punishment, all there had covered their heads with their robes, and in the dark assumed that I was punishing one of them. Some must surely have peeked and seen what I was doing, but all the rest in the assembly hall through which the noise of the beating reverberated could only have supposed that I was inflicting extraordinary punishment on one of their number. When done, I walked conspicuously and sternly back to my throne. For days later, I heard with great satisfaction whispered criticisms of my conduct. "We always thought of Khyongla as courteous, compassionate, and pious," said some; "instead he has turned out to be a merciless, short-tempered brute." And thereafter for the whole period of my "servitude," the rules of the Vinaya were marvelously maintained by this illusory image of myself, their defender, as a tyrant.

During my term as prior only one extremely unfortunate, and to me very painful, incident occurred for which I had to exercise my authority to its fullest. When walking back to my apartment one evening, I saw two of our monks quarreling in the street. They had had a fist fight and I saw blood on one of their faces. In the Gyudpa colleges it was a rule that if any monk attacked another physically, or if two or more fought and blood was drawn, the penalty would be immediate expulsion. One of them in this quarrel was a good friend of mine, and it was extremely unfortunate that I happened to see this, for I had now to return directly and report the matter to our leaders— a clear case of misconduct, and our decision was for expulsion. The caretaker was sent to talk with the two to learn what had brought the quarrel about. He found that there had been an auction in the marketplace, where the monks had bid against each other on a rug. Both finally claimed ownership, and with that the quarrel began. The monks would never again be permitted to become Gyudto members; their sponsors would be required to make prostrations publicly in the assembly hall, at all ceremonies, for three days; and the prior of the khamtsen to which they belonged would be required to make prostrations for one day. Needless to say, the monk who had been my friend was no longer my friend. He always avoided me after that; and I was sorry, very sorry, but my duty had been perfectly clear.

When the Monlam season arrived that year, my duties as prior permitted me to see it from yet a third point of view. There was for me little joy in it, only the hardest season of work of my whole life. As prior, I not only had to rouse the monks as usual in the mornings and be the last to go to sleep in the crowded assembly hall at night, so that my working hours were from 3 A.M. to 10 P.M., without holidays; but I also had to act as a proctor for the annual examinations of lharampa geshes in the Jokhang. All two hundred of our Gyudto geshes were required to attend these examinations and to participate in the questioning of candidates, and along with the abbots and lama unzes of both Gyudpa institutions, we priors had to be present to see that our geshes behaved as they should. We had to stand the whole time to make sure that every one of our charges participated. After the first session it fell upon me to deliver a disciplinary lecture at the Ramoche, chastising those who had not done their part. As a result of all this service to my brother monks, I was getting no more than three to four hours sleep a night, with no time to retire for a brief daytime break to my rooms in Phala's place. I borrowed the use of a little room over a nearby butter-and-cheese shop, to which I might, when the chance arrived, retreat for a moment's rest. But as it turned out, even there I found myself still on duty—the priors of the khamtsens learned of the sanctuary and not only came themselves for talks and advice but sent any monk of theirs who would have to miss any part of ceremony to me for permission. This was one year when the end of Monlam signalled relief to me, rather than a return to routine.

My term as prior ended a month later, and to my very great relief, it was judged that while I had been in office the discipline of the college had been satisfactory. It was customary for the outgoing prior to make a short speech to the assembly, his last morning in office. This was an entirely formal piece, which I had rehearsed and which I now delivered: "If you feel that I have done anything wrong in the period of my office as prior, please forgive me. But if you feel that I have acted in good faith to the best of my ability, then give me, please, your blessing." When the subsequent ceremony of installing the new prior had been concluded, I proceeded alone to a meeting of the council, over which the Lama Unze was to preside.

No one but the abbot had had the right during the season of my term to criticize or call me to task, whereas now the members of the council were to pass my conduct in review and make in my presence whatever criticisms they wished. If I had been lax, negligent, too stern, or in any way inadequate, I might be required to go into seclusion for a time, or even be expelled from the college. The four khamtsen gegens and the Lama Unze invited me to sit down when I entered, and the Lama Unze then addressed them. "If you have criticisms of Khyongla's term as prior, state them now," he said. I was a little nervous, but all spoke in my favor. "Are you sure?" he kept repeating; but no one said a word against me. Given a sign, I rose with real relief and stood before the Lama Unze while he draped a silk scarf around my neck as a sign of appreciation. I walked happily to my rooms, where even more friends arrived to congratulate me than had come when I became prior, for word had already gotten around: the council had approved.

One afternoon, shortly after my retirement as prior, one of Konchog's students came to my apartment to tell me that the abbot was seriously ill. Because I was the disciple who had been the closest to Konchog over the years, they sent for me immediately. Alarmed at the news, I hurried to the state Medical and Astrological College in the city, and requested the services of the chief state doctor. Though he cautioned me that since there were many in need of treatment he could not remain at Rato, the doctor accompanied me to Konchog's bedside. I was distressed by the abbot's frail appearance, but he was smiling and tending to the many students who had come to ease his illness. The doctor examined him and prescribed some herbal medicines. Konchog thanked him, but then added a little sermon on death, which only increased my anxiety for his life. If he died of this illness, he said, he would have no regrets: he had practiced religion all this life, and death would be its fulfillment. "To be born is to die," he concluded. "The Lord Buddha himself passed away, so what is important to bear in mind is that nothing is everlasting."

His condition seemed to improve and, though I remained at Rato to be near him, I began to hope that he would be able to accompany me back to my labrang after his retirement, as I had planned. But ten days later he had a relapse, and barely a week after that, I was summoned with the news that his condition had become critical. I rushed to his apartment, but he had already died. His body was sitting as ever on a cushion facing a picture of his teacher, the Thirteenth Dalai Lama. I was told that before his death he had asked those present to help him face in each of the four directions. No one had known his reason for this request, but immediately after they had helped him, he turned to the Dalai Lama's picture and expired.

The attendants and students were crying when I entered, and I could not restrain my own tears. I made three prostrations before the body and told my late teacher that I could not remember ever having seriously offended him, but that in case I ever had, I prayed him to forgive me. Three days later, after traditional funeral observations, at an hour determined by astrologers, a monk carried the corpse to a cemetery near the mountain hermitage of a celebrated teacher, whose monks I had invited to assemble up there and to pray while the body was being cut up and offered to the hungry birds.

I no longer wished to remain at Rato—my grief was intense whenever I passed Konchog's apartment. I thanked each of his helpers and attendants, and with sorrow in my heart returned alone to the city.

16.

A Last Visit Home

For a few weeks after Konchog's death, I retreated to a hermitage owned by two friends of mine, an elderly couple named Mene Thang. The peace and serenity were exactly what I needed after the shock of my teacher's death. I read and meditated, and although I remained deeply affected by this loss, the seclusion and relaxation were just what I needed.

Several months later, at the end of 1955, two messengers arrived from my labrang in the Kham with a bundle of letters and with news of my parents and friends. Nearly twenty years had passed since I had left the Kham as a thirteen-year-old boy with my guardian, Dongye, and I was now thirty-two. Dongye's letter informed me that the monks of the labrang wanted me to return immediately. The Chinese were already in control of the Dayab, but the region was a bit out of their way and so had not yet been subjected to the oppressive measures already being applied elsewhere in eastern Tibet. The members of my labrang had heard that our properties might soon be confiscated and divided, and they wanted me to see, before all their labors were destroyed, what they had been doing during the period of my absence. Dongye himself was preparing to retire and wished to give me personally an account of his activities and turn responsibility over to my hands. I would have to find a new administrator to handle our financial and practical affairs, and no one knew what new developments I might also have to deal with.

On reading this alarming letter from my old instructor and guardian, I went immediately to consult with the senior tutor of the Dalai Lama, Ling Rinpoche, whose student I had once been. He received me cordially and agreed both that it was important for me to visit my labrang and that this was the time for me to do it.

However, no sooner had this decision been made, than, on returning to my place with the Mene Thangs, I received a message from the Yigtsang, our Secretariat for Religious Affairs, inviting me to appear before them. The Yigtsang was a council of four monk officials, residing with the Dalai Lama during the summer in the Norbulingka, and I was both curious and anxious to know what they wanted.

When I went to see them the next day I was told by the second official that I had just been appointed head of the faculty of a new school that the Chinese had already opened in Gyaltse, the third largest population center in Tibet. Its students were young Tibetans who had been induced to study there; although they were being taught to read and write Tibetan, the real purpose of the place was to indoctrinate Tibetan youth in Communism. The teachers, I was told, were both Tibetan and Chinese, but the curriculum was strictly supervised by the Chinese. The Tibetans not only had no say in what was taught, but also were very closely watched by these supervisors, who believed that young people growing up in Tibet in that period of transition should neither receive religious instruction nor be taught any of the true facts concerning their own history and traditions. The entire program was designed to prepare their uninformed minds to accept Communist ideals attractively presented. There would be no serious attempt to convert members of the older generation who already better understood the materialist philosophy and motives of the Communist world. Meanwhile, our Tibetan government, well aware that a lack of public schools was a great weakness of our system and that our private schools, private teachers, and monastic schools could not cope with the new situation, could neither openly oppose the Chinese plans to found free public schools nor expose the motives behind this apparently generous act. They would try, however, to have at least a few loyal and serious Tibetan scholars appointed to the new posts.

I was not pleased to hear of this uncongenial assignment. The year before, when the Chinese had been looking for someone to teach Tibetan at Peking University, I had been asked if I had any interest in the job; but fearing that the aim was simply to use our language for

Chinese propaganda in Tibet, not for Tibetan scholarship in China, I had refused. Approached now by the Yigtsang, I hesitated, for though I greatly wanted to refuse, I had a number of things to consider and could not give an immediate answer. Following the old Tibetan custom of polite acquiescence without definite commitment, I stalled for time.

First, the announcement of my appointment had been signed by the Dalai Lama, but I did not know whether the idea had originated with him or with the officials of the Yigtsang. If His Holiness wished me to go, I felt that I should do so; but if this was someone else's idea, that would be a very different matter. It would not be easy, however, to ask directly about the circumstances of that signature, so I decided first to pay my visit to the Kham, and then see when I returned to Lhasa how things would in the meantime have developed.

The appointment, on the other hand, had already been made, so I had to get permission for my visit from both the Yigtsang and the Chinese commissioner at Gyaltse. To my great relief, I received both within a few weeks and was given three months for the round trip. I began my preparations for the trip, planning to leave in early 1956, and the two messengers from my labrang in the Kham joined in helping me to get ready. Presents had to be bought for my family and friends and ceremonial offerings for the monasteries I would visit in Dayab. And it was during this period, also, that I had my first private interview with the young Dalai Lama, already renowned for his wisdom and compassion.

He was living at the time in Lhasa, in his apartments in the Jokhang, where he was to spend the period of Monlam. I had arranged for the interview through Phala, the lord chamberlain, and received in due time my invitation, naming both the day and the hour. Going early that morning to the temple, I climbed to the top floor, where His Holiness's apartment had been recently rebuilt and adorned with a golden roof. The stair was heavily guarded; but Phala, who had been watching for me, motioned to let me pass. I was ushered into a room, decorated sumptuously with heavy Tibetan carpets and many beautiful thangkas, which I had once visited when it was being built and the public had been allowed to view it. As I now entered with the lord chamberlain, it was aglow with the early morning light filtering through the yellow silk curtains at the windows.

At the far end of the room His Holiness sat on his cushions, facing the door through which we approached. There was a long bank of windows at his left, and on his right, a shrine with butter lamps softly burning. The golden images and rare ritual objects all about were dazzling. Standing in their official positions around him were the master of chanting, master of robes, and master of ceremonies. I made the customary three prostrations and held out a long white silk scarf to the master of ceremonies, who presented to me, one by one, the usual "three gifts," which I then presented to His Holiness. When this formality had been accomplished, the Dalai Lama graciously bade me sit on a cushion by one of the windows, and opened the conversation by asking when I would be leaving for the Kham. He told me that he was pleased with the reports that he had been hearing of me. He understood that I had been diligent in my studies, and had been regularly attending the sermons of his tutors and other good authorities. He was also pleased to have heard, he said, that I seemed content to live simply, with a humility to which merit would accrue, such qualities being essential to the practice of religion, and conducive to inner contentment and profound peace.

In response, and to signify that I was hearing and accepting his words, I breathed in loudly through my mouth and stuck my tongue out, the Tibetan way of politely signifying compliance. The masters of chanting, of robes, and of ceremonies then departed, and for a moment we were alone. There were certain obvious questions I should have liked to ask, but having been trained in our rules of politeness, I said nothing of politics, and spoke only of religious matters. The tea master appeared presently, and served tea. After some more conversation, His Holiness picked up a white scarf and protection cord in sign of the end of the visit, and said, "With every action of your body, voice, and mind, dedicate yourself to the service of others."

Very early the next morning, I set forth on my trip to the Kham. When I had first come from the Kham to Lhasa as a thirteen-year-old boy, it had taken thirty-five days of rugged traveling by muleback with a large caravan. I could now go as far as Chamdo by bus on a road built by the Chinese with Tibetan labor, and the trip would take just three days. The two messengers from my labrang would be coming with me; also a few monks from my khamtsen in Rato, returning to their homes. On the outskirts of the city we boarded our bus—a big, new, yellow, Chinese bus for thirty passengers which seemed to me to represent the very height of modern elegance.

Because we were delayed by an avalanche the trip took five days instead of three. Arriving in the village of Kyi Dam, some three hours before the end of the line, my two companions and I got off, to spend the night as guests of a family I had known and visited when a boy. I was overjoyed to see them again, and it was a special pleasure when I met my brother, who had been sent by my parents to greet me. He had been born after I left for Lhasa, yet I recognized him at once, for his features resembled my father's and his husky voice was like mine and my mother's. He had recently become a monk, in keeping with our father's wish, but still spent a great deal of time with our parents and was very helpful and close to them. He had brought with him some pastries that my mother had prepared for me and said that she and my father were waiting for me anxiously. Two members of my labrang were also in the village to receive me, and next morning we set out early by horseback on the rugged two-day ride to Yendum.

I remained at Yendum a week, for there were so many visitors to see. Many were monks who, like myself, had studied in Central Tibet. Many more were lay people, some of whom I had known in Lhasa, and these came for various reasons: some, out of friendship; others, out of curiosity; many, to have my blessing, or to ask for a protection cord. I had brought many of such cords along from Lhasa, and it was a pleasure now to distribute them to my guests.

Protection cords can be of any color, but generally are red for monks, white, green, or blue for lay people, and they are worn around the neck to protect the wearer from illness and demons. They can be made of cotton or of silk and they have three knots in them, to represent the Mind, Speech, and Body of the Buddha. When presenting such a cord, the donor meditates on the union (the knotting together) of the knowledge of Bliss and Emptiness, Compassion and Loving Kindness. There is also a special Tantric meditation on the fact that the knots, having been made by man, are not self-originated, and that, although they look like knots, each in reality is a union of emptiness and a blessing. We believe that loving kindness is the best protection against all enemies, particularly Lord Mara, whom the Buddha conquered by the power of love, and it is with love that a protection cord is made and bestowed.

People in our district liked to have these cords, and their friends returning from Lhasa would usually bring back a few as gifts, those from the city of the Potala being thought of as more effective than others. People liked to have cords, also, that have been breathed upon by holy or famous lamas, and since there were in the whole Dayab only six or seven incarnations, I, as one of them, was famous and was thought to be a holy man. Actually, I was no more fond of giving protection cords than of bestowing a blessing by hand, which made me feel uncomfortable, but since our people so enjoyed receiving them, I had known there would be a demand upon me. Some Tibetans wore a number of cords together, as necklaces; many kept them in their homes; and still others just threw them away.

My labrang was two days' ride from Yendum, and our party set out early one morning, stopping the night in the home of relatives of mine in a village along the way. When we woke the next morning we saw the whole country beautifully covered with a blanket of snow. Again we started early, and when we had ridden an few hours, saw before us a large, mounted, welcoming company composed of representatives of every family from the neighborhood of my monastery. I did not know a single member, but they were all wonderfully friendly. When I asked if it had been unpleasant for them to wait for me in the snow, they laughed, declaring with many voices that it had not been unpleasant at all. Then they wheeled their mounts, and when we had ridden a little way further, I saw on a snow-covered hill far ahead the building of my labrang—which, when I was a child, had seemed so large, but now looked small and rather poor. Yet it was my home, and I felt happy to be back.

At the gates, when we arrived, there was a considerable crowd assembled, and I smiled as we trotted in, bowing to them as we passed. Dismounting in the courtyard, I went directly to the reception room where Dongye was waiting at the door. Four years had passed since we had last been together, and I immediately noticed that his hair was white. It was a real delight to see him again. We greeted each other by touching foreheads, and he led me into the room where there were assembled all the members of my staff. Many of the villagers followed us in; and there, in a formal ceremony with very little conversation, the labrang served tea, droma, and cakes to all.

That general occasion attended to, I retired to my own apartment, and in a little while my family came in: father, mother, brother, three sisters, and a nephew. I had not seen my father since that visit of his to Lhasa in 1941, when I was eighteen. He looked old and wrinkled now, perhaps because of his anxiety for the family and great worry over the Chinese invasion of the area. My mother, whom I had not seen since 1946, did not appear to be much older. She was completely happy; and when she said with tears of joy that now her whole family was reunited, except for the little son who had died when he was seven, her words caused me, as well, to shed joyful tears. My oldest sister wept for joy too, and asked whether I recognized her. When I told her that of course I did, she reminded me of my brief visit home, just before I had been taken to Lhasa. I had offered her milk from my cup and we had drunk from it alternately. Mother introduced me, next, to my youngest sister, a smiling, pretty girl of thirteen, who was now a nun and spoke with me very familiarly. She begged me to stay for at least a year, and I had to explain to her, sadly, that the leave I had been granted was for no more than three months. My second sister, who had been only two years old when I left, was a pretty young matron now, the mother of a little son. She said she did not remember what I had looked like, but she had seen a picture that I had once sent home, and I was exactly as in that picture. Her child, my seven-year-old nephew, to whom I was next introduced, though at first shy and very quiet, soon ran back and forth about the room, getting into mischief. He was evidently a spoiled child, but bright and endearing. I had already unpacked my gifts for them all, mostly cloth or ready-made clothes. We had so much to talk about that the time passed all too quickly with our exchanges.

The next day I distributed presents to Dongye, the fifteen members of my staff, as well as to every family in the village; for when I had left at the age of thirteen many had given me farewell gifts, which had been duly recorded, and I was now returning those favors. The most popular of my offerings were silks and other small gifts from India, all of which were received in the spirit that they were given, with warm, sincere expressions of long friendship.

Meanwhile a special festival had been prepared for the welcoming party, to which about sixteen people came. All stayed with us two days, and since there was no rule in our labrang about women remaining for the night, the guest rooms were full. Two great meals were served each day, one at noon, the other in the evening; and having in Lhasa gotten used to fresh vegetables and meat, I realized at these banquets that I was now going to have to adjust again to the fare of my native village, where the meat might be a few weeks old or more, and in winter there were no fresh vegetables. Chang was served both evenings, and in a lively mood the young people got up and danced. When it all ended and the guests had gone back in high spirits to their villages, my family remained three more days; and when they too departed, the labrang settled down to its normal routine.

From my window I could watch the people in the mornings, passing along the road with their cows, goats, and sheep to pasture, and in the evenings returning to the village. The middle of the day was so quiet, I might have been living in a hermitage; and I felt completely at home, wishing only that I might remain there, enjoying the peace in study and meditation.

There was now ample time for me to explore the labrang's fine library, where I soon discovered a surprising number of beautiful, handwritten manuscripts and important printed books: Nyingmapa, Kagyudpa, and Sakyapa, as well as Gelugpa texts, many older handwritten volumes illuminated with richly colored miniatures and designs. Since the great Tibetan printing presses had always been many long days' journey away from this rural part of our country, hand-copied volumes had been turned out here in great number. I also found a packet of poems that my predecessor had composed when a student at Dugugen Monastery in Chamdo, and I read these with especial interest, discovering with surprise that he had been a better poet that I could ever hope to be. I had assumed that since he had not become a geshe, I must surely be the better scholar; but now reading his actual writings, I found, with a curious mixture of humiliation and pride, that they were truly beautiful, lucid, and inspired.

Four families of nomads had charge of the four hundred yaks and dris of my labrang, and since they also had yaks of their own, they were responsible altogether for a herd of about a thousand head. All had come to my welcoming party, and the labrang had arranged for them at that time a special banquet, in return for which I was invited to pay them a visit in their camp. Remembering how much I had liked their yogurt as a child, one or more of them brought me a fresh supply every morning. When I tasted it again I remembered why I had been so fond of it—it was thick, creamy, and delicious.

One morning those coming with the yogurt brought me also their invitation to pay my promised visit to their camp the following day. Dongye joined me and with half a dozen others we rode up the mountainside early in the morning. It was a perfectly windless day, and the warm winter sun made the five-mile ride to the winter pasturelands a delight. They were on a lower slope of the mountain, protected by the foothills, not nearly as extensive as the summer grazing lands on the higher slopes, and so the herds were held close together. As we approached we saw the four large family tents made of yak hair standing in a row with their backs to the mountain.

I formally entered each of the four tents, to greet individually the members of each family. They asked me to perform an incense ceremony, and so together up the hill we climbed to a highland tract above the tents, where they built a fire of fragrant juniper boughs while I read the appropriate prayer. I had brought along some consecrated pills called *jinten*, which we now dissolved in water. When everyone had tasted this drink the herders set out some in buckets for their yaks. Such pills, of barley flour mixed with medicinal herbs and the ground-up relics of saints, fragments of their garments, holy objects, and consecrated by a special Tantric ceremony, were popular throughout Tibet. It was thought that if eaten just before death they would help one to a better rebirth. I had therefore brought from Lhasa a good number, many of which had been given to me by the Dalai Lama himself, and there was a large stock kept in the labrang as well, with records of their sources and the particles they contained. I was told that some held relics even of Milarepa and Marpa. Anyone asking at the labrang for such pills would be given them in an envelope bearing a wood-block stamp testifying to their contents and their source.

That day with the nomads in their camp was idyllic, reminding me of the summers of my childhood, when I would live with my father for days in a nomad tent in the upland camp. Sitting now with Dongye in a sheltered spot on the high mountainside, gazing down into the valley, I discussed with him plans for what we hoped might be our future. The peaceful setting was so inspiring that we could only regret that the labrang itself had no such view. Lightheartedly, we decided that when next I returned to the Kham, we should build a hermitage on this very spot. It would be a rather large establishment. The courtyard would be large enough to accommodate big audiences for my lectures, but there would also be a number of smaller hermitages, built here and there for those wishing real seclusion. We tried and almost managed on that beautiful afternoon to forget the Chinese now in our land. Only a few had been seen in our district, and so we could imaginatively ignore them, even though the fate of Tibet had already been decided. The enemy had already taken

Chamdo, and their threat to us was in fact imminent. Yet Dongye and I went on developing our vision of imagined buildings, selecting furnishings for each room in turn, and dreaming that serious students and lamas would one day come here from all over the Kham to study, meditate, and enjoy this peace.

The next day, accompanied by a servant and two monks from the labrang, I left for a brief visit home. It was a ride of but half a day, and as I approached, nothing seemed to me to have changed. It was as though I had never been away. The house did not look as grand as it had when I was a child, but it was my home and I was happy to be back. My whole family was there to greet me—father, mother, brother, three sisters—and again we spent our hours talking. My father, I now learned, was no longer working for the district in Yendum, and could remain at home in Ophor. My mother, active as ever, was fully occupied in the household. Though my stay was to be for only three short days, every family in the village had invited me to visit them, and in a lively round of celebrations the time passed very quickly. Two of the most enjoyable occasions were visits to the homes of the two young men who, when I was first taken to the labrang, had been brought, as boys, to be my playmates. They were now married, with youngsters of their own, and when I came into their homes they paid me honors. It seemed to them quite wonderful that their boyhood friend had gone on to live in Lhasa and earn degrees. They assumed that I must now know pretty much everything about this world and the next; they introduced me proudly to their children, and then we all played games.

However, in time, and all too soon, I had to terminate this holiday and return to Yendum, where I had promised to ordain two young monks. When I arrived, I was shocked to learn that about four hundred others wanted to be ordained as well. It was a formidable occasion, but not the last nor even the most fatiguing of those into which I was drawn during that memorable visit to Yendum. Years before at Rato, I had met a monk from this town who before returning home had invited me to deliver a series of lectures when I, too, should return home. I had agreed to do so, and he took this opportunity to remind me of that reckless promise. I was to lecture on the lamrim, and it was arranged for me to begin immediately after the ordinations. The series would run for three weeks, with sessions daily in the assembly hall, from noon to six in the evening; and the commentary I chose to use was that of the Third Panchen Rinpoche. The weeks passed faster than I thought they would, however, and over three thousand people attended the last lecture.

Following a brief visit to the "Son Monastery," I left for a second and last visit to my labrang. With the end of my stay approaching, I was feeling more and more at home. These were my people, the labrang was my place, my parents nearby, and I could see them whenever I wished. Wherever I went, people begged me to remain permanently in the Kham, or at least for a few years. But I had been given only a short time (my permission for a three-month stay had been extended two months), and was soon to report for my task as teacher in that Communist school. When I bade goodbye to my newly found friends, I believed I would be back in a few years. We had no idea that the parting was to be final and that I would never return.

The labrang made all the preparations for my journey, and this time there would be no need, as in the old days, to carry a great load of food or to hire men and mules. I had only to go by muleback to Chamdo and there catch the Chinese bus to Lhasa. Two monks from the labrang had been assigned to accompany me that far, to see that I and my two companions from Rato got safely aboard.

Our first stop on the way was Ophor for a farewell visit to my parents, whom I earnestly urged to consider moving to Lhasa, where the Dalai Lama's presence would be—as I then thought—a protection. They replied that they would like to come, but would have first to decide what to do about their house and properties. The situation had reached such a point that it was going to be difficult, if not impossible, to sell, and they had their children to consider. They had heard rumors of people in some of the outlying districts packing off to Lhasa to escape the increasingly repressive measures that the Chinese were imposing. The move would be a big undertaking; if I had only had the foresight to realize what the future held, however, I would have insisted that my family come with me immediately, leaving someone in charge of the properties. Travel would soon be impossible.

When it came time for me to leave, I said goodbye to my mother inside the house. She was weeping, and her last, helpless words to me were, "Come back soon!" I asked her to pray for me—we believe a parent's prayers are exceedingly efficacious, and I said to her as I left, "I'll be returning soon."

Outside I bade farewell to my three sisters, all of whom were in tears, and to my brother. I looked around for my nephew, but he had gone off to the pastures with the shepherds. His mother, my second sister, had asked me to take him to Lhasa to be with me in the monastery; but my father had objected to this, insisting the child was too young and so he remained with the family in Ophor.

My father was standing by the horse that I was to mount, and as he put his hand to the stirrup his eyes filled with tears and he began to recite: "Long life to the lama, Lord of the Doctrine . . ." With that, tears came to my own eyes; I joined in, and we finished together:

"May there be everywhere adherents to the Doctrine;

Prosperity to the patrons of the Doctrine:

The Doctrine, everlasting!"

We were both recalling a fabled incident from the life of the Third Dalai Lama. He had been summoned to Mongolia by a powerful chieftain, Altan Khan, who later became king, and when he was mounting to depart, a high officer, with his hand to the stirrup, quoted the first two lines of this poem, but stopped, overcome by emotion. The Dalai Lama completed the verses, mounted, and they never again met, for in Mongolia he died.

I mounted, wheeled, and as we rode away gazed continually back until Ophor was out of sight, my little village, with my father, mother, and all, standing there at its edge watching us go.

17.

I Must Teach in a Communist School

As soon as I arrived in Lhasa there came a telegram from the Gyaltse Committee, ordering me to report immediately for duty in their Chinese school, and enclosing my bus fare. I had hoped that they would have found somebody else for the job when I remained in the Kham longer than planned, but it was evident now that they had followed my movements closely. The best that I could do was to persuade them to postpone my trip for a fortnight, while I rested and tidied up my affairs.

The bus (actually, it was more like a truck) that I finally boarded for Gyaltse went only as far as Shigatse, a jouncing two days' ride. There were no seats, and the passengers and baggage were tossed together, with everybody scrambling and fighting for a place. I contrived to wedge myself and my own baggage into a corner at the rear; the road was not as good as the main line to China had been, and as we jolted along I became miserably carsick. The bus stopped at every major village and at the second stop I became violently ill. A Tibetan army officer sitting in a front seat, on noticing my misery, very kindly exchanged places, and from there on I was able to endure the ride.

After I arrived in Gyaltse, I installed myself in a nearby monastery and soon the day arrived for my appearance in the Chinese camp. I was to call on the head of the Chinese governing body of the town to report that I had arrived; and since this was to be my first contact with the Communist bureaucracy, I did not know what to expect. The officer received me, not in his office, but in his living room, and I found him to be a very courteous but unimpressive man of about fifty, wearing the grayish-tan uniform that had been assumed by all

Chinese military servants. His attractive, long-haired wife was there, too. Our conversation was interpreted by a young Tibetan from Kham.

When we exchanged scarves in the Tibetan manner, the officer told me he was pleased that I had come and hoped I would be of help to the people in his school. I replied that since I had studied nothing but religion and had no knowledge of politics, I was afraid I would not be very useful either to the government or to the people, but would try my very best. He declared that he liked me for giving that forthright answer and not trying to curry favor with him, assuring me that whenever I required advice I could contact him directly.

To my surprise, when I reported for work next day, instead of being introduced to my class, I was told that I had been appointed to the Propaganda Office. At that time, the Chinese were using Tibetans, wherever possible, to explain to villagers all the fine things our new rulers were going to do for us, and it appeared that they intended to use me for public speaking of this kind, persuading my trusting countrymen to collaborate in their program. When I reported the next day to the office, the first thing I saw on entering the room were blown-up photographs of Stalin, Mao Tse-tung, and Lenin, staring out from the walls above the desks like supervising spirits. I was greeted by a number of smiling young Chinese, formerly of the military service, now assigned to civilian work, and they were all extremely friendly. Only one, however, spoke Tibetan. He asked me to let him put my robe on over his jacket, and another photographed him that way. In exchange, they put a green civilian jacket on me and I, too, was photographed—it was as though they were playing a game. One had been badly wounded in the head during the war against Chiang Kai-shek, and he proudly showed me his scars. They pointed to the pictures and explained that those were very great men and that it now was our privilege and duty to study their lives and to emulate them. This too was done in a joking way, with good humor.

After I had been about a week in that office, having had very little to do, they asked me to make a public speech. They had set up a loudspeaker on a housetop in the center of town, from which speeches were being broadcast several times a day. They also wanted me to go to the monasteries and proselytize the monks. I responded as I had to their superior, saying that I had no knowledge of politics since my life had been spent in religion; but they assured me, as their superior had, that that would make no difference. They would gladly compose a speech for me that would say what needed to be said, and all I would have to do would be to read it aloud. I argued that I had such a low-pitched voice that it would not carry very far; but that, they said, would be easily taken care of with a microphone. Then I told them I had never had any experience whatsoever in delivering public addresses; that the idea of doing so made me so nervous I would make a bad public appearance; and that that would be embarrassing both to me and to the Peking Government. This seemed to persuade them, and they dropped the whole affair for a couple of days.

Meanwhile, as I had found, there was next to nothing for me to do in that Propaganda Office. Under direction, I wrote speeches that were then delivered by two Tibetan women who were serving as interpreters. One was an ex-nun, now married; the other was the sister of a distinguished gentleman, named Ngabo, who was serving at the time as secretary general of Mao Tse-tung's Preparatory Committee for the Tibetan Autonomous Region. The husbands of both women were also in the service of the Chinese, all of whom then governing our country had undergone intensive training at home and were being very careful not to offend Tibetans unduly. They had been taught Tibetan etiquette and were not to smoke in temples, comment on our religion, or criticize the Dalai Lama. The speeches that I wrote emphasized the advantages of the Communists' social reforms, the ideals of Communism, and the importance of achieving freedom from foreign imperialist aggressors. I could not possibly have written a word against my religion or the Dalai Lama, and fortunately was not required to do so. But all of us forced to work this way were in extremely difficult positions; for if we resisted overtly, we risked not only imprisonment but also the immediate loss of whatever national freedom we still had.

After a month or two of this, news came by way of Lhasa that the Chinese had decided to slow the march of modern progress and delay for the next six years the political and social reforms which they had been pressing us to effect. Perhaps part of the responsibility for this sudden reversal of policy lay with the people of Amdo and the Kham, who had resisted when the new rulers sought to introduce their measures by force. Hundreds had been imprisoned, many others put to forced labor; monasteries had been destroyed and looted for their treasures; property had been seized and all the main food supplies appropriated, giving rise to a famine in our land for the first time in its history. The peak of the Kham revolt came while I was in Gyaltse in 1956, when the people rejected and resisted fiercely every Communist promise of a liberation that had already brought starvation, and was threatening to deprive them of their religion and everything else that they held dear.

Soon after this I learned that the new school season had at last been scheduled to open in about three weeks, and that I had been listed in the curriculum as a teacher of Tibetan grammar and poetics in a course designed for the teaching staff and advanced students. No Chinese would attend. My pupils would all be Tibetans and most of them, as I soon found out, had a real interest in the subject. We would meet twice a week, sometimes in the afternoon, sometimes in the evening, in class periods of two hours. But I would still have to appear daily at the Propaganda Office for whatever assignments they might have prepared for me.

On the opening day of the program all the students of the new school were gathered in an assembly hall that was not yet finished and had the look of a makeshift shelter. We staff members sat on a low platform at one end of the room. Before us, in rows, were some three or four hundred students on bare benches.

The meeting began when a Tibetan girl, mounting the platform, raised her hand and everybody stood. She began to sing the Chinese Communist anthem, gesturing all to join in, after which one of the staff members rose to introduce the new teachers, pointing to each of us in turn. I heard myself for the first time described as a representative of the Tibetan Government in Lhasa. A few were asked to make speeches, and I was called upon last. Fortunately, I had already prepared a few notes, to be ready in case such a thing should occur.

"Our country," I said with my husky voice, "is highly developed in the fields of religion, religious culture, literature, and the arts. In this respect we are, perhaps, the most enlightened people in the world. But we have not developed our country to an equal degree on the secular side, and the time has now come for us to repair this situation, approaching in our secular life the standards of other countries. We have lagged far behind in our economic development and in the application of scientific methods. We must now catch up. But in order for us to do this, a new and modern type of education is required.

"Tibet," I continued, "has never had a compulsory public school system, and although there have been many private and district government schools, their enrollments have never been large. We have for centuries maintained a high degree of religious scholarship, but today that is not enough. Our task for today must be to abolish illiteracy in our land, so that our people may participate in the modern world and its culture. We shall have to cultivate exchanges of knowledge between ourselves and the peoples of other countries; for although we have had for centuries our own unique and precious culture, what is now required is that our younger generation should seriously study the secular sciences of this century, along with the great classics of their own religious heritage, the values of which will still be vital in their lives."

I then expressed my wishes for long life to Chairman Mao, to His Holiness the Dalai Lama, and to the Panchen Rinpoche, concluding with a hope that the friendship of the Tibetan and Chinese peoples might prove lasting and fruitful to all. Everybody applauded, the meeting closed, and I was relieved that I had found something appropriate to say that was not contrary to what I believed.

Two days later I gave my first class in Tibetan grammar. The text that I used for this course was that composed by Thumi Sambhota, the prime minister of the thirty-third king of Tibet. For the first evening session about two hundred were present, including all the members of the college staff, both Tibetans and Chinese. But from then on the attendance greatly varied. Usually all the Tibetans were present, which meant about twenty regular students—sometimes more, sometimes a little less. But not a single Chinese ever returned— evidently they felt no need to learn Tibetan.

A few weeks after I had begun to feel that both of my courses were going pretty well, the Communist Party chairman of the Gyaltse district came to pay me a visit in my room in the monastery. After we had sat down and tea was served, the chairman came to the point.

"What is your opinion," he asked, "about our postponement of the reforms for another six years?"

"It is important," I said, "and obviously necessary to press for reforms in this country. We are far behind in our economic development and in the living standards of our people. But it seems to me not wise to try to reform Tibetans in the same way as the Chinese in their motherland. Tibetans are quite different. In the first place, they have never been really dissatisfied with their way of life; they are conservative by nature and know little of the ways of the outside world. It would seem best to educate them first in new ideas, and that will take time. They will have to be made to understand the purpose of these reforms and what they will do for the people. I would say, therefore," I concluded, "that postponing the reform for six years is an excellent idea."

He listened attentively as his interpreter translated, and though I hoped my words would be effective, he made no comment. The visit ended, and I escorted him downstairs and to the monastery gate.

The year 1956 was the Buddha Jayanti, or twenty-five-hundredth anniversary of the Parinirvana, the passing away of the Lord Buddha. Many of us had known for months that the Dalai Lama had been invited by the Mahabodhi Society of India to be present at the celebrations, but letters from friends in Lhasa now told of all kinds of maneuvers by the Chinese to prevent him from accepting. He had himself already made clear his desire to attend, and all Tibetans felt very strongly that he should represent our country, for this was to be a major event in the history of Buddhism and there would be representatives present from every part of the world. The Chinese senior commissioner of Lhasa, no doubt acting for Peking, advised His Holiness to appoint a deputy, arguing incongruously that since the Mahabodhi Society was merely a religious organization, it was not important enough to invite and receive a Dalai Lama. Later we learned that when the Indian Government intervened at this juncture with invitations to both the Dalai Lama and the Panchen Rinpoche, the Chinese tried to keep the news from reaching the Potala. However, the Dalai Lama did learn of it through the Indian commissioner in Lhasa; and so, we got word one day that his senior and junior tutors, Ling Rinpoche and Trijang Rinpoche, would soon be passing through Gyaltse, going to India one day before His Holiness. They would be stopping overnight in Wangchug Phala's residence, the younger brother of my friend Thubten Woden, and since Wangchug was going to be in Shigatse at that time, he asked me to help arrange things and welcome the two when they arrived.

A servant admitted me to the mansion, where I found Wangchug's cousin already waiting. He was an elderly monk from Sera, full of fun, who helped to pass the time after supper that evening with comical imitations of the manners and sermons of the Drepung and Sera priors. It grew late, but since we were not expecting our guests until morning, we were still laughing and joking together when the servant returned to announce that someone had just pulled up in a car. We both hurried out to welcome the two arrivals, and after a brief but cordial exchange they retired for the night, having to rise next morning early to continue on to New Delhi.

Both the Dalai Lama and the Panchen Rinpoche were to follow that very day, and an official team of Chinese and Tibetans had hurriedly set up a large tent by the road just outside of Gyaltse to receive them. My name having been numbered among those to be in attendance, I was there with the others, waiting, when the Dalai Lama and Panchen Rinpoche arrived in the latter's car.

This amazing automobile, lacquered a golden yellow, its hood covered with a tiger skin, was followed by a long retinue of less spectacular vehicles, not all in the best condition. They discharged their passengers; and when the Dalai Lama and Panchen Rinpoche together entered our tent, proceeding to seats prepared for them, we ceremoniously paid them our respects. But they could remain only for a moment, having to press on to Siliguri to catch the New Delhi plane. So they soon rose, returned to their car, and as it started away, many of the Tibetans present flung white scarves containing money before them and the attendants of the Dalai Lama and Panchen Rinpoche gathered up the scarves. To my embarrassment, not having expected the two together, I had brought along only one scarf and an envelope with but one gold coin. I felt particularly guilty since the Panchen Rinpoche was not popular at that time in Tibet, and my action must have seemed a deliberate slight.

The Dalai Lama returned alone from the Buddha Jayanti celebration—staying at the Gyaltse Monastery for two weeks on his way back to Lhasa. The Panchen Rinpoche took another route to his own seat in Tashilunpo. Loving preparations had been made at the monastery for the Dalai Lama's visit for he had been asked to celebrate the New Year there. The event would be less elaborate than it would have been in Lhasa, yet it proved to be by no means unimpressive. His Holiness gave a sermon in the large assembly hall, and although it was indeed large, it was not big enough for all attending. A loudspeaker had to be set up in the court for those standing outside, and the number present must have been at least ten thousand.

The second major event arranged for the occasion was a debate in the tsog lang style, for which I was named by His Holiness one of the contestants. My opponent would be a friend of mine, a lharampa geshe from Gaden named Zeme Tulku, who I knew was a considerable scholar. We were to perform once on the first and again on the second day of the New Year, our first theme to be "The Middle Way of Nagarjuna," and the second, Pramāna.

We had little time to prepare. On the day of the ceremony, to clear my head, I went out for a short stroll, but had hardly got down the hill when I heard drums beating and realized it was time for me to be in the hall. Turning quickly and running back up the hill, I entered just in time, considerably winded, and proceeded to take my place. The Dalai Lama was already on his throne and people were filing up to receive his blessing. I took my seat and had hardly recovered my breath when the time arrived for me and my opponent to rise. We stood, facing each other, and debated for an hour, with only one brief pause while a mime troupe of young Tibetan boys in silken robes performed to the music of drums and flutes.

The next day we faced each other again, both of us exceedingly pleased to be proving ourselves in the presence of the Dalai Lama and his tutors. It was a fortunate way to be opening the New Year, we thought, and since Zeme Tulku was a respected friend, I had invited him on both days to have lunch with me in my room. He had gone with the Dalai Lama to India, and as we ate we talked of the immediate situation. He had also accompanied His Holiness to China in 1954 on that historic trip made with the Panchen Rinpoche. His observations greatly helped to clarify my thoughts about the current state of affairs. What I learned about the attitude of the Chinese both toward Buddhism and toward the character of our government did not seem to augur anything good either for the Dalai Lama, or for the future of Tibet.

In most of the larger towns of the country the Communists had by now set up committees under the general supervision of the Lhasa Preparatory Committee. The appointed chairman for religious affairs of the local Gyaltse body was a young woman named Dorji Phagmo, who was the highest female incarnation in all of Tibet, and now completely under Chinese control. She was a tiny, pretty, nineteen-year-old with long, flowing hair, not really a nun, yet not allowed to marry. Her religious rank was very high, yet now her office had really nothing at all to do with religious affairs. It was concerned only with the propagandizing of monks and wooing them to Communism—as I too found out when I found myself appointed second chairman of the same religious committee.

Shortly after my appointment, Dorje Phagmo accepted an invitation to Peking and I became the acting chairman for religious affairs in Gyaltse. The only authority I was accorded, however, was on paper—though I did receive an agreeable increase in salary. A minor Communist official in our office actually ran things and I could make no move without first receiving his approval. On the other hand, our section had actually very little to do. I cannot recall having attended more than five meetings during the whole period of my office. In the course of one of those meetings I did manage to put through a suggestion, unwelcome to my Chinese overseer, that we should immediately organize a meeting of representatives from all the monasteries of our district, of all sects, and invite the Dalai Lama's tutors (who were still in the city) to lead the meeting and speak. They were respected, I argued, by all sects and would therefore be a force for unity. The fellow was not pleased at all with this idea, but could find no reason to oppose it, and so it went through.

The meeting was held in the Chinese camp, and was attended by about seventy representatives from the monasteries. Both Ling Rinpoche and Trijang Rinpoche addressed the group, and I followed, all three of us emphasizing the necessity for the sects to stand united, now more than ever in these troubled times; for monks to devote themselves to their religious studies, abiding scrupulously by the monastic rules established by the Lord Buddha. I added the suggestion that it would now be necessary for us to study democratic principles and the procedure of the secular world outside of Tibet, to familiarize ourselves with the advances of modern science. As I had never spoken into a microphone before, it took several minutes to find the right distance from it, and I was disconcerted to hear my voice so magnified. Yet I made my points; and my overseer, who was the only Chinese present and understood our language fairly well, must have been surprised not to hear me say one word about the benefits we were all to derive from the Chinese Communist reforms. He said nothing, however, and afterward people told me privately that I had shown great courage in not glorifying Communism. Others, however, declared that in not doing so I had made a big mistake.

The morning of His Holiness's departure, I was brought an invitation to his apartment, and found there a number of others waiting to be received. When called to him, I was asked about my tasks in Gyaltse, and gave a brief report of the situation. He listened without comment, then presented me with six tea-bricks and a roll of Tibetan wool, so that I might have a new monk's robe made. I thanked him, bowed, and made my exit. A little later he left by car for Shigatse.

Gyaltse, the following day, seemed to me empty. I felt altogether alone, now that the Dalai Lama was gone; although, even in Lhasa, I had seen him only rarely, I was used to living near his presence and had often visited his tutors. In the mood of this feeling of loss, I went on a sudden hunch to the Chinese office to ask for a two-month leave. I had already been six months in their service. They replied that they would consider the request, and within two days my permission came—with the understanding that I should return to Gyaltse when the leave ended to resume my work both in the school and on the committee.

That settled, I left next day for Shigatse to stay with a family I knew. The Dalai Lama was there, at the Shigatse Dzong, a sixteenth-century fortress built by one of the Tsangpa kings, where in 1642 the great Fifth Dalai Lama was consecrated as the supreme ruler of Tibet. While stopping there, His Holiness would be paying visits to four famous monasteries in the neighborhood: the first, of course, Tashilunpo, which had been founded by the First Dalai Lama and became later one of the Panchen Rinpoche's principal residences; the next would be Shalu, one of the best-known monasteries in Tibet; the third, the ancient Narthang Monastery of the Khadampa sect; and the fourth, a half day's ride by car from Tashilunpo, would be Ngor.

I went along on the second tour in the company of the junior tutor, in a government car that broke down completely on the way, but we were brought a jeep for the remainder of the trip and arrived in good time for His Holiness's sermon. The third monastery visit was one to which I had been looking forward with the greatest of interest, for Narthang had in early times been especially renowned for its scholarship. Its editions of both the Kanjur and the Tanjur (known as the Narthang Editions) were standard works, which I had studied. In those days there had been hundreds of monks in residence, but in our time the number was not great. Many beautiful treasures of the monastery, never exhibited in public, were brought out for His Holiness's visit, and I was present when they were shown. They included many chortens containing relics, as well as extraordinary images and thangkas.

After a visit to Ngor, the Dalai Lama and his aides left for Lhasa, and three days later I went with my aide to the bus station to buy tickets to follow them. They were sold out for that day and we had to wait another twenty-four hours, which greatly annoyed and upset me—little did I know that fate had been very kind to me at that juncture. For when we arrived in Lhasa next day, I heard the horrifying news that the bus I had missed, in which there were riding some of my closest friends, had tumbled down a mountainside, killing all thirty of its occupants. There were no survivors, so we never learned the cause. An old Lhasa merchant and his wife, who were very dear to me, were among the lost, and some of our friends in Lhasa who had been expecting me on that bus, were in mourning for me when I arrived, and were astonished to see my face.

The news of the calamity greatly saddened my homecoming, but I was relieved to be back and away from the watchful eyes of the Gyaltse Communists, with whom I had been sparring for the past six months. I had no reason to believe that I would be excused from returning to their supervision after my holiday; yet for the moment I allowed myself the illusion of a taste of freedom, hard as it was for me to believe that any Tibetan could ever again be free. That was in March, 1957, and everybody in Lhasa could feel that our already desperate situation was steadily becoming worse.

18.

Between Two Worlds

Some weeks after my return to Lhasa a brilliant scholar from Rato, Lo Ten by name, who was a few years younger than I, came to my door, and when I rose as usual to greet him, to my astonishment, sank to the floor and began to make prostrations. I was uncomfortable and said to him sharply, "Don't tease me this way!"; but he finished the three salutes, rose without a smile, and explained that a number of members of the monastery wanted me to come and interpret for them a text by the great seventh-century philosopher Shantideva that was not in the curriculum. Since I had just settled down to lunch, I asked him to share the meal with me and discuss the matter at length. The work in question was the profoundly inspired *Bodhicharyavatara* ("Entering the Path of Bodhisattva Conduct"), in Tibetan, *Jangchub Sempe Chyopala Jugpe*, or for short, *Chyojug*, which is one of the most important and sublimely poetic Mahayanist texts of any period.

I suggested to Lo Ten that a student of his caliber hardly required help from me in the interpretation of such a text. Some of its passages were obscure, but surely he and his friends could resolve them. He replied that they had already encountered serious difficulties, and pleaded so persuasively that I finally gave in, promising to join them all at Rato as soon as I had had time to prepare my talks. He left, greatly pleased, and I, a few days later, moved out to live with my friends the Mene Thangs in their hermitage. There I could find peace and quiet for the considerable task before me.

For some reason never explained to me, Shantideva's *Bodhicharyavatara* was a text not taught in any of the monasteries in which I had studied. In fact, it was only after passing all of my examinations in the Sutras and Tantras that I had begun, with private teachers, the serious reading and memorization of its verses. I had reviewed it twice each year since, and so had its phraseology well in mind. Yet, though I had memorized it all and could explain its literal sense without reference to the commentaries, I could not yet claim to know the text well enough to unfold its deepest meanings. Furthermore, it was going to be a great challenge for me to deliver before an audience of advanced scholars and perhaps hundreds of theological students a long series of formal sermons, even on a text so well held in mind. At the Mene Thangs' I reviewed very carefully the Indian, as well as all of our Tibetan, commentaries, made extensive notes, and finally wrote a commentary of my own—not only to reinforce my memory, but also to improve my grasp of the deeper levels of meaning. The Mene Thangs, meanwhile, were again, as always, the kindest of hosts—going about their own daily routine of religious practices without any disturbance to me, and yet managing to provide for all of my needs.

Over the years I had so often stayed with the Mene Thangs that I could now feel completely at home with them. From the late spring to midsummer of 1957, I dwelt in peace at Dagna Lubug, oblivious of the mounting Communist peril, even forgetful of my charge to return in two months to that school in Gyaltse. That was indeed a wonderful time for me. I could study and practice my religion of eternal light to my heart's content, without losing myself in the temporal world and its terrible upheavals. I felt as though I had escaped from time and returned to that tranquil Tibet of the Lord Buddha which I had always known, and which for so many centuries had existed peacefully in accord with the beauty of its skies and snow-capped mountain ranges.

My sermons had been scheduled for the break between semesters, when the monks would be absolved from attendance at daily ceremonies. When I arrived at Rato, I discovered, to my astonishment, that absolutely everybody, from the abbot to the youngest monk, came to ask permission to attend my series of talks. Ordinarily it would have been my duty to pay my respects to the abbot, but in this case it was he who came respectfully to me, as a private person wishing to be my student. And his appearance at my door gave me a real sense of the serious challenge of my responsibility. Every day for three weeks, from noon to 5 P.M., I reviewed for my audience in detail every line and phrase of the ten chapters of our text. Occasionally, I realized acutely that I was not taking them the whole way, to the ultimate reaches of Shantideva's thought. But then, when reciting aloud his beautiful poetic verses, I felt somewhat reassured that my conduct was correct and that I was communicating, at least a good part of the time, the sense of the author's meaning and intention.

The monks were now treating me as their lama, which had the effect of making me want to improve greatly both in my knowledge and in my practice of the faith; for I had had an uncomfortable feeling ever since delivering my first public speeches in the course of my visit home, that unless I practiced what I was preaching, I would be shamed before my pupils and undeserving of their respect. It was becoming increasingly apparent to me that a teacher should not presume to advise anyone coming to him for counsel, unless he is himself strenuous in his effort to embody the Perfections. With what I could regard as only limited success, as the weeks passed, I earnestly tried to make myself worthy of the honors and respect now showered upon me.

The two months of my leave passed swiftly, but I had no word from the Communists ordering me to return to the school at Gyaltse. And I, as one might imagine, did not write to them to inquire about my position. I gladly returned to my life in Lhasa, after the series, and again took up my studying and teaching. As it turned out, I never did go back to Gyaltse.

Shortly after the series ended, I was saddened to learn that a gentle seventy-year-old nun who had lived in the building for years and of whom I had been very fond, had died during my absence. Thubten Woden then graciously offered me her apartment rent-free, saying that now that I had begun to lecture publicly, with pupils of my own and many visitors, he felt that I needed more living space. I was overwhelmed by this generous offer and accepted with delight. The elegant suite occupied one whole side of the second floor and I soon realized that my simple furnishings would be hardly even visible in such a spacious home.

Studying the situation, I decided, after considerable thought, to have a large shrine with many images made for the sitting room. We believe that it brings great merit in future lives to have images of the Buddha, deities, and saints, all those in whom we take refuge. I had been dreaming ever since leaving that of my childhood of having another really beautiful shrine. I ordered from an image-maker three large figures of clay: the Lord Buddha in the center; Atisha the great Indian reformer who had taught and died in Tibet, at his right hand; and on the other side, Tsongkhapa. I also ordered two smaller images of Gyelstreb and Khedup. The fee that was asked for all five was about equivalent to two hundred U.S. dollars, of which I paid half in advance; and in a few weeks notice came that the images had been made. They were brought to my apartment and, when uncovered, I beheld them with the greatest excitement.

They had been beautifully made; and no sooner had all been arranged upon my altar than a dear old friend from Rato, the lama Te Chung, offered to do the *Lung Bul* for them—that is, the selection of secret mantras, relics, stupas, and other such religious tokens, which would be sealed into the sacred images. I was, of course, delighted. And next day, with enough money of mine to cover a bill of some ten to fifteen dollars, he went to a bookshop where mantras of various kinds were sold to buy many little rolls of long narrow paper strips with prayers printed by wood-blocks on them. Returning happily with these to my place, he first dyed them golden yellow with saffron, then rolled selections together in tight bunches, attaching labels to each. I went out to collect from my teachers tiny images of the Buddhas, Bodhisattvas, and yi-dams, as well as fragments of cloth from the robes, not only of ancient saints, but also from those of my teachers who were recognized as spiritually advanced—Pabongkha Rinpoche, for example. I also went to the Treasury Office to procure such lucky objects as would be given for the asking: old coins no longer in use, pinches of various grains, and ground-up precious stones. People sometimes would ask also for tokens from families who had been rich for generations, imagining themselves fortunate in the possession of objects formerly owned by people who had been able to hold onto wealth. When I returned with my prizes and the preparations were complete, Lama Te Chang and I on the first anniversary of my dear teacher Konchog's departure from this world, began placing all of these collected objects inside my images, in a special ceremony and in the proper canonical order and way.

We first inserted in a special opening at the base of each image a long splinter of red sandalwood to represent the *brahmananda*, a channel of the psychic body that in the physical body runs parallel to the spinal column; and on each of these sticks the words *Om A Hum* had been written to symbolize the Buddha's Body, Voice, and Mind. Two blades of *kusha* grass were next inserted, one on either side of the sandalwood stick, representing respectively the left and right psychic nerves (known as *idā* and *pingalā*) which wind about the brahmananda in a double helix. Then we filled the hollow images with the rolled-up mantras in proper order, tucking in, at the base of each, printed copies of the eight symbols of prosperity and seven symbols of royalty, and pinches of earth from various sacred sites that I had myself collected during my pilgrimages in India.

I now began to find myself increasingly interested in the study and collection of paintings and images. My altar was a beautiful thing to behold, yet lacked, it seemed to me, a certain grandeur; so I decided to order from a very great master craftsman a silver image of the Goddess Tara, with necklaces, earrings, and headdress of pure gold, to be dedicated to the health and well-being of the Dalai Lama and his tutors, since my debt to them was so great. In her white form this gentle goddess was one of the most popular in Tibet. She is the patroness of longevity, and many, wishing long lives, recited diligently her mantra and meditated on her form.

When I was starting out on this lavish adventure in the arts, one of my students exclaimed: "Khyongla, you are simply crazy. Keep your money! The Chinese are going to drive us out of our country, and when they do, you will only be able to take your silver and gold with you—not your images. And you'll need every bit of it, not only to get out of Tibet, but also to exist wherever you may go." I replied that if I could now build up merit while I had the chance, my life would not be difficult wherever I might go. "But if I don't go on with this work," I said, "I shall be poor, even if I own a kingdom." My young friend replied, with a shake of his head, "From the point of view of religion, you may be right. But from any practical standpoint, you're making a big mistake." I had nothing to say to this last remark, and he added, while turning away, "But then, it's your money, after all!" Realizing that basically he was not unsympathetic to my project, I let him have his say; and when the work was done and he saw what a beautiful altar we had, he not only apologized for his earlier statements, but even declared with real feeling, "Now we have an image of the goddess such as everybody dreams of owning one day."

I have never regretted having had those thangkas and images made during my last days at home. When we were forced to flee and suffered real hardship and poverty, I never once wished for my money back—though it surely would have made my life easier. In this complex and turbulent modern world the gaining of spiritual merit through the practice of religion is very much harder than it used to be in our country; and what I most want for my next life, much more than material goods in this, is spiritual merit.

Shortly after the shrine had been completed, two Rato administrators arrived to ask me to let my name be put in nomination for the office of abbot of the monastery. The present incumbent, Losang, who in 1955 had succeeded Konchog (and who, just now, had become my pupil, auditing my sermons) was, after three years' service, about to retire, due to failing health. Only a few months later there came to me a letter from a friend in Dayab, informing me that my name had been proposed for the post of chogzed of the district. According to our ancient system, the few district heads, or rinpoches, were like local petty kings. All were high-ranking incarnations, and directly under them were the chogzeds. Each rinpoche functioned as the highest authority of his district, submitting to the Dalai Lama only in larger, national contexts, and the chogzed, meanwhile, took in charge all local secular affairs, reaching his decisions generally without even consulting the rinpoche. The office of chogzed was of the secular order, and yet often held by an incarnate lama, since many believed that a religious man would be more conscientiously devoted to the public welfare than others, and more considerate, consequently, of the poorer families in his district.

All of this was to me extremely unsettling news. I felt that in both situations my training and studies had not equipped me to deal with potentially explosive situations. In the case of Rato, I knew that I did not want to return to the confines of life in a monastery, now that I had established myself outside of it. As far as being chogzed, I was inexperienced in administration, and so felt that I would be unable to handle effectively any of the more serious problems that might develop. I knew nothing of practical affairs, and even less about the local politics of Dayab, and thought that I might even unwittingly bring harm to the very people who would be looking to me for guidance.

My wish to decline both posts was granted and I learned later, on reaching India, that the second candidate on the list for chogzed was appointed, and that he was then thrown into prison by the Communists, where he died.

The future seemed already upon us, but as though time could wait, there was to be one final Monlam during which, until the last minute of our way of life, the ancient traditions of our land would be honored.

In the middle of August, 1958, our young Dalai Lama took the first of his geshe lharampa examinations. Since he was a member of all three of the major monasteries, there would be three preliminary examinations, the first to be held in Drepung. On the first day, yellow hat in hand, the Dalai Lama listened carefully to each question and then putting on the hat, replied with quiet assurance; he would then remove his hat and again listen attentively to the next one.

The examination continued for some four to five hours, during the course of which fifteen challengers arose with questions. For me those hours passed quickly, fascinated as I was both by the Dalai Lama's answers and by the questions he himself posed. It might be argued that a Tibetan would naturally say that the incarnation of Chenresig was an extraordinary youth; but it is a fact that we were all struck by the wisdom and precision of his answers and by the composure and natural grace of his manner throughout at Drepung, Sera, and Gaden.

Inspired by these memorable events—undoubtedly the last of their kind that would ever be enacted in this cycle of time—I returned to my now beautiful apartment, to my teaching and to writing; for at the request and suggestion of the government I had lately begun the composition of a new Tibetan history, to be edited by His Holiness's junior tutor; and so I had much to occupy me in poring over rare and interesting old chronicles, histories of the country, as well as biographies of our early kings, Dalai Lamas, and Panchen Rinpoches. The Fifth Dalai Lama himself had composed a history, and before his time a number of other works of the kind had been written by learned Sakyapas and Kagyudpas. However, these had all stressed the religious side of our culture, whereas my own book was to emphasize the social and political parts and would be addressed to foreigners as well as to Tibetans. Such a work, it was hoped, would contribute to our struggle to maintain our independence. But since I had never in my life so much as seen a foreign book of any kind, I had no idea what approach to take, and my task was consequently extremely difficult. Indeed, it was not only difficult, but also possibly dangerous, since the Chinese now were attempting to prove that Tibet was historically and properly a province of imperial China. The last thing the Chinese would have liked would be for anyone to put forward an honest history, showing Tibet to have been from the beginning a very different land from theirs, occasionally invaded by foreigners, as in T'ang and Mongol times, but geographically, traditionally, spiritually, and politically an independent region. There were many ancient records in both the Potala and Norbulingka, including day-to-day accounts of the reigns of each of the Dalai Lamas; but since it would be dangerous and extremely unfortunate if the Chinese ever got wind of what I was doing, none of those precious documents could be delivered to my rooms. The most important, indeed essential, research materials were thus unavailable, and I had to pursue what researches I could mainly through secondary sources. But in the end, my history was not to get very far, after all—as events were soon to make known.

One morning, not long after His Holiness's preliminary examinations had been finished, one of the Rato administrators arrived to invite me to be one of the two scholars of our monastery who would serve as debating challengers of the Dalai Lama in his final examination at the Jokhang during Monlam. I was immensely pleased but hesitated for a moment, doubting whether I was up to the assignment. Having attended many of His Holiness's sermons, I knew how vast and deep his knowledge was. However, I also realized how rare an opportunity this would be for me—debating with the Dalai Lama was an experience not to be missed. There would be eighty of us, from ten colleges: three of Drepung's colleges, two of Sera's, two of Gaden's, mine at Rato, and the two great Tantric colleges, Gyudme and Gyudto. After a little thought, I plucked up courage, accepted the assignment, and a week later went out to the Norbulingka to learn what my charge was to be.

On the big day, the Dalai Lama was at ease. He smiled calmly at the monks in the great hall and again his answers were impressive. I was so caught up with my own anxieties, however, that I could not pay very close attention. When my turn came at last, I went forward, almost unconscious of everything but His Holiness, and my own confused state of mind. Striving to have a steady voice, I asked how meditation draws together all the Mahayana paths. This was a question that had always been most difficult for us all. It was also one of the most profound. The Dalai Lama, however, did not hesitate. He responded immediately, then clarified his points, which made me more uncertain of myself than ever. It reconfirmed my faith in him, however. The ease and clarity of his answer revealed to me, unquestionably, his innate knowledge of the truth. For half an hour our thrilling interchange continued until the senior tutor, my good friend Ling Rinpoche, raised his hand and I returned to my place, exceedingly joyful and relieved. I could now sit back and enjoy myself. At the end of that splendid afternoon His Holiness was as cheerful and fresh as he had been at the beginning. Long white scarves were presented to us all, and the multitude of people dispersed.

I returned for the evening event, which went on from five until ten; and the talk that I heard among all of the most important scholars present was entirely in praise of the Dalai Lama. "We have devoted our lives," they were saying, "to the study of the Doctrine. His Holiness is young and had many responsibilities that keep him from his studies. He receives visitors, gives lectures, travels to India and China, and is now deeply involved in this situation with the Communists. Yet he was able to answer every one of our questions correctly and with clarity, precision, and even elegance. For an ordinary man to have responded that way would have been impossible." "We are convinced," was the general verdict, "that he is truly the incarnation of Chenresig."

When I told the scholars I met in Europe of His Holiness's performance, many refused to believe me. They pointed out that in his autobiography he states, himself, that temporal affairs had made it impossible for him to pursue his studies properly, in the way of those great saints of the past whose entire lives had been devoted to the search for spiritual knowledge and enlightenment. I would reply—but to no effect—that he had said that simply because it was our custom, in the Gelugpa and Khadampa sects, not to write or talk about our own attainments, but to celebrate only those of others. We are to speak of our own qualifications only when the information contributes to the advancement of others, or of the Doctrine. For true knowledge can be attained only when sought for its own sake, not for the gaining of wealth, power, or renown; and I knew that the young Dalai Lama had grasped that true knowledge.

19.

My Flight to India

On the fifth day of March, 1959, the Dalai Lama, at the head of a long procession, left Lhasa for the Norbulingka. At the request of a wealthy merchant from Phari, who had ridden to Lhasa expressly to witness the Dalai Lama's examination, the Dalai Lama had graciously consented to deliver a series of sermons on Tantric themes in the residence known as Takten Migyur Phodang, the "Everlasting Unchanging Palace" at the Norbulingka. The palace had been expressly built for His Holiness at about the time of his visit to China in 1954 and served now as his summer home. I remember well how we had all wanted to contribute to its building, and how monks and lay folk alike had transported stones to the site to gain merit.

On the seventh of March, therefore, having received permission from His Holiness to attend, I walked out to the Norbulingka and the palace we had all helped build, to be present for the first of the sermons and to remain for a visit of three days. My two nights there I slept in the court chamberlain's apartment, and on the evening of the ninth of March, following the last sermon, walked back to Lhasa alone, meditating, as I strolled, upon all that I had heard and learned. That was the last event and stroll of that kind in my life.

For that evening, when I went to the Jokhang, I met in one of the top-floor chapels a company of my friends in a state of considerable agitation. One of them, an official who in the late 1940's had been our envoy to Nanking, explained to me that he had just received terrible news; that the Chinese general, commandant of their military post in Lhasa, had invited the Dalai Lama to attend a theatrical performance to be presented inside the encampment, requesting him to arrive without his usual retinue and with no more that two or three unarmed men as bodyguards. All members of the cabinet had also

received invitations, though not Thubten Woden nor any of our other
high officials normally in attendance on His Holiness wherever he
went. All Tibetans except the Dalai Lama and a few cabinet members
had always been forbidden to cross the stone bridge into the Chinese
camp, which in the past year had grown very large and was scarcely
two miles from the Norbulingka. Moreover, since no Dalai Lama had
ever been known to leave his residence without an armed guard and
retinue, this invitation seemed additionally ominous. We all realized
that it represented a real and serious breach of diplomatic protocol,
and my experienced friend greatly feared that His Holiness was in
danger of being kidnapped. For in Eastern Tibet, as he told me, those
high lamas who had accepted Chinese invitations to attend parties of
this kind had never again been heard from. No one knew what had
become of them, whether they were murdered or taken to China. I
had never heard of such things before, and when I returned that night
to my apartment I was so frightened I could not sleep, but tossed
about thinking only of what might happen the next day.

That morning the little twelve-year-old novice who had lately
been staying with me went to the market, and when he failed to return
after a couple of hours, I became anxious—there were now so many
rumors about as to what was happening in the city. At last he
appeared and told me that he had seen hundreds of people leaving
the city, running toward the Norbulingka. Somebody had told him
that they were going to try to stop the Dalai Lama from crossing the
stone bridge into the Chinese camp. And on the Barkor he had seen
hundreds of marching women, shouting: "Tibet is for Tibetans!"
"Let the Chinese go back to China!" "We are an independent
country!" He had also seen some *rajyapas* ("outcast undertakers")
bearing off the body of a young Sera monk who had just been beaten
to death. As I later learned, this young monk, Phakphala Khenchung
by name, who held a minor post in the Norbulingka, had been riding
his bicycle on the way to his job, disguised in a Chinese uniform,
when the crowd, mistaking him for an enemy soldier, fell upon him
and killed him. I had not known the young monk personally, but had

seen him many times. His brother was a high-ranking incarnation from Chamdo with whom I had occasionally attended lectures. Hearing his name and all this frightening news, I was deeply shocked and though I knew that it was now dangerous in the streets, I could not remain indoors but went out repeatedly on exploring trips—seeing nothing, however, of the terrible events of that day but only people running through the streets. A little later I learned from a neighbor that Samdup Phodrang, a distinguished member of the Seventh Dalai Lama's family, who had recently been appointed to the cabinet but was not well-known in Lhasa, had driven to the gates of the Norbulingka in his own car, accompanied by a Chinese officer. The crowd, assuming that the car was Chinese and the officer coming to take the Dalai Lama away, began hurling stones. Samdup, struck in the head and knocked unconscious, was hurriedly driven to the Indian Consulate, where he was treated and in a day or two recovered. Then—as I learned some time later in India—he gave speeches over loudspeakers, warning our people that if they continued to resist, the Chinese would destroy our temples.

Hatred of the Chinese had in fact now reached such a pitch in Lhasa that an attack on their occupying soldiers might have occurred at any moment, which would have set off a chain reaction of the greatest violence. The Tibetans had a few modern guns, some cannons and machine guns, but would have been no match at all for the occupation. There had been some fighting between Khampas and Chinese the year before, in southern Tibet, and at that time we had all been heartened on hearing rumors that firearms had been dropped to our people from an airplane. We had no idea who might have sent the guns, but imagined that some big country was helping us. Now, however, it was clear to us that there was not going to be any help of that kind and, furthermore, that there were just too many Chinese and Chinese guns.

I was so upset that day that I continually paced the floor, my mind shot through with questions: What now would happen to the Lord Buddha's teaching? What would happen to our nation? What fate would befall the Dalai Lama and my friends, his tutors, if actual fighting broke out? And what could any one person do to prevent the clash of these explosive forces now confronting each other?

I had no answers to those questions, nor had anyone else in Lhasa; but by the next day I had come to the realization that for the Dalai Lama at least there were only three possibilities: either to escape from Tibet, or else, on being taken to the Chinese camp, either be killed or be sent as a prisoner to Peking. But where might he seek refuge? I had a vague idea that he would be welcomed in the United States, which was, at that time at least, the strongest opponent of Chinese Communist aggression. But the United States was on the opposite side of the globe, so far away that its daytime was our night. Furthermore, as I had been told, it was an altogether different civilization, a completely different world from ours.

In a mood of utter desperation, realizing that I might never again lay eyes on the Dalai Lama, I decided to go at once to the Norbulingka and seek his blessing and that of his tutors. I also thought that I might learn something there about the actual situation to help me decide what I myself should do. All the high officials, including Thubten Woden, had been out there since the trouble started, and all that we in Lhasa were hearing were rumors. It was too dangerous for our leaders to appear in the streets. As I hurried anxiously along the streets I heard the loudspeakers, which had been mounted on buildings occupied by the Chinese, warning our people not to revolt against their true friends, the same Chinese; not to listen to reactionaries like Thubten Woden and the Minister Surkhang.

While still some distance from the Norbulingka, I could see that the crowd which had gathered before the gates the previous day was not only still there, but had grown to several thousand people. It was rumored that the Dalai Lama had declined the Chinese invitation mainly because the people would not have allowed him to leave the palace. When I reached the gates, after forcing my way through the gathering, I found Tibetan soldiers on duty and the regular bodyguards of His Holiness, along with a great number of volunteer civilians and an efficient-looking troop of Khampa insurgents.

At first I was refused entry, but I patiently stood my ground until some of the soldiers of the bodyguard finally recognized me and, after a brief consultation, let me pass. I went directly to Ling Rinpoche's apartment, whom I found putting on his robes to join the junior tutor in the palace, to pray there to Mahakala and the other protective deities for the preservation of our religion. When he left, I hurried over to Trijang Rinpoche's apartment, but he too had gone to the palace and would not be back for several hours. I called next on Thubten Woden. His reception room was crowded with relatives and friends who had fled from the city, fearing that the Chinese would soon be firing on Lhasa, and had imagined that they would be safe within the walls of the Norbulingka. These people felt protected in the presence of the Dalai Lama, and in any case wished to share his fate. Before I could ask any questions of my friend the chamberlain, he turned to me and said seriously: "The situation is very grave. We do not even know what the immediate future holds." As there was obviously not only nothing that I could do, but also no place for me in the palace, I left, to hurry back to Lhasa, and had no trouble at all passing out again through the gates.

The crowd was restless and anxious, but nothing much was happening. On the way back to the city two people stopped and asked me: "Is it true that the Dalai Lama has already left the Norbulingka?" I was suspicious, thinking they might be spies, for it was well known that I was close to Thubten Woden and the tutors. I answered that because of all the confusion within the compound I had heard nothing, and hurried on.

I had to get back before dark, when the doors of our building would be bolted. Every night great wooden beams were fixed across the door, and in the courtyard there were now heaps of stones to be hurled in case of attack. Somewhere in the house there might have been a pistol or two, but those stones were the only weapons I knew about. Nor was there any definite plan of action for those within the building, should there be an attack. I knew that as a monk I could not participate in acts of violence, but had no idea what else I might do. Sometimes I imagined that since I had never participated in any anti-

Chinese or political activities at all, I might perhaps be safe; but at other times I was simply frightened, remembering stories I had heard of the violent things the Chinese were doing to monks in the Kham.

I reached the Phala mansion without incident, but next morning the first thing I heard was that the Chinese now had trained their big guns on the Norbulingka and Jokhang, ready to be fired at the slightest provocation. "They can completely demolish Lhasa in an hour," I was told. In fact, just after I had left the Norbulingka the night before, two shells had actually been fired, but had landed harmlessly on the palace grounds. I realized that the attack had really begun, and it would only be a matter of time before they started shelling Lhasa. I made up my mind to head immediately for Rato, which would at least be on the road of escape to India.

I hurried first to warn the Mene Thangs, who immediately declared that they would come with us. Then I ran back to my apartment, where my attendant, Tenpa Dargye, urged me to take along the golden headdress, earrings, and other ornaments of the White Tara figure on my altar. I at first agreed to this and we removed them, thinking that later, when hungry, we might sell them: but then I reconsidered, for our religion teaches that it is better to go hungry than to sell the sacred images of those gods in whom we take refuge. So I put all the golden ornaments back where they belonged. In that excitement, possessions seemed meaningless. I packed almost nothing and—unfortunately—left every bit of my research materials, notes, and the few pages already written of my history of Tibet just where they were. Only when I reached Rato did I realize that I had forgotten all of that material, and that I had now to get away entirely before the Chinese found it. Escape was no longer a matter of choice for me.

Before quitting Lhasa I had gone for a last visit to the Jokhang to pray for all Tibetans, for a long life to the Dalai Lama, and that the angry Chinese might be somehow prevented from wiping out all of our culture. Returning to the apartment, I found a company of my friends there, who had come to say goodbye. It was a heart-sickening separation. They were all in tears, fearful of the future, quietly weeping while Tenpa Dargye and I gathered up our things. The

Mene Thangs had arranged with a villager who had come to town with his produce to take us and our baggage in his wagon as far as Nyethang, about twenty miles west of Lhasa on the road to Rato; and he was already waiting outside. When we had loaded, we had him drive on ahead to Dagna Lubug, while Tenpa Dargye and I kept a little distance behind. We passed a number of houses with Chinese faces at the windows, anxiously watching the street. When we came to the Mene Thangs' gate we stopped while they and their servant clambered aboard with their one small box of clothes. Tenpa Dargye and I then climbed in too and we all rode together for a while. But at Dungar Pass we all got down and walked, letting the wagon go on well ahead; for we were approaching the huge Chinese camp. I wondered how many big guns they had. We casually sauntered past the camp, as though out for a stroll in the suburbs. Some of the soldiers kept their rifles pointed at us, but they let us pass without incident. The road then became narrow and along the cliffs above us we could see Chinese soldiers building pillboxes. Though we were now walking quite separately, as though strangers, trying not to hurry, I was terribly afraid that soldiers would stop us. Far ahead of us, we saw the Chinese stop and search the wagon, opening all the baggage; but when they found no weapons, or anything else suspicious, they let the driver go on. And when we had gone about a mile further, we realized that we had passed the Chinese lines. What a relief! But though we had passed through, we were still anxious for Lhasa, for the Dalai Lama and our friends.

Just before reaching Lha Chenpo (a name meaning the "Great Image," for there is a huge figure of the Lord Buddha there carved into the living rock), we were brought to a full stop. The road there was narrow, with a small tributary of the Kyichu River running to one side of it and on the other a steep ridge rising. There was a barricade before us, formed of hundreds of large rocks. Our hearts sank—we were trapped. It was impossible for the wagon to go on.

At a loss, we discussed what to do. The Mene Thangs suggested turning back and heading for Drepung. I was a member there, and they themselves would find shelter somewhere close by. That seemed our best alternative; and the wagon had just turned when suddenly we heard, beyond the barrier, a galloping rider coming our way from Lha Chenpo. At the wall he drew to a quick stop and, dismounting, scrambled over. Running after us, he called in Tibetan to ask our destination. To our relief, he was not Chinese, but a heavily armed Khampa, and we told him that we had been trying to get to Nyethang but because of the blocked road had just turned back. He sharply sized us up, then warned us not to attempt any such thing. No one was being allowed, he said, to travel now toward Lhasa; the Khampas guarding the mountain ridge directly above us had orders to shoot anyone who tried. (As we later learned, the Dalai Lama was escaping that night from the Norbulingka, and these were the native arrangements made to protect him.) The man who had thus saved our lives began pushing some of the big rocks away, and we helped him pile them by the side of the road until there was room for the wagon to pass. We then put them back into place and thanked the good man, going our way relieved but heavy-hearted. For that barrier, temporary and makeshift though it was, symbolized the finality of the step we had just taken. We all knew at that moment that we should never again see Lhasa.

A little further along we came on a group of thirty or forty mounted Khampas. I recognized among them two monks I had known in Rato, now in Khampa dress, bearing guns and swords like the rest. Monks, unless they have renounced their vows, cannot enter armies or bear arms, and in general the renouncing of vows and then taking them up again is forbidden. However, when conditions make it impossible to continue as a monk, this may be justified, and these two had renounced their vows to help repel the Chinese. They recognized me at once and told the company that I too was from Rato, whereupon all the Khampas immediately became very friendly, asking for my blessing and for protection cords, images, or any other religious articles I might have—though I had nothing of the kind. The two monks ultimately escaped to India, as I learned when I met them a few months later in Assam.

Having been permitted to pass on, we were presently approaching a little temple to the Green Tara, Dölma Lhakhang, when we met a villager I knew who invited us to his home. We were extremely tired, all having walked most of the way, for with six people, and but one mule drawing the wagon, each had ridden only a little part of the journey. Moreover, we had all lifted and rolled those heavy stones, and all of this under the greatest tension. With heartfelt thanks we bade goodbye to the owner of the wagon, who, when he had discharged us, turned to drive to his own village. It was with a real sense of relief that we entered the villager's house to sit down awhile in safety. As we rested he confided to us that he was about to join up with the Khampas, and two days later I learned that he had actually left and joined the resistance.

We rested only an hour, then again set off for the two miles to Rato. On the road we encountered a large party of about a hundred Rato monks coming from the direction of the monastery. They told us that a government messenger had, the day before, arrived from Lhasa, warning that the Chinese might be coming through that night and must be stopped at all costs. The reason, of course, was to protect the Dalai Lama's escape, but none of us at the time knew this. The monks had simply obeyed official orders, not really knowing what was expected of them, and had spent the night at watch on the road, some in monk's robes, some in lay clothes, others in a strange mixture of styles. The only weapons among them were some heavy sticks and a few old-fashioned guns. Luckily for them, the Chinese did not come through that night for if they had, these monks would surely have been slaughtered.

When at last we arrived at the monastery, everyone was in a state of great excitement and uncertainty. Some asked whether I thought they should remain or try to escape, to which I could answer only that I knew as little about the situation as they, but that it was clearly dangerous and each would have to decide for himself. The one thing of which I could be certain was that in my own case my reputation was such that I simply had to escape, by whatever means.

I found rooms in the village for the Mene Thangs, and thought I would pause a few days in Rato to gather strength and courage for the journey. But when a couple of my students only two days later went out to reconnoiter for news of Lhasa, they got only as far as Lha Chenpo. They returned in a great fright to report that they had heard the big guns of the Chinese and seen many monks on the road in flight from Drepung. Wanting to make sure, I walked down to the main highway to India from Lhasa, and I saw there hundreds of fleeing monks, many of whom I knew. They told me that the shelling had started the morning of the previous day (March 20) and that they had seen the Norbulingka under fire. Some had climbed to the mountain summit behind the monastery, where they had a good view of Lhasa, and had seen the Ramoche Temple burning and the city itself being bombarded by heavy guns. They had then escaped, going down the back of the mountain and cutting cross-country to this road.

Hearing that, I returned in the greatest haste to Rato, where I heard a rumor that the Chinese were approaching the monastery from the rear. Fortunately, it proved false, but it confirmed me in my decision to flee. Tenpa Dargye begged to go with me, whether for better or for worse, and my cousin Nyima, a novice, pleaded, weeping that he would not be able to bear being left behind. I agreed to take them both. A married couple from Dayab, Dawa Apho and his wife, whose sons were members of the monastery and who were living in the village below Rato, presented us with a mule. A number of friends advised us not to bring along any valuables, since in situations of this kind there might be robbers who would murder us—but others suggested that we should take as much as we could. As it turned out, since we had only that single mule, we could carry little more than our food supplies: a supply of tsampa, dried meat, tea and butter, some paper money, and our warmest clothes. I had also a box of gold jewelry that the wife of a Khampa in Lhasa had entrusted to my care, and a gold-lined wooden drinking bowl that Thubten Woden had one day left in my apartment (when we later met in India I was able to return these to their owners). Abandoned were all my beautiful images and thangkas, ceremonial robes, soft rugs, and books. When I applied to the abbot for permission to leave the request was immediately granted, and we set off about four o'clock that afternoon.

I had sent word to the Mene Thangs, who joined us on the road, and that night we stopped at a farm belonging to my khamtsen, about ten miles from the monastery, not far from the Tsangpo River. The abbot of Loseling College, Drepung, arrived on horseback with a company of his students, so exhausted they had to lift him from the saddle. The caretaker of the farm, shocked by the news we brought of Lhasa, was wonderfully helpful to us all and sincerely concerned to help us on. He gave me a second mule to ride, to which we transferred our luggage, taking turns riding the other. But most of the time, at Nyima and Tenpa Dargye's insistence, I rode since not only was I considerably older than they, but also—and this was decisive—I was their teacher. I often argued to let one of them take the mule while I walked, but usually they refused. I have had in my time a great many students, but those two were the kindest: completely loyal and selfless when my life was most difficult and in danger.

Together with the abbot of Loseling and his party, we left the farm early next morning, and with a villager whom we had hired to be our guide, crossed the Tsangpo. He brought us to a shallow place, where the river could be forded, and we rode on mule and horseback, two on each mount going over, so that one could return to pick up another rider. In a village nearby we had breakfast, trading dry tea for fresh-brewed. When we had been there about an hour some of those who had been fighting in the Norbulingka arrived, a number of them badly wounded, with horror stories of the devastation they had left behind. They told of how they had escaped when the Norbulingka lay smoking in ruins, and of how many had been killed while they crossed the river at Ramagan Ferry. There had been no boats, and since Tibetans generally cannot swim, they had crossed as a human chain of about twenty people holding hands, wading with the water well above their waists. The Chinese spotted them from a hilltop and opened fire with machine guns, killing most of the party outright, while others drowned.

Our next problem was to climb "Sandy Mountain," Mount Chela, and we reached the summit in about three hours, where again we rested. The descent was a good deal easier than the climb, since the trail was sandy and we slid down on foot—I was reminded of this when I saw my first movie of people on skis. We again arrived at the banks of the Tsangpo, where about a hundred people waited to be ferried across. Khampa soldiers were helping load the coracles, of which there were a good many on the river, and it was not long before we all found space. The mules and horses swam across, and we were all constantly on the lookout. But there were no signs anywhere of the Chinese.

After trudging along the bank a few miles, we reached a village called Happy Valley, Kyishong, where there was a monastery of the Sakyapa sect known as Ramad which had always had an informal "mutual aid pact" with Rato. We asked them for shelter, and they made us welcome in comfortable quarters, and told us, furthermore, something that we were relieved and delighted to hear—namely that the Dalai Lama and his party had crossed the river there on the way south and stopped the night at the monastery. It was a large party, they said, and they had not known which was His Holiness, for to prevent recognition he was wearing Khampa dress in his flight and assumed no special privileges. So far so good! That was our first news from actual witnesses of the Dalai Lama's escape from the Norbulingka, but there was still a great way to go, and we were all as much concerned for his safety as for our own.

Two hard days of travel brought us to the town of Chong Gye, where the Fifth Dalai Lama had been born. Mene Thang knew the district officer there, but on going to his residence found only the officer's wife at home. The officer had left on a mission with the Khampa soldiers, but the good woman received us and arranged for Nyima, Tenpa Dargye, and me to stay in the nearby Riwodechan Monastery, where I knew a number of the students. The Mene Thangs remained but one night at the district officer's home, then found a room in the Peri Monastery, which was one of the Nyingmapa sect. For several days we all rested in comfort.

Each day monks from every part of Tibet and lay people of all classes arrived, many with news of terrible looting and slaughter in Lhasa. One of the Norbulingka chapel keepers gave an account of the horrible battle there, where so many Tibetans were killed. He had himself escaped by jumping into a canal that ran through the park, which he then followed to its source in a river outside the walls. Hiding in various shelters along the increasingly dangerous route, he had had next to nothing to eat, and so I shared with him some of our dried meat, barley flour, and tea. He was an older man and altogether exhausted. He declared he could go no further, and I fear he never reached the border.

The second or third day of our stay in Chong Gye we paid a visit to the little village of Tradug, a few hours' ride away, to see a famous temple built by King Songtsen Gampo in the eighth century. A Khampa leader from Dayab who was there said he was pleased to see me in monk's robes, it being unusual now to see a monk. Most had changed to laymen's clothing, so that if the Chinese came they should not be put to torture. I explained that I had had to flee in haste and had no laymen's clothes. On the way back to the monastery we stopped between Tradug and Riwodechen at one of Thubten Woden's estates, where the very friendly manager who invited us to remain a few days brought out laymen's clothing and strongly advised us to put it on; so we all changed.

Back in Chong Gye at the monastery, one night we heard the sound of big guns from the direction of Tsethang, the next district eastward. Then we heard guns from the other direction, and, feeling that we were in danger of being surrounded, we prepared to set off next day at sunrise, again heading directly south. Soldiers who had escaped from Tsethang, some recovering from wounds, were staying in many houses in the village. We learned from them that a big battle had begun there when the Khampas trapped about a hundred Chinese who had dug in on a hill. We asked about the road south, and they advised that when passing through their lines it would be safest for us if I carried a letter from the office of the Volunteer Khampa Association, whose present center of operations was in this town. Nyima sought the place out and got the pass without difficulty; but he was gone about two hours, during all of which time I saw many Khampas hurriedly leaving the houses in which they had been staying and heading for the road south. By the time Nyima reappeared with our pass, the village was all but empty, and I felt strongly that we too should begin moving. However, when the villager in whose house I had been awaiting Nyima's return saw my attendant with our pass, he declared that he and his family wished to escape with us, and started packing their belongings. Hours passed and night fell as we waited impatiently for them to finish. During that time the Chinese sent messengers, mostly Tibetans, through our lines, telling everyone that the Communists would not harm any of the villagers but were only fighting the armed forces. Hearing this, the villager for whom we had been waiting suddenly decided that he and his family would do better trusting the Chinese than chancing it with their possessions on the road.

It was now very late and dark, so we asked the villager to find someone who could show us the way to Peri Monastery, where the Mene Thangs were staying, and he found us a deaf-mute. When we arrived so late at the monastery, the monks, not surprisingly, were afraid to let us in, declaring that the Chinese were very near and that our presence might endanger them. We pleaded that we could not go on that night since we did not know the roads and might run into the Chinese. So they let us stay, but only on the porch; nor would they let us see the Mene Thangs—whom we did not see again until weeks later, far to the south.

The monks sent us away the next morning before dawn, and we traveled all day with our two mules as fast as we could over steep rocky hills and mountains; when night fell we had not yet seen a village. The air at that altitude was chilly, and all three of us were very tired. We searched for dried cow dung for a fire, settled down to sleep on our single rug, and woke the next morning for another such difficult day. Two evenings later we reached the village of Zurbud, where there was a large mansion owned by an aristocratic Lhasa family. We did not know them, but luckily, when we introduced ourselves, they had heard of me in Lhasa and hospitably took us in, offering not only a night's lodging but also a substantial meal. Hardly had we settled down, when someone arrived with the news that the Chinese had now reached the village of Degug, only a few days' journey away, where the Khampa volunteers had first met to found their organization. We knew that we could not stay. The Lhasa householders themselves began packing, and abandoning even the idea of a night's sleep, we bade them a hurried goodbye and set out again at about ten that night with our two fatigued mules.

A strong wind was blowing, and snow began to fall as we climbed another steep mountain, in the extreme cold. Not only were we exhausted, but Nyima and I had developed fierce headaches, and presently seized with cramps, both of us began to vomit violently. Alternating riding on the mule, we nevertheless pressed on, and halfway up the mountain came upon a shepherd's camp, where the family, roused from sleep, took us in and immediately made a fire in their yak-hair tent. The heat did us wonders and soon we began to feel life returning. They served us buttered tea and such a delicious soup that I can still recall its flavor. In the morning we gave them our heartfelt thanks, and some money to repay them for our visit. All that day we climbed still another mountain.

Not very far along, we overtook a large group of Tibetan refugees who had a few spare donkeys, and when I asked if we could have a couple to get ourselves up the mountain, one for Nyima and the other for Tenpa Dargye, they agreed to let us have two for a fee of six Tibetan dollars. However, Tenpa Dargye now refused to ride, insisting that there were thousands of refugees on foot and that he also preferred walking; besides, said he, the weather was cold, and walking kept one warm. So Tenpa Dargye walked while Nyima and I rode to the summit, where Nyima declared that he would wait to return his mount to the group from whom it had been rented. Tenpa Dargye and I continued down the other slope; and after a few hours— as Nyima later explained to us—when his party failed to appear, he rode back down to see what had happened. He found that the donkey owner's wife had stopped by the roadside to have a baby. It was still snowing heavily and two men held a blanket above her for protection. Nyima returned their animal, walked up the hill again, and then rejoined us in the Tsona Valley.

There were many small villages in this area, and that night we stopped in a house with a hot spring running underneath that kept it comfortably heated, so that when I spread our old rug out on that floor we had a bed that was snug and warm, and the best night's sleep we three had had in weeks. No one by now would have taken me for a monk in my bedraggled chuba, and it was only when I spoke to the villagers that they realized I was not one of them but a refugee in flight. In the morning, I learned from our host that one of the chief governors of the southern districts, a monk official I had known in Lhasa, had a residence nearby. I called upon the man, hoping for information concerning the region through which we would have to pass. He gave us excellent directions, even providing us with dry tea, some meat, fodder for our mules, and best of all, he assigned two villagers to guide us to the top of the great ridge that now rose before us, directly south from the valley.

The snow had been falling for two days and was so deep that it would have been extremely difficult, indeed probably impossible, for any stranger to find and follow the dim trail. It proved to be no more than a winding path used by local herders to bring their yaks down from the high pastures. It was not only invisible, but also extremely steep and slippery, so that without these knowledgeable villagers we should never have found our way. Great drifts lay to either side, and the snow continued to fall.

In one place our baggage mule lost her footing and tumbled into a deep snowbank. We all five struggled to extricate the helpless beast, but every moment only sank her deeper. One of our guides pulled stoutly at her head while Nyima pushed at her rump when suddenly the sole of Nyima's woolen boot fell off and disappeared into the snow. This was a very serious matter. His whole foot was bare, and all he could do at the time was to wrap a scarf around it and keep pushing at the mule. After a lot of huffing and tugging, the beast was finally brought safely to her feet, with none of our meager baggage lost. This cheered us and our spirits were further lightened when the snow stopped. Nyima rewrapped the scarf securely about his foot, we rested briefly, and were off again.

Several times we had met others on the way to the top of the mountain, villagers with yaks heading down the slope, and refugees like ourselves climbing up. But we were alone when, at last, we approached the summit, and saw its cluster of tattered prayer flags. The usual pile of rocks, or *latse*, was nearby, to which we added one of our own, calling out as we set it in its place, "*Lha gyallon*," "Victory to the gods." Our guides then bade us farewell. We paid them for their valiant help, they turned back down the trail, and once again we were on our own.

Gazing southward from our great height, we discovered in the distance far below, a broad valley where Nyima declared he could see green trees. Suddenly the sun broke through the clouds and the sky became a brilliant transparent blue. The light reflected from the untouched snow, however, was so harsh that both Nyima and Tenpa Dargye soon suffered from snow blindness. They tried to save themselves by tying their protection cords over their eyes, but Tenpa Dargye was soon so severely afflicted he could scarcely see to walk. By a miracle (as it seemed), though I had left so much behind, I had taken along a pair of sunglasses and could lead them down; and as we gradually, painfully descended, the snow on the ground disappeared, rain began to fall, and the air became first warm, then almost tropical. There was green grass all about and there were thickets of bamboo. Although my two friends' eyes presently cleared, they were both in pain the rest of the day.

We reached a village at nightfall, where the houses stood on stilts and were constructed of interwoven strips of a light and pliant wood. We asked at one of these for shelter and were admitted by a Tibetan who gave us a comfortable room, warning us, however, not to let our mules eat any of the foliage round about as it would make them sick. They should be given only fresh leaves of bamboo. Nyima, borrowing

Tenpa Dargye's shoes, went out into the forest to cut bamboo for our mules' fodder, while Tenpa Dargye busied himself preparing a meal for us in the family kitchen. When Nyima returned, he was covered with blood and we jumped in alarm, but he reassured us—the blood was from the hundreds of leeches in the saturated forest, and there were plenty of them clinging to him still. He asked for snuff. Someone had just told him that snuff sprinkled on leeches would make them fall off. We dusted him with snuff, and we washed away the blood. I had meanwhile bought at a nearby inn a pair of soles for Nyima's boots, and that evening our host himself kindly stitched them to the cloth tops.

The next day's trek brought us to Mong Mong, where we put up in a little temple. While Tenpa Dargye and Nyima rested there, I went for a stroll around the village and ran into a monk I knew from Namgyal Datsang, the Dalai Lama's college in the Potala. He was draped in a ragged brown peasant's chuba, and when he told me that he had fled with no possessions but his wristwatch, I invited him to come eat with us. Though our supply of tsampa was low, Tenpa Dargye made buttered tea and added dried meat to the soup. It was not much of a meal, but it used up all our tsampa, and so next day we did without breakfast. Nyima went to the village to buy barley from the farmers and came back with a small supply, which he and Tenpa Dargye then roasted and took to the local mill, where it was stone-ground into flour.

We spent one more night in the little temple and next day set out in the rain, taking our new friend along with us. Between us we had one umbrella which somebody in the village had given me. The ground was soggy, our feet were sopping wet, and the lower parts of our chubas clung thickly to our legs. One of my shoes completely disintegrated; some time later in a village through which we passed, a sympathetic man, noticing my problem, handed me a substantial pair. Most of these people of the Mon district were poor, and their villages small and humble, but they had very generous hearts and we received welcomes wherever we paused. Their territory had been divided by the so-called McMahon Line into a northern part, assigned to Tibet, and a southern, to India; but the people themselves were Tibetans, and their friendliness was the same when we had crossed the invisible line as it had been before.

We had become, of course, more and more excited as we neared the border. It seemed to me that we had escaped, but my friends were still afraid for they thought that even in Indian territory we still could be in danger. At the border there would be only a few Indian guards and the Chinese could easily capture and drag us back. Indeed, at Chhutangmo, the first Indian outpost, all that we found was a bamboo hut and we had to wait several days there before the officer in charge got in touch with New Delhi and issued us an Indian pass. The entire area was crowded with Tibetan refugees. A few lucky people slept under waterproof sheets or tent covers, but all the rest slept in the open. Rain continued to fall heavily; for the monsoon season in Mon for that year had just started.

One of the minor officers in the Indian bamboo hut, a Tibetan serving as interpreter, invited me to sleep in his quarters while he and his wife moved to the office. Nyima took shelter in a nearby cave, one of many in the neighborhood, while Tenpa Dargye, like so many others, slept under a tent cover outside. We worried constantly about our food supply. Our tsampa was diminishing daily and if the Indians held us up much longer we should have nothing at all to eat.

One morning the sun came out for a few hours, and at last we could dry our clothes. Every day we asked if there were news of our families and though there was never anything, the interpreter did pass on to us one day a welcome report: the Dalai Lama had arrived safely in a hill station, Mussoorie, north of Delhi, in the foothills of the Himalayas.

The Indian government had been quick, we learned, to make arrangements for His Holiness and his retinue, providing him with a large mansion belonging to a wealthy family. His first act, on arrival, had been to request aid for the refugees now pouring over the border in flight from pursuing Chinese. We were greatly heartened to learn that the Dalai Lama had himself reached safety and that his first thought had been for his people. By the end of the week there were indeed thousands of Tibetans camping miserably in the vicinity of Chhuthangmo.

The problems of shelter and food were acute, and everybody was anxious to get well beyond the border, deeper into the safety of India before the Chinese army arrived. We divided into groups of about a hundred, each with an elected leader, and gathered to discuss who should be the first to leave when permission finally was granted. There were only a few families with children, but there were many wounded from the battles in Tibet, and there were also many monks. Everyone agreed that the wounded and sick should be moved first, and then high officials, abbots, and incarnations, since these would be in the gravest danger if they fell into Chinese hands.

Nyima took a long walk one day to a place from which he could see the escape route from Tibet and watch for the Mene Thangs. He talked with some people who had just arrived, and was told that a large group of our countrymen had lately been trapped and massacred not far from the Indian border. A couple of Chinese masquerading as Khampas had offered to guide and help them as they were approaching the line. The Tibetans, deceived, followed them, and when they had gone a few miles, a Chinese company attacked, slaughtering most of them and taking the rest prisoners. On hearing this, we could only fear for our friends, who might have been among that unhappy lot.

Meanwhile, the Indian officers, through interpreters, were taking notes on everybody, asking who we were, by what route we had come, what fighting we had witnessed, and, above all, for what reasons we had fled. One day, the welcome news arrived at last that I, as an incarnation, was to be included in the first group to depart, and to our great relief, both Nyima and Tenpa Dargye would be coming with me. We had been worried that we might be separated, and so lose touch with each other. India is so vast and populous that it might have taken weeks, months, even years, before we met again, if ever.

Early next morning, we left with our group of about a hundred, some riding, others walking. As we passed through the village its kind inhabitants who had assembled gave us butter and tsampa and distributed twenty Tibetan dollars to each abbot, geshe, and incarnation. The interpreter, who had been acting as our host, then took pictures of us all, and for the next five days we trudged unendingly over mountains and through valleys, attended by Indian guards. The air was hot and wet, the trees and plants were tropical, and all the way there was a plague of leeches that wriggled into our clothes and even into our boots. We slept usually in shepherds' camps, or found rooms occasionally in villages. Sometimes Nyima and Tenpa Dargye, who were both among those on foot, lagged far behind, for it was a long and miserable march to Tawang.

Along the way there were frequently friendly Monpas by the roadside offering butter and tsampa as we passed. At one point an old monk, who had been educated in Tibet, awaited the passing of one of the members of our group—the young reincarnation of Pabongkha Rinpoche, whose predecessor had been not only my own teacher but also the teacher of this monk. He stopped me as I rode by and asked me to point out to him the seventeen-year-old successor of our teacher. When I did, the young Rinpoche joined us, and we found a green spot by the road, settled down, and together enjoyed a marvelously refreshing occasion. The old monk had generously brought with him a supply of prepared buttered tea, cooked rice, cooked vegetables, and meat. Afterward we rejoined our company, and later that same day arrived in Tawang, not far from where the Sixth Dalai Lama had been born. There, we were conducted to a famous monastery, which had been one of thirteen founded and established by the great Fifth Dalai Lama. The monks came out to greet us and invited our abbots and incarnations to stay. Together with Nyima and Tenpa Dargye, I was assigned a place in the chapel chamber.

The day after we arrived, we heard a helicopter flying overhead and were told that the Indian Government was delivering rice to us. But the day was very foggy, and evidently they could not see us; the plane failed to drop its cargo, and we soon heard it fly away. Next day, however, the helicopter returned and, since the weather had improved, they could now see us and bags were let fall, containing rice enough for us all. Furthermore, many Monpas kindly came to us with food and distributed coins; so that we were now actually being very well taken care of.

One morning I was startled to see a Chinese in Tibetan dress appear suddenly in my chapel room. He could speak a little Tibetan and immediately told me that the Communists were very bad, and that he had joined the Khampas who had given him his clothes. He had come to beg from me something to eat, and complained that since he had no bowl he could never get hot soup or tea. Then he asked for mine, and though at first I hesitated—for I had only my monk's bowl—he began to weep so bitterly that I let him have it. When I told my two companions of this visit, they laughed, asking me to show them how I was going to drink tea with my hands. Later on my generous Tawang hosts presented me with a large wooden bowl, and so my case was not so desperate after all.

Refugees were pouring in every day and the district of Tawang was becoming crowded. Many could find no shelter and were sleeping in little tents or under protective sheets; those who had nothing more would hang a raincoat up on sticks. We found it extremely hot, and the ground was damp from the incessant rains. Thousands arrived on mules or horses, which they sold at very low prices just to have a little cash (one of my friends, for example, let his horse go for only five rupees). Most of those who had left Chong Gye after our departure had been forced to take an even more difficult route than ours, through extremely mountainous country, avoiding all roads and trails; for the Chinese had now gained control of a great part of the South and were trying to prevent our people from escaping. Hundreds arrived completely exhausted by the hardships they had endured. As for myself, I had now lost both of our precious mules. We had pastured them outside the monastery walls, but when I one day went to look for them they were gone.

And then one fine morning the Mene Thangs appeared. They had just reached Tawang and came directly to visit me, and though it was an immense relief to see them both alive, it was saddening, too, since the old man wept continually from sheer exhaustion. They had left four weeks after us, had had a very rough trip, and were now camped nearby in the open.

Exactly one week after our arrival in Tawang, Nyima, Tenpa Dargye, and I were informed that we were to take off next day with the first group of one hundred for Assam. I would now greatly miss our mules, for the road went up and down rugged hills, sometimes over steep mountains, and I had never been much of a hiker. Among the refugees I had a number of generous friends, however, and one of these, Gyalsay Rinpoche, had three horses. He rode one, his attendants two, and every so often he would himself dismount and allow me to ride a while. But since he then had to walk, I was uncomfortable in his saddle and never rode longer than an hour.

One day, under these conditions, another monk and I became so tired that we asked to be allowed to remain overnight in a village that we were passing. Here and there along the way bamboo huts had been built for the refugees, but the next set were miles ahead, and we felt that we would never make it. However, the members of our group were not permitted to break ranks, and so permission was denied us. On and on we trudged, until at nightfall we arrived before a small house in which there were some Indian police quartered. We asked if we could remain there for the night, but this plea too was denied. The others had already passed on, far ahead, and so two Indian guards were detailed to us, for the night was dark, and the path, by moonlight, difficult to follow. But the guards set a hard pace. Neither could speak Tibetan, and when my friend tried to make them understand that we wanted to stop just a moment to prepare some tea and rice, they only strode faster, until at last we simply lay down on the ground by the side of the road. The two Indians prodded us to get up. Altogether our number had now increased to eight, all completely worn out, and I didn't care if they killed me. I simply could walk no more. Nyima, who was now one of the group, discovered a little cave. We offered the guards some of our food and a few coins, but they refused to take a thing, and could only watch while everybody went into the cave, built a fire, prepared some rice and tea, and presently began to feel and act a bit livelier from the nourishment. The two Indians, then finally relenting, shared with us our tea and rice and let us remain where we were for the night.

At dawn they woke us and we shambled on, coming at about eight o'clock upon the rest of the group, who had become worried about us and were waiting. "We have been waiting for you here for a long time," a surly old abbot whom I knew complained to me. "We so many, and you so few! What has delayed you? Why could you not have kept up with the group, when you are all so young?" At which I lost my temper. "I'd have liked to have kept up with you," I said angrily; "but I couldn't; I just couldn't!"

Four days later we entered Bomdila, a large village with very nice houses. Some four years later the Chinese captured it, but withdrew after a couple of days. A good road begins there that can be used by trucks, but there were no trucks waiting for us. We had two days of welcome rest there, and then were off again for Assam.

All in the group were feeling a reaction from the long flight and the constant, terrible fear of falling into Chinese hands; always tired, sometimes very thirsty, and generally hungry, we found our anxiety beginning to focus now on what was to become of us in the future, now that we were safely over the border. I had never dreamed of being so helpless, but the happiness of being free, out of Communist hands, was compensation enough for all of these comparatively small discomforts. More than once, when I lay down to take a short nap on the ground, leeches fastened themselves to me but I scarcely noticed them. Nyima and Tenpa Dargye teased me, saying that even a leech could attack me, I was so weak.

On the flat plain near Assam, a small group of us saw a truck coming, which we hailed. We were a company of about ten, and when we asked the driver to take us all aboard, he kindly did so. The ride to our destination then took us no more than half an hour; walking, it would have taken half a day. On the way we saw two elephants with their keepers and I was reminded sadly of the pair behind the Potala, which I used to watch being taken to drink and bathe at a pond near the Mene Thangs' house. As we were approaching

Assam in the truck, we saw sitting by the roadside a group of eight Tibetans, and asked our driver to let us out. They were a delegation that had been sent by the Dalai Lama to greet us, and among them were two cabinet ministers who had accompanied His Holiness in his flight, Surkang and Kundeling. There was also an interpreter, Phunsom, who for years had lived in India. We thanked our driver and climbed down from his truck, our eyes already wet with tears, moved by the kindness and everlasting concern of the Dalai Lama for his broken people.

20.

My New Life

Surkang, Kundeling, and Phunsom told us of the Dalai Lama's remarkable escape and his presence now in Mussoorie, two or three days by train from Assam. They spoke of his deep concern for the refugees in India, Bhutan, and Sikkim, as well as for the lives of all those left in Tibet in Communist hands. The combination of grief at the loss of our country with the joy that overwhelmed us in renewing contact with our spiritual leader, was for all a profound experience. Together we walked, talking, down the road about a mile to a group of houses where the Indians had prepared for us sweet tea, and where we could pause for a brief rest. Then suddenly, a group of some forty or fifty reporters and photographers from all over the world surrounded us and began questioning us relentlessly on the situation in Tibet and our own plans for the future. Our first experience with Western news coverage left us bewildered. Depressed and fatigued, none of us could find anything to say, and we let one spokesman do all the talking, with Phunsom and a few others interpreting into English while the cameras clicked and flashed around us.

After this grotesque interlude we were loaded into a fleet of trucks and transported three miles to a broad plain, where two long bamboo houses roofed with grass had been built. In these the hundred or more of our party were to make themselves at home. Our evening meal that day was of tea and a thin rice soup, prepared and served by Surkang himself, the Dalai Lama's gracious cabinet minister. That was the first time in any of our lives that such an honor had been bestowed on us—here rendered so unexpectedly, simply and compassionately, without show. The order of life as we had known it in Tibet was already overturned on all levels. His Holiness's representatives next counseled us to go immediately to sleep; we could talk and discuss our situation in better spirits in the morning. So we all stretched out, at about 9 P.M., on the long narrow benches ranged along the walls, and were so relieved to be in safety at last that sleep soon overtook us all.

The next day about twenty Indian volunteer workers arrived to help us. Their curiosity had been aroused, I was told, by the rumor, soon proved false, that one of our party spoke ten languages. In addition to the disillusionment that the workers suffered in this expectation, they had the unpleasant experience of coming upon us in the early morning, after our long, hard journey. One could feel that our stench repelled and embarrassed them. But they remained, to do for us what they could.

We soon learned that we would have to remain close to the camp. Indian soldiers and other officials were stationed around the compound to keep us in, which made us feel watched and confined. Surkang and the other representatives of the Dalai Lama advised us to bathe twice over and to throw out not only all our remaining meat and butter, which by then had spoiled, but also our clothes, which were filthy and rotten from rain and sweat. Representatives arriving from an Indian charity organization provided each of us with a clean cotton shirt and pair of trousers, and with whatever food we required. They inoculated every one of us (against what, I did not know); since that was the first time in my life that I had received an injection I was a little frightened, as were many of the rest. A few experienced slight but painful after-effects, and that night I was wakened by the unconscious mutterings of a sleeping neighbor lamenting our sad predicament even in sleep.

Our next experience was an interview with Indian government officials who questioned us on what were thought to be relevant data: age, occupation, and so on. None of us had passports, since there was no such thing in Tibet; and the reason my name is now spelled Khyongla, though pronounced as if spelled Chungla, is that *kh* was the way one Indian official chose to render in roman letters the consonant *ch*. Our weights, heights, and other statistics were recorded meticulously and we were then provided with papers. I was one of those who could write his own name; for some others a thumbprint sufficed. For days thereafter, more and more refugees arrived, each with his own variant of the same woeful story of terrified flight, together with a new bit of horrible news about the state of our disintegrating country.

One of my biggest personal problems was finding time and relative serenity for saying my daily prayers. Having studied with more than seventy teachers, and having received initiations from many of them, I had been pledged, not only to meditate, but also to recite daily certain texts, amounting to about two hundred pages of my prayerbook. Most I could repeat from memory, and when in a recollective mood, with enough time, I could complete the whole assignment while meditating. But if I had to be finished in a hurry, it was easier to read from the book, which I had kept with me throughout this entire adventure. In Assam, however, when I drew aside to open it, I found that, so unsettled was my mind by the shock and disorientation, a whole day might pass before I finally turned the last page.

After what had become a timeless season of endured discomforts and routine, one day the Dalai Lama's representatives brought to us papers to be signed by those wishing to receive an education in India. Many of the young lay folk and a few of the younger monks signed immediately. One young lama, however, made a very strong case for all of us monks to remain together and found in India a new Tibetan monastery; and there were many who thought this a fine idea. But it seemed to me that, for myself at least, the old Tibetan way of life was finished. We could never go back. It was time to learn the ways of the rest of the world. And so I decided, after long and serious consideration, to try to learn to read and write in other languages, and to make myself somehow useful (if possible) in the world into which I had been thrown, rather than to live in a monastery as I had in Tibet. My life would be radically changed by this and when I spoke of it to my friends, many responded with real anger and the strongest opposition. They told me in no uncertain terms that I was crazy, and insisted it was my duty to remain within the monastic fold. But I replied no less strongly that the finding of a new place in the world was my actual duty now; and so I stuck to my resolve.

Eventually, after two months, the oppressive heat and continuous buzz of mosquitoes became unbearable in the camp, and I considered moving to Kalimpong, to start my new life there. Many incarnate lamas and their aides were already talking of that area, where a person would at least be out of the heat; but the Indian Government required that anyone contemplating such a move should first procure a sponsor, who would guarantee to support him if he failed to find remunerative work. A number of my friends had relatives in Kalimpong, and their problems were easily solved. I too had friends and a relative there, but did not want to ask them to undertake such a responsibility for my future; so I wrote, instead, to the Abbot Dardo Rinpoche of the Tibetan monastery in Bodh Gaya, whose summer residence was in Kalimpong, assuring him that I would never give him any trouble if he would only sponsor me. I would clean floors, collect garbage, or do anything at all, to be self-supporting. After a short delay I received his kind consent. I thereupon invited both of my two loyal disciples to come with me. Tenpa Dargye declined, declaring that he preferred the security of the refugee camp to life on his own in a completely strange world. And so Nyima alone accompanied me when I left our barrack in Assam for Kalimpong.

Tenpa Dargye came as far as the train to wave goodbye as we boarded, and I felt terribly sad on leaving him; he had been my good and very kind friend, at my side through all those years. Some months later he left the refugee camp for Sikkim and worked on the roads there, occasionally sending me money from his toil; and when I visited India in 1966, he helped me with a lot of money. I had, meanwhile, been sending him presents, which (he argued) meant as much to him as the money meant to me. His attitude was unique. Whereas other Tibetans in India were forever receiving and expecting help from their friends in Europe and America, he was the opposite, always giving his money away. Every time he sent me something I refused it, and he would then refuse to receive it back. One does not often meet with such a person, infinitely generous and absolutely loyal, maintaining through years a timeless friendship regardless of changing conditions.

Two days of crowded train travel brought us to Siliguri, the nearest station to Kalimpong, where four of us hired a car and from there were driven up a steep mountain road that was rough, narrow, and perilously winding; again I became carsick. It was a long, two-hour drive. When we came to the cab stop in Kalimpong, we were met by a Tibetan whom I did not know, but who had lived a long time in India and very kindly took us to his home, where his wife served us tea and pastry. But I had no idea where to go, or what to do, beyond that. We did not have with us enough money for a hotel.

I thought of one of my teachers, Serkong Tsenshab, who, as I knew, had reached India through Bhutan a few weeks before, and now was staying in a friend's room in a monastery. So we called on him, were decently received, and taken in for the night—though his room was very small. He said in the morning that if we wanted to remain he would speak to his friend; but four of us in that one room would have been extremely uncomfortable and an imposition besides, and so Nyima and I decided not to stay.

We went instead to the marketplace, where I searched out the residence of my old friends, the owners of a store known as the Pearl Shop in the Barkor in Lhasa. Acopoli was still living there, who ten years before had been my interpreter in Nepal. He responded to our knock, was amazed to recognize us, and actually wept when he saw how ragged and bedraggled we both were. I told him our tale and asked if we could stay with him a few months, to which he immediately agreed. There were plenty of rooms in the house, and the only residents were himself and a couple of Nepalese merchants. He opened a large room to us with a separate kitchen for our cooking, and himself, for the first few days, provided us with our meals. Indeed, he helped us in every possible way, even giving us a few rupees with which to start our new lives; and at last we were able to feel, for the time being, comfortable, well off, and at home.

Some merchants from Dayab who lived in Kalimpong came to visit us, and when they saw me in laymen's clothing, were displeased.

Hiring a tailor, they bought material and had a monk's robe made for me, and invited us to dinner every evening. They also gave us money, and when I protested, they insisted. Tsiwang Gyatso, a distant relative, was also in Kalimpong, and though I knew that he was there, I did not get in touch with him right away. When I did, he insisted on giving me a couple of shirts, trousers, and some money, asking why it was that I had not written from Assam for him to sponsor me. The Abbot Dardo Rinpoche, whom I also visited, admitted that when he had received my request for his sponsorship, he had at first hesitated. The future had not looked too promising, but on reconsidering, he had decided to take a chance, and was now exceedingly pleased to have done so.

I thought that I had now better begin learning both Hindi and English, so I asked a Tibetan student, who had been living for some time in Kalimpong, for lessons. He suggested that English would be the more important language for me, so I started my ABC's, but found it all extremely difficult. My mind was still in Tibet. I was unable to concentrate. My patient young teacher gave me the English spellings for *left* and *right*, which I wrote out one hundred times and pronounced out loud one hundred times—but the next day, when he asked for the spellings, I wrote down *left* for right and *right* for left. Hindi I found easier, but all I learned in English for a while was to recognize such simple words as *man, table, chair,* and *face.* It took me nearly a week just to learn the alphabet.

Many of my friends thought it odd of me to be studying English instead of practicing our religion. I answered, at first half jokingly, that the time had come for me to teach Buddhism in English; since the Buddhism of Tibet had gone into exile, it was important now to introduce its teachings properly to the English-speaking world. My study of this language, therefore, would be turned, I argued, to religious action. Were I studying merely to overcome enemies, or for my own living, this action might be termed wrong; but since I was actually preparing to bring the teachings of the Lord Buddha to the inhabitants of the world in which I too was now living, showing the way to Enlightenment, my study was the act of a Bodhisattva.

Presently this argument no longer was a joke, but actually became inspiration for me. Every morning, therefore, before sitting down to my primer, I would pray to my lamas, Buddhas, Bodhisattvas, and yi-dams, that my study of the English language should contribute to the teaching of the Doctrine of the Lord Buddha and to the good of all sentient beings.

During my six-week stay in the house belonging to the owners of the Pearl Shop many former high officials and aristocrats whom I knew came to Kalimpong as refugees. Some were old friends, others former pupils. They frequently came to visit me and as a result my affairs took a bad turn. Our talks were never of politics or the political situation, but were chiefly about the circumstances of our harrowing escapes, and of how we got to Kalimpong. Someone, however, informed the family of the owners of the Pearl Shop that I was meeting government officers in their house, and they sent me a letter in Nepalese, which Acopoli translated, stating that they feared that my stay in their building might jeopardize the business they were still running in Lhasa. I did not think that that would be so, yet saw that I had better leave. So friends began looking for a place for me and presently found a room in the home of a Tibetan, Amdo Gyeltong by name, into which Nyima and I immediately moved. It was a very small room, with no kitchen, so we cooked in the garage. The rent was twenty-five rupees a month (about three American dollars at that time), and though I had not known Gyeltong before, he and the members of his family were very friendly and good to us. They even shared with us some of their food. But we stayed with them only one month; for even twenty-five rupees was beyond our means. In only a few months all of our money would have run out.

It was suggested that we might move into the Tharpachoeling Monastery, where I should have to pay no rent at all, and since I knew the acting abbot of Tharpachoeling, friends of mine got in touch with him. He had been a pupil of one of my own teachers, Yeshe Loden, and though I not know him well, he offered the guest room of his own apartment, and Nyima and I moved in. We were, of course, not members of that monastery, and yet a number of the donors contributing money for its monks gave something also for us, as well as for several other refugee lamas who had recently been taken in. Sometimes, we were included in tea ceremonies. (Not a few of those donors providing for us would ask me to offer up prayers for them; and occasionally my own friends, too, would invite us to join them in prayers.) But I was now feeling extremely uncomfortable in all this, since I had already firmly made up my mind that this monastic type of life was no longer for me. I never asked for money myself, and many of my friends thought me stupid to take that attitude. There were plenty of other monks, they pointed out, who, even though they already had money, were still asking for more; and there were many lay refugees in Kalimpong, as well, who were accepting support from relatives. I was determined, however, to try to learn to stand on my own two feet, and so, while accepting of necessity whatever help came my way, I was at least no longer going to play the part of the begging lama.

The history of Tibet on which I had started work in Lhasa had been far from finished when I was forced to flee, and I had left behind both the manuscript and my notes. My dear friend, the Lord Chamberlain Thubten Woden, arrived one day in a town on a mission for His Holiness, and asked me to try now to write a shorter version of the work I had started, suggesting that I might go to Sikkim and pursue my researches at the Namgyal Institute of Tibetology in Gangtok, which had been founded only in 1958. Nyima and I made the trip together by car and found lodging at an inn close to the Institute, where we had to do our own cooking and pay one rupee a day. A Tibetan friend introduced us to the librarian, who received us respectfully and helped me to find what I wanted. There were many books from Lhasa, but not many of the rare texts from Mongolia and Amdo that I required. Yet I was able to read, once more, the life histories of the Dalai Lamas and many outstanding lamas of our other sects. However, having studied them all before, all I now wanted was to refresh my memory of details, and so I went through the books rather fast; and as the number of texts increased that I was leafing through, the librarian, with whom at first I had gotten along pretty well, became annoyed at the frequent trips he was making. He was used to people who read his books more slowly, and was glad to see us go when Nyima and I left after a month. I should have liked to have stayed longer, but our money was running out, and we had to get back to Kalimpong, where we could again put up in the monastery. Once there again, I set to work in earnest, and with Nyima's help as copyist, completed in about two months a shorter version of my history, which I immediately sent to Thubten Woden. He presented it to the Dalai Lama, and many of its pages are included in the textbooks being used today in our Tibetan schools in India.

Meanwhile, I continued my study of English. The young student who had been teaching me had had to return to school, but a monk helped me find another instructor, whom I had to pay, however, two rupees an hour. Formerly I had been able to exchange lessons in Tibetan grammar for my English, but now, with two lessons a week and no more than two hundred rupees left, I was beginning to wonder how long I could keep on. I studied hard and a little desperately, but my progress was extremely slow.

About this time, an Australian doctor who was operating a free clinic in Kalimpong came to visit my host, the abbot, who brought him to my room. I offered them buttered tea, which our visitor refused; he picked up my yellow rosary which was lying on a table and offered to buy it. I replied that I required it for my prayers, thinking it rather bold of him to offer to buy a monk's rosary. He stayed only a short while, because we soon ran out of words, even with the abbot acting as interpreter. That was my first contact with a Westerner.

My second followed a few days later, when the abbot took me to meet an English monk named Sanga Rakhita, who was living in a small temple that he himself had built a short way from the marketplace. I presented him with a scarf and he said he was glad to meet me; the abbot told him of my life and studies in Lhasa, and explained that, now that I had left Tibet I was eager to learn English and required someone to converse with. The abbot suggested that I might some time later move in and share the temple, to which the monk readily assented. However, it was evident that since I could not yet speak or understand one sentence in the language, I would still have to go on working for some time with someone who could speak Tibetan.

Returning from that visit, while passing through the marketplace, I recognized a Nepalese named Maitrana, who was a member of the family that owned the Pearl Shop. Greeting him familiarly, I asked how things were going, when he had arrived in Kalimpong, and so on, but his answers were very short. It was obvious that he did not want to talk with me. At first, I was annoyed, for I had known this man for years and in Tibet had known him well; in fact, both his brother Bodhiredna and his whole family had been patrons of mine. But then it occurred to me that he was perhaps afraid that I might ask him for a handout; or possibly, since I was a refugee from Tibet, he might think it dangerous for his business if he were seen with me. In any case, at the close of that curt encounter, I made up my mind more firmly than ever to find some way to support myself without leaning on friends.

That was easy enough to say, but not so easy to accomplish—I had not had experience before in living on absolutely nothing. I had not been rich in Tibet, but neither had I been poor. I had not had money to give away; yet if I had only been able to bring with me some of my possessions, I should now have been able to sell them, which would have been a very great help. It began to seem to me that in some past life I must have acquired pretty bad karma of some kind and that that was the reason why in this life I had become so desperately poor. But, on the other hand, Buddhism teaches that as long as we continue our wandering in this world, in some lives we shall be rich, have property, and be able to enjoy it, while in others we shall be (or become) poor as beggars, even die of hunger and thirst. Hence, if in this life I did not free myself from delusion, and thus from good as well as from bad karma, I should have to go on being reborn, in some lives rich and able to enjoy life, and in others poor and a beggar. In another mood I would think, musing on my lot, that everybody was really meant to be rich and happy in this world. But since some were born poor because of bad karma, I prayed that in my own poverty, I should absorb everybody's bad karma to myself, so that no one should ever have to suffer or be poor again.

Meanwhile, even though without a rupee, and perhaps with a lot of bad karma, I nevertheless had a basic feeling that everything was somehow as it should be. Many of my friends thought me a little crazy, because though destitute I was still in some way happy, telling them not to worry, since worrying is no help and only adds mental to physical suffering. So let us all now try to get jobs for ourselves, I counseled, work hard, and pull ourselves out of this pit—though it was evident to all that I myself was not fit for any job whatsoever in this world into which we had all been thrown.

One week after my encounter with Maitrana, I went, on a friend's suggestion, to the home of a Christian clergyman from Lhadak named Tharchen, who ran a Tibetan-language publishing house. He had had a Tibetan wife who had died, and he had then married an elderly, very gentle and kind Austrian lady. They obviously loved each other; and when I visited them, they were both friendly, wanting very much to be helpful. But the great problem was that I was unable to speak any language but Tibetan, and besides, had no usable skills. When I suggested that I might be of help to them, Mr. Tharchen promised that though he needed no one just now, he would surely keep me in mind. That was the end of that—I was at an impasse.

There were half a dozen families from Dayab who occasionally invited me for dinner to their homes and helped me out with money, but this was not the life I wanted, and I was deeply embarrassed to have to continue subsisting on gift-giving of this kind. It was to my great relief and delight, therefore, that a few months after my disheartening session with the Tharchens, there appeared one evening at my door one of the Dalai Lama's representatives. He gave me a letter from His Holiness's chief secretary, which I opened with a trembling hand in considerable excitement to read that His Holiness was inviting me to Mussoorie, his new headquarters, to assist in the planning and writing of a textbook series for use in the Tibetan schools in exile. It was as though a dam had burst. I was thrilled, but on further thought, quite uncertain. For the books were to be planned according to modern teaching methods, and I knew absolutely nothing about modern methods. I did need a decent job; and here, it appeared, I had one. Also, I had the honor of having been chosen from among thousands of refugee scholars. Yet, was I fit even for this kind of work? Would it be honest of me to accept?

I held a consultation with Nyima. He suggested that I should go to Mussoorie and learn about modern methods from the people there who would be attending modern schools. He would like to be with me, but thought that he should go instead to Benares, having just received from the Indian Government a scholarship to the Sanskrit University there. We talked all of this over carefully, again and again, and it seemed to me, finally, that he was right. With that, we parted ways. We had made up our minds about my job and about his career as well, and we bade each other farewell, each to go his own way in an open world.

When I left Kalimpong, Nyima helped load me into the taxi that brought me to Siliguri, where I found the whole third-class section of my train already full and crowded when I arrived. A number of Tibetans already inside one of the cars saw me helpless on the platform and suggested that I should give a porter some money to hoist me aboard. I had little baggage, and when I had handed one of the red-turbaned chaps a few annas, he did the trick by lifting me up and pushing me through a window. Between his shoving from behind and the others pulling from before, I had quite a time, and when I finally fell into place the car was both so crowded and so hot that I presently became miserably sick and was unable to eat for two days.

The day after I arrived I had my interview with His Holiness. When I had made the customary three prostrations, he greeted me very kindly and, bidding me to sit down, asked when and how I had left Tibet. I found it difficult even to speak. I had on a brocaded monk's jacket, which I had worn all the way from Tibet, and he asked me where I had gotten it. I then realized that he, like me, was adjusting to this changed world, and did not want incarnate lamas to be any different in dress from other monks. When I asked what sort of books he wished prepared, he told me they should be composed as modern textbooks in grammar, literature, and the religious and political history of Tibet. When I left he invited me to return and talk of these matters with him again when the work had progressed and we could discuss it in more detail.

My next business at Mussoorie was with my two revered friends, the Dalai Lama's tutors, in consultation with the principal of the new Tibetan schools being founded in exile for the children of refugees. I was told by the principal that I was to be in charge of the entire project and that he would supply me with all the help I needed. However, what I needed most was an idea of what the program of instruction in the schools was going to be, and it was not yet quite clear to anybody how the programs were to be organized. Next day, consequently, the principal conducted me to a meeting of the Dalai Lama's cabinet, where some Tibetans were to be interviewed who had lived for some time in India and attended English schools. I confessed that although I wanted very much to write the sort of textbook required, I knew nothing of foreign methods either of teaching or of writing books. The principal and other cabinet members had nothing to reply to that, but the others wrote down suggestions; and with nothing but those to guide me I started work.

No such texts as were then required had ever existed in Tibet. They were to be composed, not only according to modern teaching methods, but also for Tibetan students of all sects. One of my first suggestions to the principal, therefore, was that it might be a good idea to have representatives of all the major sects collaborate in the work. He replied that the Dalai Lama himself had already had such a thought, and that he would now discuss the matter with him again; which he presently did. But meanwhile, His Holiness's headquarters had been transferred from Mussoorie to Dharamsala, and we joined him there.

When I arrived I found three of the others who had been appointed to the project already present and waiting to begin. One, Zeme Rinpoche, from Gaden, whom I had known for a long time, had been my opponent in the tsog lang debate held in 1955 at Gyaltse before the Dalai Lama. I also knew the brilliant Sakyapa scholar, Ngor Thartse Rinpoche, having met him in 1956 at Ngor, when I was there with His Holiness's party, just after leaving the Communist school. I had never met Dudjom Rinpoche, the third member of our team, but found him to be a very fine person indeed, and an excellent scholar besides. He was married, the father of three children, and one of the best known Nyingmapa teachers—now considered by many to be the leader of that sect. Khunu Lama Rinpoche had been selected for the Kagyudpa sect, but because of ill health, he had not been able to come. This was a real disappointment to me, since he was a truly formidable scholar, and I had been counting heavily on his advice in the projecting of our uncertain task.

With the exception of Zeme Rinpoche, who would be living somewhere else, all of us were to be housed together in an old building that had been rented for our use, and we were to work there from nine to five, six days a week. There would be two clerks to take notes for us and prepare the finished manuscript. Our procedure was to first compare and discuss each other's plans, making corrections and adjustments; then, to divide up the work; and finally, to get going. We assigned Ngor Thartse Rinpoche and Dudjom Rinpoche to the text on our political history; Zeme Rinpoche, to Tibetan grammar and an anthology of poetry; and me, to the religious history of Tibet. The little series was to serve as an introduction to our language, poetry, songs, folklore, and political as well as religious history, for study from the first to eleventh grades. Since, of course, none of us knew anything of the style of a modern textbook, we ran into all kinds of trouble. Yet we did lay a foundation for the works of this kind that have been published since.

When we had finished our task in three months' time, Dudjom Rinpoche returned to his home and family in Kalimpong; Ngor Thartse went to Japan; Zeme Rinpoche remained in Dharamsala; while I departed for Europe and, later, America. Another group has since taken over the task of preparing more such books and revising those that we composed. The texts are being used today throughout the world, in the new Tibetan schools that are being set up outside of our country; and our great hope is that they may be useful, not only to the exiled children of the Land of Snows and all interested in Tibetan studies, but also for the propagation of the teachings of the Lord Buddha, and as a memorial to the spirit and majesty of what once was Buddhist Tibet.

Epilogue

In 1962, I was informed by the exiled Tibetan Government that Rechung Rinpoche and I had been chosen to go to Holland. Many scholars were eager to go abroad at that time and there were not offers enough for everyone, so I felt fortunate.

We worked in Leiden with Mr. V.A.N. Verwey, curator of the Indian and Tibetan section of the Rijksmuseum Voor Volkenkonde, in cataloging the many Tibetan books, thangkas, and objects in the museum's collection. Mr. Verwey's kindness to us was immeasurable. He and his wife and children were always willing to help us with our difficulties with English and with our adjustment to the Western world and its customs.

After four years our work was completed and I went in 1966 to visit my old friend, T. W. Phala, in Geneva, where he was the first representative to Europe of His Holiness the Dalai Lama. During our warm reunion a letter arrived from the Tibetan Government in exile in Dharamsala, requesting that I go to Argentina for six weeks to give a series of lectures on Buddhism and the Tibetan refugee situation, and to explore the possibility of establishing a Tibetan settlement there. I went immediately to New York, spending only one week there, but liking it immensely, and then went on to South America.

At the completion of the lecture series I returned to New York, since it seemed that establishing a Tibetan settlement in Argentina would be a very long-range project, without certainty of success.

For some months I looked for a job in New York, aided by T. T. Liushar, former Tibetan Foreign Minister, then Representative of His Holiness the Dalai Lama in New York. Also, I was able to spend some time with Geshe Yerphel Lharampa, whom I remembered from my earliest days in Lhasa when he often visited my teacher, Konchog.

During this period I thought a great deal about my future. My way of thinking had undergone many changes in response to new experiences and ideas. I had lived away from the monastery for many years and, while I still followed all the many monastic rules, I was attracted to the layman's life. I knew the time would come when I would be tempted to break some of those rules. Rather than do this, I reluctantly concluded that my long career as a monk was over, although I had always expected to live out my life as a monk. I wrote to Geshe Tsultem Gyaltsen telling him of my decision, and thus giving up my vows made so long ago, in the homeland I might never see again.

Mr. Liushar received a request for a teaching assistant of Tibetan language from the University of Minnesota, and offered me this opportunity. Eager to have a job and to be in another place for awhile, I gratefully accepted. After a year, still restless, I went from Minnesota to a teaching position at the Crowell Collier Institute of Continuing Education in Arlington, Virginia, where Kunga Thartse Rinpoche (later founder of the Sakyapa Center in Berkeley, California) and I taught Tibetan language to American servicemen. We loved visiting the famous buildings and sites in Virginia and Washington, and I began to learn something about the history of my new country.

In mid-1968, I returned to New York to make my home there. With the help of friends I found an apartment and a job at B. Altman & Co. as a stockroom clerk, which I thoroughly enjoyed. For the first time I could go to a job, do whatever I was told, and come home at the end of the day with no further responsibility. My co-workers and my boss, William Berriel, treated me as one of the guys—a pleasant feeling.

With my mind at ease, I began to think more and more about my autobiography and other books I wanted to write. After working a year and a half, I took a leave of absence to visit India and to work full-time on my autobiography. In 1971, I received a year's grant from the John D. Rockefeller III Fund to write the history of important Tibetan monasteries.

In 1976, I founded the Tibet Center with the help of Philip Glass, a musician; Tenzin Tethong, Acting Representative of His Holiness the Dalai Lama; my friend Marjorie Mortensen; Richard Conover, our lawyer; and my cousin Nyima Dorjee, whom I had managed to bring from India a few years earlier. The purpose of the Center is to assist Americans and Tibetans with their study of Buddhism, and to help preserve the culture, civilization, history, and arts of Tibet.

In 1980 Geshe Wangyal, one of the first teachers to bring Tibetan Buddhism to America, invited Ling Rinpoche, senior tutor of His Holiness the Dalai Lama, to visit his monastery in New Jersey. Due to this invitation, Ling Rinpoche, who had been traveling in Europe, came to visit me in New York City. Since my apartment was very small, my dear friend, Chojey Lama, volunteered to trade his spacious apartment in Queens for mine, for the duration of the visit. This kindness, along with the help of many friends and students, enabled me to make Ling Rinpoche's stay comfortable.

During his time in New York, Ling Rinpoche gave several teachings at the Tibet Center. He also gave the Center its religious name: Kunkyab Thar Dö Ling (Land Pervaded With Liberation Seekers). In addition, he presented the Center with a thangka of Buddha, with his own hand impression on the back. We took him to see the Metropolitan Museum of Art, the World Trade Center, Chinatown, Macy's, and even a movie. Although he himself would not have had any interest in seeing one, a number of friends invited him to *Star Wars*, and he was quite delighted at being able to please his hosts. All in all he spent two weeks here in New York City. After his return to India, he wrote me twice to say how much he had enjoyed himself.

In 1983 I was fortunate enough to attend Ling Rinpoche's last major teaching, given at Sera Monastery in Bylakuppe, one of the Tibetan refugee settlements in South India. For over one month he taught Tsongkhapa's *Lam Rim Chen Mo* (The Great Exposition of the Stages of the Path to Enlightenment). Although I'd heard discourses on this text many times, this particular teaching gave me fresh insights, and because of this, I became a better practitioner—at least during the time the teachings were taking place.

The Monlam festival then followed at Drepung Monastery, located in Mundgod, another Tibetan settlement in South India, and shortly thereafter, we celebrated the 25th anniversary of His Holiness's obtaining his Geshe Lharampa degree. Since I had been one of the debaters during his final examination at Jokhang, the central cathedral in Lhasa, I was invited to attend the ceremony, along with others who had debated with him then. We were each presented with a copy of Tsonkhapa's *Essence of Eloquent Sayings*, along with ceremonial scarves, a protection cord, and Tibetan coins. His Holiness spoke about his own education, and remarked that he would not be able to return the kindness of his teacher, Ling Rinpoche, until he himself attained enlightenment.

When the festival was over I went to Dharamsala for a short while, and then returned to the United States. I had planned to go back to India that coming winter and meet Ling Rinpoche in Bodh Gaya, where he was to narrate his life story to me so that I might write his biography. In the fall of the same year, though, I received a letter from his secretary informing me that Rinpoche had suffered a stroke. I left for Dharamsala immediately.

Rinpoche was very pleased to see me. I spent about three months there, assisting him in any way I could, especially with his prayers. Since it was difficult for him to read, he preferred that I read them aloud while he meditated accordingly. I stayed by Rinpoche's side, as his condition was very serious. His therapist, a Frenchman named Jean-Pierre, gave him vocal exercises to help him recover his speech. Rinpoche would have me do these exercises, loudly and carefully forming the vowel sounds, which caused him much amusement. Since it was difficult for him to speak, I refrained from asking too many questions, but on a number of occasions he imitated my husky voice. The stroke had rendered him unable to move very well, and when he wanted to be moved we would all assist him. During one of these moments, as we were lifting him up, I farted, and he burst out laughing. In spite of his grave illness and the severity of his condition, he was lighthearted and did not complain at all.

My visa was expiring. I had to return to America, but I promised to come back to help him in a couple of months.

About a month later, one morning in my apartment in New York, I heard a loud and awful shriek from a woman. It sounded as if she had screamed "Khyongla!" That very day I received word that Ling Rinpoche had passed away. Recalling the shriek, I realized that it had been a bad omen. I felt as though my heart was broken; I could not restrain my tears. I cried, knowing that I and thousands of others had lost a great teacher. But I also prayed for his wishes to be fulfilled, and for his quick return.

Two weeks later I received a letter from the secretary of the Dalai Lama, requesting that I gather information about Rinpoche's life for His Holiness, who would be writing his biography. I immediately left for Dharamsala. Shortly before Rinpoche's passing, he had been moved to the very comfortable new home of a disciple of his called Kelsang Yeshi, in the warmer climate of lower Dharamsala. It was here that I went, upon my arrival, to view his body. That night I stayed in Kelsang Yeshi's home and, as I was still very sad, I was not able to sleep much. During the night, strangely, I heard the sound of footsteps, a door opening, and water being thrown out. The next morning, though, no one admitted to having done anything that would have produced these sounds.

Because Rinpoche was a unique and peerless lama, His Holiness asked that his remains be preserved through a long and traditional process of mummification. Lisa Heath, a friend of mine and student of Ling Rinpoche's, did all of the necessary work, and upon its completion, His Holiness consecrated the body.

For two months I tried to question Losang Lungrig, Rinpoche's secretary of over 40 years, about the details of Rinpoche's life. But I could get little information from him because, whenever we began to speak of Rinpoche, he burst into tears. Eventually, though, over the next two years, relying upon my memory and that of Losang Lungrig, as well as records kept by His Holiness's private office, I was able to collect sufficient information for a biography. When this task was completed it was presented to His Holiness, who then wrote the biography of Ling Rinpoche entitled *Norbue Doshal* (Garland of Precious Jewels), which was published in 1989.

I am extremely fortunate to have been associated with Rinpoche over such a long period of time—since the age of 25. I have come to realize more and more of his profound qualities and attributes. He acted only according to the teachings he so skillfully presented. I realize now that his spiritual and scholarly qualities parallel those of Nagarjuna and Tsongkhapa, two of the greatest saints and scholars in Buddhist history.

In 1987, after over a year of searching, Ling Rinpoche's incarnation was discovered, and recognized by His Holiness. I traveled to India to meet the young child. Before I was introduced to him he greeted me by name and offered me an apple. When his predecessor departed from New York in 1980 he had left his official yellow hat at the Tibet Center. I had thought, at the time, that he would be returning there to teach again. After his passing away, however, and on meeting his new incarnation, I realized that leaving his hat had been an auspicious sign that this young lama might some day come to spread the Buddhist teachings in the West.

Over the years I have traveled to India about twice annually in order to continue receiving teachings from His Holiness. These trips make it convenient for me to stop over and visit several countries in Europe, where I am often asked to teach. While in New York City I teach at the Tibet Center at least once a week.

Now, with the help of my students, and especially my friend Richard Gere, the Tibet Center is sponsoring and organizing the Kalachakra Initiation, to be given by His Holiness the Dalai Lama here in New York City in October 1991. The spiritual benefits will reach millions of people. I consider myself very fortunate, and feel very happy, to have the opportunity to take part in this extremely rare event. I am confident it will be memorable and successful.

Khyongla Rato
June 1991
New York City